CREATING AN ECOSOCIAL WELFARE FUTURE

CREATING AN ECOSOCIAL WELFARE FUTURE

Mary P. Murphy

P

First published in Great Britain in 2023 by

Policy Press, an imprint of
Bristol University Press
University of Bristol
1–9 Old Park Hill
Bristol
BS2 8BB
UK
t: +44 (0)117 374 6645
e: bup-info@bristol.ac.uk

Details of international sales and distribution partners are available at
policy.bristoluniversitypress.co.uk

The author would like to credit Niki O'Brien for creating the spider-web images and
acknowledge that the author has copyright over these images.

British Library Cataloguing in Publication Data
A catalogue record for this book is available from the British Library

ISBN 978-1-4473-6355-2 hardcover
ISBN 978-1-4473-6356-9 paperback
ISBN 978-1-4473-6357-6 ePub
ISBN 978-1-4473-6358-3 ePdf

Cover design: Nicky Borowiec
Front cover image: Adobe Stock/Cienpies Design

I dedicate this book to three people. First, my late mother, Olive, who died during the latter stages of writing this book, and has always supported, nurtured, cared for and loved me. Second, my now adult children, Emer and Dan, critical advocates and early readers of emerging drafts. It gives me great hope to see them care about, and play their part in, creating a sustainable future.

Contents

List of figures and tables

Figures

Tables

Acknowledgements

This book is an outcome of years of conversation and discussion in many places, formal and informal, classrooms, seminars, meeting halls, marches, kitchen tables and bars. Thanks to all those who shared with me their heartfelt enthusiasm for transformative change. Many are convinced we can create a better life for not only all humanity, but also other sentient beings with whom we share our planet. Thanks, in particular, to a wonderful group of colleagues who commented on early (painful) drafts and steered me along the journey of writing this book, from civil society: Siobhán O'Donoghue, Orla O'Connor, Niall Crowley, Mike Allen and Ruth Lawlor; and from the academic world: Peadar Kirby, Pauline Cullen, Michael McGann, Matteo Mandelli and Fiona Dukelow. Thanks also to colleagues and students in the Department of Sociology and elsewhere at Maynooth University. Special thanks and sincere gratitude to Research Assistant Shane Gough and his invaluable editing work. Thanks also to Damien Ó Broin for the title, to Niki O'Brien for her graphic design of the spiderweb images, to the anonymous reviewers for their encouraging feedback, to Laura Vickers-Rendall and Jay Allan and the rest of the team at Policy Press, and to Thea Watson for all their wonderful support and work. All errors and claims are mine alone.

Introduction: The case for a welfare imagination

This book contributes to the growing number of arguments for a new ecosocial form of welfare and examines the politics of making ecosocial welfare a reality. The problem the book addresses is structural and the solution is ultimately political. My aim is to bring together accessible arguments about the need to recast the welfare state to meet the challenges of achieving sustainability and equality, and to address the politics of making that happen. A key theme is the integration of ecological and social arguments in identifying the problems and solutions, and the political strategies to make change happen. While intentionally light in its presentation of theory, an eclectic range of theory informs and develops the work.[1] It draws on key concepts including globalisation, sustainability, institutions, services, income, imaginaries, transformation and power. These concepts and ideas are brought together to map a welfare reform project, grounded in the transformational potential of social policy, and applied in the context of specific reform proposals across institutions, services and income supports.

An ecosocial solution to climate change and inequality forms part of global agenda that unites poor and rich countries in a new economic and social settlement, the financial responsibility for which must be borne by the Global North (Gough, 2017). Future welfare policy must develop in this international context but will more often be implemented nationally. The more detailed discussions in Chapters 4, 5 and 6 apply predominantly to developed nations' welfare state reform. The same principles, but not the same policies, may be relevant for the Global South, while global redistribution of resources is essential. The author acknowledges the Global North bias of this book, which results in a relative absence of focus on issues more relevant to the Global South including debt and reparation. The need for different strategies for different regions, and the role of global and regional institutions including the EU, are beyond the scope of this book. This short introductory chapter first outlines the problems, solutions and strategies that inform the underlying argument for ecosocial policy. It then justifies the case for imagination and hope, my motivation for authoring the book and the choice of Ireland as an anchoring case study. Finally, the chapter outlines the structure of the book and the content of each chapter.

Ecosocial welfare

Identifying the problem

Part I focuses on problematising the shared origins of inequality and climate change. The cumulative scientific evidence is unequivocal: global warming, caused predominantly by human action, causes climate change – an existential threat to human wellbeing and planetary health (IPCC, 2022a, p 37). The window of opportunity to secure a liveable and sustainable future for our planet is rapidly closing. If you are reading this book, you likely know and accept this. But you are also wondering about what this means for the future and more precisely what you and I, or we, can do about it.

At the same time, we know the globalised model of financialised capital leads to greater inequality of wealth and income (Picketty, 2017). Capitalism and neoliberalism, with the imperatives of privatisation, marketisation and commodification, are driving the destruction of society and ecology. Related processes including imperialism, patriarchy and racism impact differentially on women, racial and ethnic minorities and those belonging to precarious classes and castes (Folbre, 2021). These impacts are discussed annually in Oxfam's *Global Inequality Report* and include widening inequalities in wealth, income and power; lack of access to public services and related consequences; climate migration; the global care crisis; and gender and other intersectional and particularly racialised inequalities. The impact of globalisation on societal wellbeing and vulnerability is overwhelming in and of itself. It becomes existential when combined with climate change.

Identifying the solution

The solution, the focus of Part II, lies in progressing equality and environmental sustainability as interlinked goals and identifying relevant tools, including social policy or welfare policies and practices (Mandelli, 2022). Achievement of each depends on the other and both are cojoined in the book's ambition, analysis, solutions and strategies for action. Ecosocial welfare can enable values and behaviours to evolve (Mandelli, 2022). This includes a shift from production and consumption towards other forms of participation and ways of experiencing and contributing to the world, to achieve 'both social and environmental protection' (Gough, 2017). The book argues for a transformation of the entire socio-economic system – 'system change' as called for by activists in COP 26 and COP 27 – as a move from economic growth as a primary mechanism to distribute resources. The focus is less on how welfare can mitigate unequal impacts of climate change and more on what ecosocial policy offers as part of a post-growth society that moves beyond societal and environmental degradation. This ecosocial alternative approach needs to govern how we redistribute carbon emissions, work, time, income and wealth (Hirvilammi and Koch, 2020, p 1827).

Ecosocial policies are explicitly designed to achieve social and ecological goals interconnectedly (Mandelli, 2022). The book explores how a palette of policies, including enabling institutions, Universal Basic Services and Participation Income, can contribute towards a society based on equality, reciprocity and interdependence, rooted in an ethic of care for our planet and each other. This creates conditions for social and ecological sustainability and supports a different political economy that rebalances power away from markets, and towards the state and society. The seeds for such change are often hiding in plain sight (Stamm et al, 2020). Ideational debates already underway need to be augmented to accelerate the path to ecosocial welfare.

The strategy

This political economy approach focuses on the relationship between political and economic systems and understands the economy as an outcome of social and political contestation and cooperation. Part III focuses on strategies for transformation. We are living through perpetual crisis generated by the combined forces of the climate crisis, inequality and digitalisation exacerbated by the COVID-19 pandemic, the Ukraine (and other) wars, and catastrophic food shortages including famine. Such crisis rarely leads to critical junctures for transformative change unless actors are ready for transformative action. The strategy informing this book understands the value in framing and articulating what is needed for transformative policy change: building from the present by developing an imaginary of new welfare architecture – institutions, services and income supports, as well as necessary taxation – to enable a flourishing society.

Even in the context of strong corporate and elite power the progress of equality and environmental sustainability as simultaneous and interlinked goals offers the foundation for coalition-building. The ecosocial paradigm can enable the emergence of a new social order, while also being an integral part of it. It is at once chicken and egg. The analysis offered is critical of the siloed nature of contemporary civil society and argues for a more vibrant public sphere in a high-energy democracy. This focus on welfare reform rather than overall paradigmatic reform is offered in part as a mechanism towards breaking down silos and building tactical coalitions across climate activists and welfare or equality activists, bringing both into each other's conversations.

Political imagination and hope

As Obama has noted, hope is a political position. It is different from optimism which springs from a personal characteristic. Ernst Bloch in *Principle of Hope* draws on the importance of imagination and action, arguing that people find hope in throwing themselves actively into what is becoming, and in belonging.

> Hope ... is the belief that what we do matters even though how and when it may matter, who and what it may impact, are not things we can know beforehand. We may not, in fact, know them afterwards either, but they matter all the same, and history is full of people whose influence was most powerful after they were gone. (Solnit, 2016, p xii)

Hope is related to our capacity to imagine. A sociological imagination distinguishes between personal troubles and public issues (Mills, 1967). Social imaginaries have critical power, enabling an examination of politics and power relations in social formations. Sociological and political imagination refer to the ability to see the contexts which shape individual decision-making, and decisions made by others (Cullen and Gough, 2022). Imagination allows people to question the prevailing composition of society. Statistical imagination, for example, allows us to interrogate what is measured, such as critiquing Gross National Product (GNP) as a measure of wellbeing and imagining better national indicators. While much of 'what we dream of is already present in the world' (Solnit, 2016, p xv), we need to develop collective socio-ecological imagination in a way that incorporates an intersectional political economy form of environmentalism (Folbre, 2021).

Social imagination allows us to identify the possibilities for transformation that are already in motion in welfare regimes – the seeds of the future already planted in the present. Many political parties have narrowed their sights to defensive, and, at times, even regressive, short-sighted policies, while progressive ecological politics is rarely focused on social or welfare policy. Universities, including Arts, Humanities and Social Sciences departments, are not the sources of creativity that they once were (Unger, 2009; Higgins, 2021), with few focusing on alternatives to the dominant ideologies. Notwithstanding this, many are contributing and innovating in engaged research on social inclusion and climate change (Robinson et al, 2022). Similarly, several creative think tanks are leading the way, for example the UK-based New Economic Foundation and the Amsterdam-based Transnational Institute (TNI) stress the importance of imagination.

As a pracademic, I work at the intersection of social policy and political sociology. Public sociology should be a leading discipline in the fight against climate change by contributing ideas, knowledge and concepts to empower society to understand the new forms of power, state, society and governance, and enable transformation and transition. Climate change is becoming a more dominant central concern of social policy which, as Hirvilammi and Koch (2020, p 1824) observe, has tended to be closely associated with employment, capitalism and industrialisation, and often works to maintain capitalism with all its inequalities.

Finding the sweet spot

COVID-19-induced restrictions fed our imagination and offered some glimpse into a future that many claim they want to see. But policy innovations to respond to the pandemic were limited, both in time and in scope, and we have largely returned to the status quo. There is little hope in incremental change when the problem is systemic; adjustment is not enough (Jackson, 2021). Unger (2011), lamenting our lack of ambition for alternatives, speaks to the importance of 'institutional imagination' or programmatic imagination, what I refer to in Chapter 4 as welfare imaginary, and the need to articulate ideas or frameworks for transformation as opposed to detailed plans. An institutional or programmatic imagination is neither trivial (practical but small ideas) nor utopian (idealistic and beyond our reach). Rather, it must avoid dogmatic oversubscribed blueprints in favour of a particular vision of the future that can find the 'sweet spot'; a practical political alliance between transformative politics and programmatic thought (Unger, 2009; Wright, 2013; Folbre, 2021).

> The trick is to have big imaginative ideas about the direction of travel and the capacity to define the smaller first steps in traveling down that route.

In that sense, this book tries not to offer a blueprint but to signpost institutional alternatives that are possible as the first steps towards ecosocial welfare. This means identifying what is possible in the next steps, and what can be achieved in a short time frame. It means using the seeds of the future that are planted in the present as tools to move in the desired direction of travel with 'non-reformist reforms' (Unger, 2009, p xxi; Wright, 2013; Fraser, 2014). Of course, who plants the seeds and who gets to exercise their institutional or programmatic imaginations is crucial, hence experiential knowledge and inclusive participation are key themes discussed in Part III.

Why this book and why this author?

I am indebted to Naomi Klein for her candid admission that she 'denied climate change for longer than I care to admit' while suffering a form of 'on again–off again' 'ecological amnesia' (Klein, 2014, pp 3–4). It was not until 2009 that she recognised the climate change emergency as a huge opportunity to galvanise humanity for social and economic transformation. She identified that the challenge was more about the 'politics of human power than the technicalities of solar power', and that climate change offers the 'best argument progressives have for a catalysing force for positive change' (Klein, 2014, p 4).

I self-identify as a progressive pracademic, someone who has crossed the boundaries between the academic world, voluntary social activism, paid work in civil society and elected positions in politics in political parties and local government. I came late to academic life and continue to be involved in and with civil and political society. Journeying through this trajectory, I have had the opportunity to test and appreciate the nuance in different pathways to power and transformation. I have often found myself on the losing side and perhaps learned more about why change *does not* happen than how change *can* happen. I am also the mother of two young adults in their mid-20s whose lives are already very different to my own and who are forging their own paths as activists trying to shape their future. My mother, Olive, died during the late stages of drafting this book. Not everything was positive for her generation, however Olive lived through and enjoyed more progressive change than I have seen in my own lifetime. My generation owes her generation a debt of gratitude for their role in bringing about this change. Through all of this I have learned to live the feminist slogan 'the personal is political', and as a woman in Ireland, I am all too conscious of how hard we fought for all the change that has happened. These changes, like much political and social change, were determined through political struggle.

Offering this personal account is, for me, crucial. In the latter stages of a multifaceted lifetime of work for change, I believe it is necessary to take risks. I am consciously 'sticking my neck out' and 'wearing my heart on my sleeve'. I do not want, as I have often done in the past, to stick to a safer land of critiquing existing institutional arrangements and the status quo. Following Wright's (2013) tradition of real utopias, I want to offer imaginative but practical alternatives as first steps towards transformation. A key influence in my activism is a practical grounding in everyday life and policy reform. I am ambitious but also pragmatic about the possibilities for social transformation. The impetus for this book comes from colleagues, students and activist peers who regularly challenge me to 'write that down'. The possibility of contributing to an understanding that challenges current policy, practice and thinking motivates me. The audience for this book is therefore broad and includes policy makers, academics, media and, particularly, the activist equality and environmental community.

The book aims to be part of a process of social transformation, encouraging and tooling readers with strategies and vocabularies to achieve social transformation (Massey, 2013). It seeks to meet the challenge by shifting conversations about climate change beyond climate science and into the social sciences (Robbins et al, 2020), and to contribute to solidarity, momentum and synergy across a critical mass of people including local communities, active citizenship and democracy movements. As an activist I know the importance of narratives, framing and ideas, and as an academic, I appreciate how language, concepts and frameworks can help people to make sense of what needs to be done and to point the compass in the direction of transformative change.

In the analysis of the problem and identification of solutions and strategies, I have tried to mainstream feminist perspectives. Inspired by the 1980s and 1990s Greenham Common Women's Peace Camp, I have adapted their logo, a symbol of the spider's web on p. ii, to unify the book's disparate content. Part of this image is used at the start of each chapter to signpost the connective tissue across climate change and social inequality. The spider's web is also emblematic of joining the dots in collective action, and of course biodiversity, directly and indirectly, for example by symbolising the magical web of communication between trees.[2] Readers, educators and activists will no doubt find and innovate other symbolisms.

Why Ireland as the anchor?

This is not a book about Ireland, and the content relating to Ireland is differentiated with a vertical line to facilitate the reader who wishes to read through the book without the Irish content. However, anchoring the argument in a specific country affords the opportunity to examine how transformative policies and strategies might be developed in a specific context. Such is the nature of the challenges explored, any state could function as an exemplar or template for an ecosocial state. Ireland is offered to demonstrate a practical model of the alternative paradigm in a particular national context.

The Irish state does offer interesting insights (readers unfamiliar with Ireland can find a very brief introduction in Appendix: Ireland). Globalisation, regionalisation and marketisation are experienced in different ways in more vulnerable political economies with smaller domestic markets. Such public administrations may have limited scope and capacity, while reliance on informal relations, a common feature of small states, offers both opportunities and constraints (Boucher and Watson, 2017). Ireland is a 'nimble state with a social conscience and potential to respond to the challenge posed by climate change' (Sweeney, 2020, p 32). While social conditions appear conducive to collective action, the scale and speed of such action appears insufficient. Barriers to urgent reform in Ireland are comparable to, and offer lessons for, similarly sized jurisdictions (Robbins et al, 2020).

As a small, open and peripheral economy in the EU and Eurozone, Ireland is of interest to similar economies in Europe and further afield. Irish society sits at the nexus of the tensions in the European project, including austerity and fiscal policy, Brexit and US corporate globalisation (Dukelow and Murphy, 2021). Ireland's model of political economy has often followed a negative form of leadership. For example, the areas of the agri-food business and data centres are characterised by poor regulatory environments allowing poor practice in those industries relative to the rest of the EU. Though often described as a laggard in both welfare state and climate change development, Ireland is also an interesting anchor for praxis. The recent past offers lessons in popular political mobilisation, particularly social transformation of bio-politics (including divorce, marriage equality and abortion).

Like elsewhere, there are challenges in translating such momentum into distributional and ecological transformation. Despite big-state pandemic interventions, a low tax effort per capita remains a core feature of the Irish political economy, resulting in poor public service provision. The low-paid and gendered foundational economy is market-oriented, with significant procurement and commissioning of services once considered the domain of state or society. Yet welfare state transfers are quite effective at mitigating extremely high levels of market inequality in Ireland. As a country in flux, the post-Brexit environment offers a unique context as British devolution may have implications for the future direction of the island of Ireland, and constitutional questions may inform climate and welfare policy in Northern Ireland (as well as in Wales, Scotland and England). Welfare imaginaries can inform constitutional conversations as the different jurisdictions explore how welfare reform might reconstitute citizenship. As such, the book has specific relevance to UK audiences, and at the same time to other open, small and peripheral economies.

The content and structure of the book

The book is structured into three clear parts, each with three chapters. Each chapter concludes by anchoring the discussion in the case study of Ireland. My hope is that you, as a reader, educator or activist, can anchor the analysis in your own national context, wherever you are.

Part I, From problems to solutions: a post-growth ecosocial political economy, focusses on defining macro problems and pointing towards the solutions that are discussed in more detail in Parts II and III. It sketches the nature of the commodified political economy as the basis of ecological and social degradation and argues that solutions lie in a decommodified and post-growth world. Chapter 1, Commodification and decommodification, contextualises the contemporary globalised and financialised political economy. It draws on Polanyi (1944) to demonstrate the harm caused by commodification before turning to decommodification as a central concept to frame solutions. The chapter concludes by discussing Ireland's commodified political economy and the need for decommodification. Chapter 2, From unsustainable environmental outcomes to a post-growth world, problematises the impacts of capitalism's unevenly distributed environmental damage. It then examines contemporary debates with a focus on the Global South and argues that system change requires a paradigmatic shift to a post-growth scenario and just transition at a global level. The chapter ends by reviewing how Ireland's model of political economy impacts on local and global ecological sustainability and biodiversity. Chapter 3, From an unequal society to ecosocial welfare, examines the impact of the global political economy on social inequality in the Global North and the Global South. It focusses on the welfare state's capacity to mitigate the worst impacts of inequality and argues that the solution lies in an ecosocial policy that redistributes work, income, time, care and democratic and ecological participation. The chapter concludes with a focus on social inequality in Ireland.

Part II, Building an ecosocial imaginary, focuses on the policy architecture of an ecosocial welfare regime, on enabling institutions, services and income support. A core theme, that pockets of the future are found in the present, is developed. Chapter 4, Reciprocity and interdependence: enabling institutions, reflects on the important role that institutions play in fostering values and norms. Building on Part I's argument for sustainability and decommodification, it unpacks the relationship between reciprocity and collective freedom, asking how welfare institutions can foster both. The chapter concludes by focusing on Ireland's hybrid regime and the possibilities of building ecosocial policies and outcomes. Chapter 5, Universal Basic Services, as the title suggests, focuses on Universal Basic Services (UBS) as a key building block of an ecosocial state. UBS offer a mechanism to transform the way in which services are provided while also enabling diverse models of ownership but maintaining the state as the regulator and primary funder. Taking care services as an example, UBS is explored in the Irish case. Chapter 6, Participation Income, discusses options for income support that can complement UBS, as part of an ecologically-oriented social model that shifts from 'commodifying' labour to promoting a greater variety of decommodified, socially valued, participation. The focus is on enabling and valuing reproduction including care, democratic participation and environmental sustainability. The chapter concludes by focusing on a policy innovation in Ireland, the Pandemic Unemployment Payment (PUP) and contemporary income support pilots as templates for a Participation Income (PI).

Part III, An ecosocial political imaginary, explores how to make ecosocial policy happen and discusses strategies for social transformation and mobilisation. It focusses on how imaginaries, ideas and values can translate into strategies and collective action, through a 'high-energy democracy' and coalitions for transformation. Chapter 7, Power and mobilisation, first explores power and examines strategic logics and types of transformation. The nature of change is explored with a focus on the mobilisation of collective interests around key ideas. The Irish case study reviews recent power dynamics in Ireland and the degree to which they are oriented toward transformation or deepening and widening democracy. Chapter 8,

Imaginaries and ideas, explores the struggle about ideas and how they prompt mobilisation but also evolve in the process of mobilising and building alternatives. The importance of language is discussed, including how effective framing can potentially mobilise and unite a wide range of actors across a common goal. The case study on Ireland offers rich examples of framing narratives, coalition-building and strategies to enable intersectional mobilisations. Chapter 9, Achieving change through high-energy democracy and coalition-building, focuses on the structure of democracy and argues for a 'high-energy democracy' in which institutions enable empowerment, solidarity, participation, community and active citizenship. Focusing on action and struggle for normative values, challenges in collective mobilisation and convergence are discussed alongside the need to join the dots across key sectoral interests as a so-called triple movement. The chapter then examines opportunities for coalition-building towards an ecosocial future.

The conclusion rehearses the arguments in the book, the cojoined problems of ecological destruction and social inequality, the solutions found in a post-growth and ecosocial world, and the strategic need to collectively mobilise towards this transformative goal. It reminds the reader that the nature of change is never inevitable, and that hope is a political position, one we can foster and find in taking action to shape the future we believe is necessary.

PART I

From problems to solutions: a post-growth ecosocial political economy

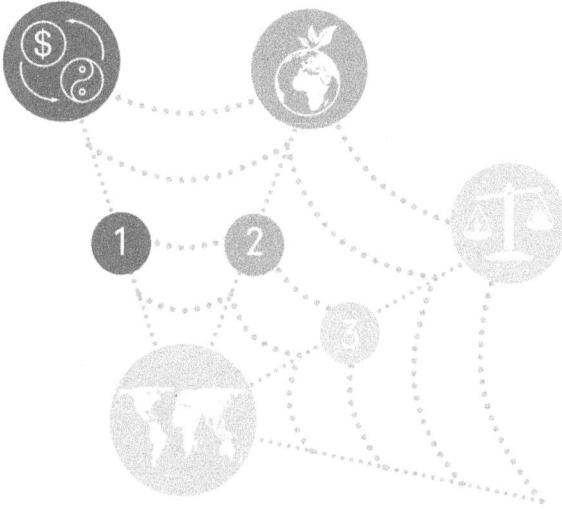

While this is largely a book about how welfare and social policy needs to change, the starting point is defining the problem: how the political economy of 21st-century capitalism impacts so negatively on both environmental sustainability and societal inequality. Inspired by Polanyi (1944), a fruitful way of understanding social policy is as a reaction and a decommodifying response to capitalism and its unrelenting commodification of labour, land and money (Gough et al, 2008, p 327; Kirby, 2021). A call for decommodification underpins the analysis throughout this book.

Contemporary political economy models and the related worlds of welfare capitalism are deficient, failing to secure gender and other equalities, socio-economic justice, health and wellbeing, social reproduction, democratic participation as well as sustainable ecologies. The case for transformation is altogether stronger from these multiple perspectives and demands a comprehensive political response. The case for an ecosocial solution is manifold, and true from the obvious perspective of climate change, as well as the wider perspective of system change.

The analysis rejects green-growth solutions that are overly productivist or techno-optimist in nature. This is consistent with a post-growth transformation to an ecosocial model that demotes economic growth as a policy objective, instead maximising human wellbeing, meeting basic needs and protecting our common eco-system. Each chapter concludes by exploring the chapter topic in the anchoring case study of Ireland.

Commodification and decommodification

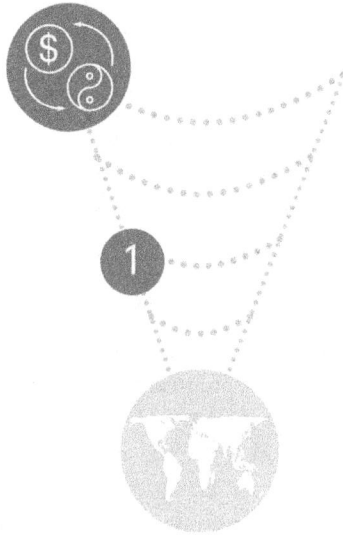

This chapter begins by examining the contemporary globalised and financialised eco-political economy and draws on a Polanyian framework and the concept of commodification. It identifies the problem, and the related social and ecological destruction, as commodification, and uses the concept of decommodification to frame potential solutions, pointing to an ecosocial project that de-emphasises the role of the market in favour of an enhanced role for the state and society. It argues that states should focus on addressing need through social, public and local mechanisms in which we care for each other and put our planet at the centre of our policy processes. The chapter concludes by assessing the Irish political economy and market, and its commodified policies and outcomes.

Capitalism and neoliberalism

While the focus in this book is on the ills of the 21st-century political economy, it is useful to recall how capitalism emerged in the 16th century on the back of organised violence, generating mass impoverishment and systematic destruction of previously self-sufficient subsistence economies (Hickel, 2021, p 48). Capitalism worked by impoverishing people in the pursuit of growth which was achieved through excessive profit and accumulation. Traditional welfare systems (granaries, communal irrigation systems, commons) were destroyed and hunger became an everyday threat, while new harsh rules forced people who had lived subsistence lifestyles to work for the benefit of others (Hickel, 2021, p 60; and Chapter 4).

The brutality of this is demonstrated in one simple statistic: life expectancy decreased from an average of 43 years in the 1500s to the low 30s in the 1700s (and as low as 25 years in Manchester) (Hickel, 2021, p 50). Through brutal processes of enclosure of the commons (which describes the accessibility of natural, cultural and societal resources to all members of the society) and the external processes of colonisation, slavery and extraction, capitalism expanded and grew. With profit continually reinvested, growth accelerated 'like a virus' (Hickel, 2021, p 87). The 1830s period of transition in Britain, known as the 'great transformation', has also been described as an 'abrupt', 'brutal shock', 'a lacerating operation' with the market mechanism eating into the 'marrow of society' (Polanyi, 1944, p 106). As private wealth increased, public wealth decreased, and relational ontologies were undermined as people were forced to change how they understood their relationship to the world. The social and psychological impacts of enclosing the commons and ending the centuries old system of Poor Law in Britain brought a loss of belonging, social exclusion, powerlessness, vulnerability and inequality (Polanyi, 1944; Hickel, 2021, p 78).

For capitalism to survive, it must consistently feed itself by finding new frontiers to exploit, as well as constantly finding new mechanisms to commodify labour, land and money across the world (Fraser, 2014; Kirby, 2020; Konzcals, 2021). Much of this happened historically though imperialism and colonialism, or sometimes through naked and violent extractivism (Polanyi, 1944). More recently it happens through hidden mechanisms of aid, trade, tax avoidance and legal or regulatory impositions, as well as culture and education. Historical and contemporary racial capitalism is underpinned by a racial state where long-standing historical racial and ethnic inequalities intersect gender, class, and other forms of inequalities (Folbre, 2021).

Globalisation

Globalisation can be understood as a transformation in the spatial organisation of social relations, transactions and power, and a process that includes movement of capital and people (Held et al, 1999, p 9). While the world has always experienced globalisation, trade and migration, over the last half-century we have witnessed a significant increase in the scale, intensity and velocity of global activity across economic, political, cultural, technological and personal spheres. This includes an accelerated pace of globalisation since the 1980s which differed in substance from other intense periods of international trade and which in an era of technological advancement generated new forms and scales of globalisation including a more networked society, the information age and more powerful all-encompassing multinational corporations.

In earlier periods of classical or laissez-faire liberalism, the state was relatively passive with respect to the market, while from the 1930s to 1970s, the state increasingly intervened to regulate markets. From the 1980s we saw an intersection between globalisation and a new form of liberalism – neoliberalism. The state became more subservient to the goal of fostering economic growth and actively facilitated capital accumulation, financialisation and profit maximisation. Neoliberalism can be understood as a transnational project with 'an ideological and theoretical agenda for a restructured capitalist economy and social system' (Held et al, 1999, p 16). This is characterised by a number of policies including: 'free' trade and capital mobility; monetary restraint and budgetary austerity; the 'flexibilisation' of labour markets and the repression of wage demands; the privatisation of public companies and services; restructured welfare states; lower taxation; increased user charges; more conditional and less rights-oriented forms of welfare (Daly, 2007, p 62).

The 'Tip of the Iceberg' image in Figure 1.1 is a useful way of understanding how the rules of the market inform and drive how capitalism works. These politically instituted systemic rules inform people's everyday experience of economic and other forms of inequality. These drivers and rules inform, for example, how privatisation and marketisation work as contemporary features of neoliberal capitalism. Marketisation processes occur where non-monetised welfare is commoditised (given a market value or a price) and delivered through private market mechanisms. Water, for example, remains a public good in many countries delivered by the state, but in the UK and other countries it is a privatised service delivered by a variety of market actors including international financialised actors. Even when the state still delivers a service, market concepts can be used to bring competition into the public sector, thus transforming how public services are managed, delivered, paid for and experienced, as, for example, has been the experience of the British National Health Service. The OECD (2009, p 7) describes the early 21st century as a 'new privatisation landscape' in which all kinds of public functions are transferred to the private market in areas as diverse as nursing homes, electricity pylons, prisons, health, parks and public transport.

The contemporary form of capitalism – financialisation – occurred as the financial sector was deregulated in the early 1980s, leading to the development of new forms of financial products and markets. These new forms of products greatly expanded credit and money supply in new types of markets that were complex, lightly regulated and highly speculative. As the financial market was left to self-regulate, new financial interests came to

Figure 1.1: The tip of the iceberg

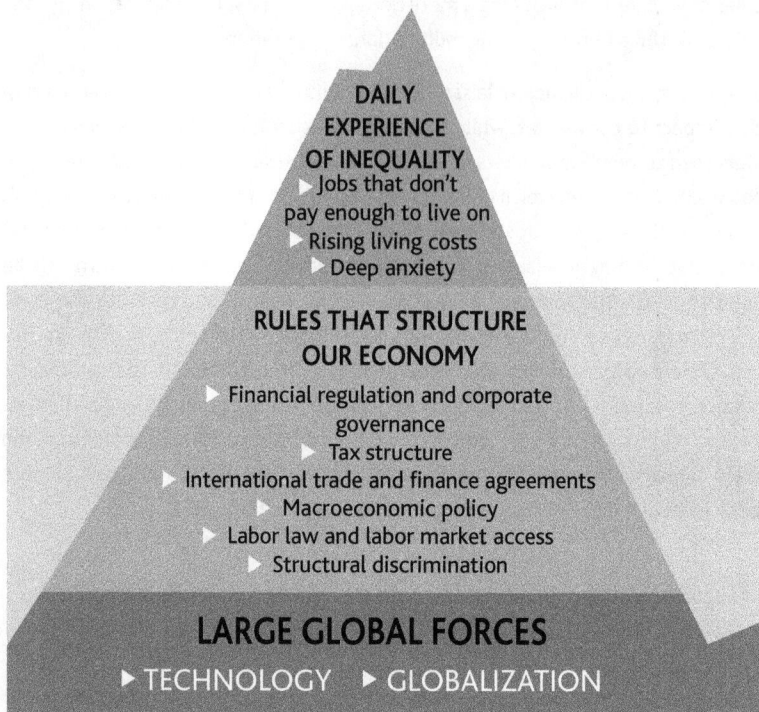

DAILY
EXPERIENCE
OF INEQUALITY
▶ Jobs that don't
pay enough to live on
▶ Rising living costs
▶ Deep anxiety

RULES THAT STRUCTURE
OUR ECONOMY

▶ Financial regulation and corporate
governance
▶ Tax structure
▶ International trade and finance agreements
▶ Macroeconomic policy
▶ Labor law and labor market access
▶ Structural discrimination

LARGE GLOBAL FORCES
▶ TECHNOLOGY   ▶ GLOBALIZATION

Source: Stiglitz, 2015, p 18, Creative Commons

dominate the sector. Large private hedge funds drove ever riskier speculative processes, eventually leading to the 2008 great financial crisis. While the collapse led to some (re)regulation, the financial sector continues to dominate the global economy and is expanding into new markets including public services, with often dire consequences for land, nature, workers and society. This happens through three distinct processes: as a new regime of accumulation; as shareholder value orientation; and as financialisation of everyday life, particularly through access to credit (van der Zwan, 2014). Increasingly, financialisation affects the welfare state as it finds its way into social care, social housing, education and homelessness, and impacts on the production of knowledge.

Today, neoliberalism appears to transcend the left/right political divide, so political and policy debate is now shaped by the same 'common sense' that the market knows best and that privatisation and marketisation are positive processes enabling true and free competition (Mudge, 2008; Murphy and Dukelow, 2016). In practice, drivers associated with globalisation, including technology and demographic change, are mediated by rules and regulations. Such laws and institutions determine how and whether markets work for society (Stiglitz, 2015, p 7). All these rules are political decisions that can be unmade. Even the biggest global trends, the drivers at the base of the iceberg which shape the economy, can themselves be shaped and pushed toward better outcomes. Rules and power matter, but there is much that can be done to change the rules governing our economic and social systems that shape daily lives (Stiglitz, 2015, p 11). Transforming the system means changing the rules and contesting the power dynamics that created and maintain the common sense underpinning the belief that capitalism is inevitable. Ever mindful of Jameson's (2003) observation, 'it's easier to imagine the end of the world than the end of capitalism', we can take hope from Le Guin's (2014) reflection: 'We live in capitalism – its power seems inescapable, so did the divine right of kings, any human power can be resisted and changed by human beings'.

Commodification and decommodification

'The capitalist mindset is a river that has busted its banks, flooding our other social interactions. Society has become transactional' (Bednar, 2023, p 2). Privatisation and marketisation in the contemporary globalised world can be understood through the lens of a relatively old concept – commodification. Polanyi's (1944) most famous contribution, *The Great Transformation*, is almost 80 years old but has enjoyed a recent resurgence. Written to understand the violent nature of the transformation to capitalism or liberalism in 19th-century Britain, the work resonates with recent social and economic dislocations and helps us to understand the nature of the 2008 global financial crisis, the climate crisis and the relationships between disembedded economies, commodification, inequality and environmental collapse. Polanyi's study about the transition from a feudal to a capitalist economy has inspired a growing global network of scholars and civil society activists who promote a 'Great Transition' to a future of equity, solidarity and ecological sustainability (Matthies, 2017, p 4). The Polanyian critique of commodification offers a central framework for understanding privatisation and marketisation, and the relationship between economy, social reproduction, economics and the political economy. The following five concepts are related and enable an understanding of how our lives are increasingly lived through markets (Kirby, 2021; Konczal, 2021):

- Fictitious commodities: land, labour and money were never destined to be market commodities. But capitalism treats them as commodities, pricing them to be bought and sold on markets, and in the process destroying societal and ecological well-being.
- Commodification: the allocation of monetary values or market prices which occurs as exchanges are turned into money transactions for

private gain. Use value is shifted to exchange value and the motivation of subsistence is shifted to profit.

- Decommodification: the process of reversing commodification, lessening the dependance of society on markets and money, often through social protection.
- Recommodification: the process of reversing decomodification, increasing dependence on the market, often through welfare conditions requiring activation or paid employment.
- Embedded/disembedded: the degree to which economic activity is constrained by non-economic institutions. Embedded economies are relevant to social needs.

An over-emphasis on market mechanisms is explained by Polanyi as the commodification of aspects of our lives that are simply not marketable. He classified land, labour and money as 'fictious commodities', which, when treated as saleable market products, can no longer serve their natural, social or ecological function, leading to destruction of society and ecology. The net effect is the commodification of the most precious fictious commodity, life itself (Konczal, 2021). By failing to effectively regulate capitalism, politics allows the market to dominate society, effectively creating a 'market society', in which humanity is subservient to the needs of the disembedded economy or market. This over-emphasis on the market as the means of our survival is at the expense of our mutual interdependence and reciprocal relationships (our society) and our ability to use political mechanisms to redistribute common or collective goods (our state). What is needed is a 'rebalancing of state, market, society to restore a trilateral interdependence' (Jones and O'Donnell, 2018, p 246).

Examples of contemporary commodification

Polanyi's original fictious commodities have now expanded in unimaginable forms such that virtually every aspect of our lives, relationships and nature are now potentially marketable. The fictious commodity of land now expands to include nature, air, water and carbon. The fictious commodity of labour now encapsulates our bodies, recreation, sport, culture, sex, love and even bodily organs, while money markets are no longer about exchange but include all kinds of saleable financial products including many forms of credit, mortgages, loans, securities, dividends and derivatives (Kirby, 2021; Fraser, 2014). These pervasive markets damage our lives and our planet, and lead to a myriad of interrelated social and ecological dysfunctions (discussed in Chapters 2 and 3).

Commodification of everyday life occurs in many different and subtle ways. Think, for example, about dating. Instead of meeting people through social interaction, in work, in a bar or through hobbies, many people now pay dating agencies, or social media software applications like Tinder, Grindr, Match.com and Facebook dating to meet people. Many of these applications have both free and paid versions but even the free option exacts a price by capturing our data. Dating in the 21st century is, therefore, commodified. As supporters of various sports teams, many of us are used to being consumers, willing to pay to watch our favourite teams. However, sports teams and even sports players are now commodities, bought and sold and subject to market speculation. Instead of becoming fans and members, we buy shares in clubs. There are more and more merchandised products at exploitative prices. We pay to watch televised matches in our homes and public spaces and there is less and less equality of access to attend and watch matches or games. Sport is commodified.

A political economy approach focuses on the relationships between individuals and society, and markets and the state. It incorporates diverse traditions, some focusing on the productive or market economy, others on the relationship between economy and ecology, while feminists incorporate social reproduction in their understanding of political economy. Folbre's (2021) concept of 'intersectional political economy' analyses not only the production of human capabilities but also the social reproduction of group solidarities based on contestation and collaboration within and between gender, class and race. This is important and this book aims to situate the discussion of welfare transformation in a feminist and ecological understanding of the political economy. The dominant contemporary form of political economy in the Global North is a globalised and financialised political economy – an international form of capitalism which, in Polanyian terms, is highly disembedded and creates havoc with our lives and our planet (Streeck, 2017). Echoing arguments by Galbraith (1958) in *The Affluent Society*, capitalism is a system of social action and a set of institutions. Globalised markets, fearful of saturation of commodities, continually stoke demand. Capitalism is increasingly dependent on marketing and advertising, and the sale of symbolic goods. The ever-present danger is that more and more of our social life is subsumed into private accumulation (Streeck, 2017).

Teaching third year politics students a module based on Polanyi's analytical framework offered me a real opportunity to see how the concepts of commodification and double movements could empower people to find words and language to explain what they were seeing in their own lives. At a macro level, students could make the connection between the crisis of the Great Depression and the great financial crisis. Exploring the different responses to the 1930s crisis, poverty and unemployment in the US (with Roosevelt's social democratic New Deal) and Europe (with the rise of fascism) enabled students to understand the potential pathways of response to austerity as Europe jostled with forms of left and right populism. At a micro level, students relayed their emotional responses to the commodification of more and more aspects of their everyday lives as music, culture, health, housing, education and information were increasingly behind pay walls, commodified and marketised. It always gives me pleasure to see past students as activists resisting the creep of markets into their lives and demanding rights to housing, care, urban spaces, reproductive rights and education.

Double movement

As a response to increasing commodification and destruction of society, Polanyi anticipated a double movement as society responds to an original movement that disembedded the economy from society and ecology. This refers to the demand from society for regulation, welfare and social institutions to re-embed the economy back into serving the needs of society. The double movement in 19th century Britain was a spontaneous, pragmatic, self-protective counter-movement by society to correct the harms of the market. This emerged from both the left and the right at the end of the 19th century and resulted in regulations around public health and factory conditions, and the establishment of social insurance, public utilities and trade associations (Kirby, 2021, p 17).

Counter-movements by market forces then sought to reimpose the principles of economic liberalism and market mechanisms. Thus, there is 'a continuous contestation of boundaries' (Streeck, 2014) between capitalist forces and social forces seeking social protection from an overbearing destructive market. The term 'rentier capitalism' describes ever increasing processes of commodification which lead to greater inequality and unequal power, limiting capacity for contestation, but crucially also creating the possibility for new forms of collective mobilisation (Christophers, 2020, p xxiv). The idea of being free from the market has inspired many historical movements relating to land, labour and money (Konczal, 2021). Many contemporary movements continue to question the balance between public and private provisioning of needs and seek reversals of the marketisation and financialisation of public services and infrastructure. We explore this collective action as a response to the contemporary social destruction of society and ecology in Part III of this book.

All of this could be very depressing, but inspiration can be found in movements that won historical victories over the market. Polanyi offers us the insight of a world living through transition, as do Jones and O'Donnell (2018). Political economic frameworks are constantly changing and renewing in the context of multiple driving forces (see Figure 1.1: The tip of the iceberg) (Levi and Ugolnik, 2023). Today, we see the political and economic structures of capitalism and democracy under intense pressure. In this contemporary moment of transition neoliberalism is not inevitable; society and democracy can influence the direction of what comes next.

Esra Klein and Kim Stanley Robinson's podcast[1] on *The Ministry for the Future* discusses a climate fiction novel that imagines how changes to the earth's biosphere will force humanity to rethink capitalism. The novel speculates that the dominant capitalist order will rupture and change and will ultimately transform to emerge as a new global economic system. This new system will still include capital, an economy and money but could also include a horizontal distribution of power and a redistribution of the value of labour. *The Ministry for the Future* affirms the importance of imagining the end of capitalism as a way of avoiding the end of the world and offers an understanding of a process of transition that is regionally uneven, dialectical, complex and adaptive to process as it emerges. While classic theories such as Marxism offer a rich set of tools, the novel demonstrates how we also need new theory, tools and imagination to interpret and interrogate new realities.

Everyday contestation of marketisation has tended to focus on ways to limit or regulate capitalism (for example, labour or environmental regulation) and/or how to protect society from capitalism or mitigate the damage it causes to society (welfare and social protection). However, we often accept the underlying premise of the market as the primary mechanism through which we access what we need to survive. The existential threats posed by the interrelated challenges of climate change and social inequalities require us to seek solutions with transformative potential and with capacity to change how we understand and distribute paid work, care, time and wealth. This means focusing on pluralism and diversity in a new economy with different forms of public ownership and economic democracy (Cumbers, 2018, p 215). The next section offers the underlying principle of decommodification as an approach to building an ecosocial form of welfare that recalibrates where and how we source what we need to survive. By limiting the role and function of the market in meeting our needs, ecosocial welfare can restore the roles of reciprocity (society) and redistribution (state).

Decommodification: reclaiming state and society

Kirby (2021, p 95) defines decommodification as part of the process of re-embedding the market into society – the process of reversing commodification, lessening the dependance of society on markets and money, and restoring our mutual interdependence on each other. He offers a set of principles as to how society should relate to nature (or land or money) rather than treating them as commodities to be bought and sold. Taking land or nature as an example, these principles include rethinking forms of ownership of, and access to, nature; socially valuing land and nature as a public resource for the community; ensuring radical egalitarian access to the local fruits of land/nature and enabling a different type of belonging and wellbeing. Effectively, an ontology of security and stability is derived from the local community and associated with access to nature, protected from profit maximisation. These principles are actively informing land use, agricultural production policies and decommodification projects relating to the other two fictitious commodities of labour and money (Kirby, 2021, p 97). The principles are, for example, visible in experiments of living without money (Boyle, 2013) and countless innovations in ownership and delivery of collective services (Kishimoto et al, 2020).

For this book, a core question is how social, or welfare, policy relates to commodification and decommodification. The objective of decommodification, in the sense of making people less dependent on paid employment in the market economy, was central to growth of the redistributive post-World War Two welfare state, although this was never fully achieved. In the context of shifting ideologies and global systems of production, this core objective changed over the last 50 years so that welfare, instead of offering a decommodified social citizenship, is now understood as recommodifying people. Through welfare-to-work paradigms of activation and workfare, an employment ethic was promoted as central to self-worth, while social inclusion is associated with market consumption. Working age recommodifying welfare seeks to insert people into the labour market and makes paid employment central to survival; however, child and elder welfare and some forms of adult welfare still seek to decommodify and offer livelihoods outside of the market.

In commodified states people are mostly reliant on the market for their wellbeing. Downplaying the role of the market means returning to the central importance of both the state and society as means of societal and ecological wellbeing. Decommodification means deemphasising the role of both paid work and the private market as the primary means through which people survive and flourish. A decommodified welfare state enables exit or non-participation in paid employment without impact on capacity for wellbeing, either through little or no loss of income, or through access to public services (Murphy and Dukelow, 2022). People are enabled to derive income from other forms of participation than paid work. Universal Basic Services (UBS) reduce the role of the private market in accommodating people's basic needs for, for example, welfare, health, housing, education and care.

Decommodification offers potential for a more imaginative way of distributing time, care and paid and unpaid work, leading to a more holistic approach to paid productive and unpaid social reproductive work or care, and a better balance between the two, while also advancing gender equality. This understanding of economic life as embedded in social relations reflects the importance of relational ontologies or belonging discussed earlier in this chapter. Decommodification offers opportunities for changes in power relations between men and women, between carers and people being cared for, and between workers and users of public services. Changing how people relate to each other and belong to communities can be the basis for new solidarities and possibilities. Such changes in subjectivities can enable further changes in values (Hickel, 2021). Enabling institutions can also reaffirm or reinforce values such as solidarity, mutual aid, collaboration and cooperation.

Getting the balance right

Transformation is not a simple aspiration; many who aspire to decommodi-fication also value other social goals including high levels of social inclusion, equality and labour force participation. Reducing the numbers of people in paid employment also reduces the state's capacity to tax labour and requires new sources of revenue to be found. It also requires renegotiation of the social contract which legitimates social support on the assumption that people who can work in paid employment will do so. Many women have achieved economic independence through labour market participation and decent employment remains a legitimate goal for many who are denied such opportunities. Commodification and decommodification are on a spectrum and neither are fully achievable or even desirable. Few seek a fully decommodified world. Universal Basic Income supporters, for example, advocate for such income to be compatible with participation in a commodified economy and society. Others advocate forms of welfare reform that support self or community development, and alternatives to market hegemony, but see these as parallel to labour markets (Murphy and Dukelow, 2022).

Decommodification of social policy brings us closer to the post-growth objective of living within limits. Seeking to decommodify requires a careful rebalancing of the respective roles of state, society, and the market. It requires a respect for the roles of each sphere and strong leadership to achieve and sustain societal and ecological wellbeing. Decommodifying housing, for example, means taking some housing off the speculative market so it cannot be bought and sold for a profit.[2] Instead, there are alternative housing models, like community land trusts and permanent real estate cooperatives, which create secure and affordable housing for generations to come. The pandemic demonstrated that decommodified income and services are not only desirable but also possible, organisationally feasible and politically legitimate.

The ecosocial state?

Despite the range of great philosophers who have considered the role, function and history of the state, we are often ill-equipped when discussing and reimagining the purpose and capacity of the state (Runciman, 2021). Political rhetoric suggests that neoliberalism causes states to become smaller and less powerful. However, globalisation and neoliberalism, rather than leading to a withdrawal of state intervention, more often leads to a dual process of 'rolling back' and 'rolling out' various aspects of state activity (Peck, 2010). While the great financial crisis (GFC) of 2008–2013 occasioned a period of austerity and rolling back of the state, the more recent pandemic revitalised and affirmed the central importance of an interventionist and strong state, a form of 'rolling out'. What kind and size of state is needed in a new non-capitalist, decommodified post-growth world?

The meaning of the state remains contested and different concepts of the state have informed classic debates in academic literature and in politics (Runciman, 2021). A common understanding is that the nature of the state emerges from economic relations and values, and the state has both capacity and legitimate authority over a given territory. State capacity is the ability of the state to pursue and/or implement official goals, while legitimacy is largely derived from the democratic and bureaucratic functions of the state, but also its legitimate recourse to coercion. The state's exclusive competence to regulate activities on national territory, or 'sovereignty', is increasingly challenged in an era of interdependence, globalisation and financialisation (de Schutter, 2010). The future state needs capacity to enable collective transition to a sustainable, equal and democratic world. The future may be located in and regulated by nation states, but also supranationally. However, most lives will be lived in local settings and the local capacity of the state will be an important determinant of the future.

The expectation is that an ecosocial state will require significant capacity. The amount and character of state capacity can vary according to the public or private composition of the political economy (Mazzcuto, 2013). Recent experiences of 'state power' were exposed as states responded to recent crisis. We can extract lessons from the GFC when we saw strong capacity in some state institutions who were able to invest in and manage debt in what was, overall, a remarkably successful intervention to sustain the banking sector (and wider economy), albeit in the context of austerity for many in society and with authoritarian hues in the context of societal resistance to socialisation of bankers' losses. During the pandemic crisis of 2020–2022 the state emerged as a strong actor, collaborating with key medical and professional elites, and innovating agile policy responses for key actors including employers and workers. Accusations of authoritarian hues were largely drowned out in a compliant society. The 2022–2023 'cost of living' crisis demanded state and collective responses, not so much requiring a large role for the state, but focusing on its policy and governance role, for example, by regulating the market in the context of price increases and supply chain shortages.

Imagining a different conception of the state as an ecosocial state requires assuming a different set of economic relations and related values. There is a challenge here in that we cannot create what we cannot imagine so we require some creative license in anticipating what an ecosocial state might be. An ecosocial state will rebalance power away from the economy, market and competition towards meeting societal needs within ecological limits. Enabling state institutions, national and local, will capacitate civil society and communities to maximise participation and support people to work in paid and unpaid roles to achieve wellbeing in caring, reciprocal and equal relationships. Democratic participation and diversity are key. The state, through its political and welfare institutions, needs to accommodate diversity and participation in different political and policy dynamics and outcomes (Cullen and Gough, 2022), discussed further in Chapter 9.

The Irish political economy: a commodified state

As a small, geographically peripheral state, a member of the European Union and the Eurozone, and well-integrated into the global political economy, Ireland provides an interesting test case for the impact of globalisation (Smith, 2005). Pressures associated with globalisation and financialisation on, for example, labour, taxation or housing, are mediated by and filtered into domestic policies in Ireland. We see competing logics of both competition states and developmental states in the Irish political economy (Kirby and Murphy, 2011). This 'openness', and its impacts on Ireland and the Global South, are discussed further in Chapters 2 and 3.

Ireland's political economy is oriented as an open export economy which is strong but volatile. As a late industrialiser with no significant fossil fuel industry, agricultural-related food production occupies a larger proportion of the political economy than the EU norm. In small states like Ireland, welfare or social compensation ensures societal protection from volatility and provides investment in building capacity for adaptability. However, agile domestic institutions – national and local – with capacity for policy coordination and learning are required in the face of constant change (Ó Riain, 2014, 2020). In their absence, marketisation through the procurement or outsourcing of the provision of services can be vulnerable to domination by a small number of societal or market actors, leading to monopoly-like quasi-markets and intensifying commodification (Murphy et al, 2020). In contrast to employment in multinational industries, Ireland's smaller, low-paid foundational domestic economy is neither highly skilled nor well paid. Strong investment in meaningful policies and institutions is needed to increase productive capacity of this indigenous sector.

Impacts on the Global South

Ireland is an exemplar of a globalised and financialised political economy and market society which has negative impacts for both local and global ecological sustainability and biodiversity. Ireland's global openness means exposure to, and dependence on, the economic actions of foreign trading partners, while immersion in global supply chains also impacts on developing countries and global patterns of trade, particularly in relation to food production (Robbins et al, 2020).

Besides being very open to capital flows, and among the most financialised economies in the world, an assessment of Ireland's trade, financial emissions and raw material linkages suggests that although a small state, Ireland's footprint leaves a disproportionately damaging imprint. Ireland is relatively unique in the degree to which agricultural-related activity comprises a significant part of its post-colonial economy. Oxfam and Trocaire's (2021) assessment of impacts on global food sustainability highlights how Ireland's export of subsidised Irish milk powder to West Africa flies in the face of local government officials, small-scale dairy owners and farmers who argue that powdered products are nutritionally inferior, environmentally damaging and undermine local markets and dairy production.

The intensification of finance and capital flows is of great significance in a small open economy like Ireland which for the last 70 years has been over-dependent on foreign direct investment. The opaque nature of Ireland's corporate tax policy has negative tax implications both domestically and internationally. Labour linkages relate historically to emigration and, in more contemporary times, to migration, in, for example, the global care supply chain. Financial linkages work through domestic taxation and regulation policy, and institutional facilitation of shadow banking. Ireland facilitates 'brass plate' financial-vehicle corporations established solely to house or trade securitised investments, the economic activity of which amounts to multiples of Irish GNP and is the subject of significant tax evasion/avoidance which impacts as revenue lost in the Global South.

Financialisation

Financialisation results in global capital having increasing influence on national priorities. This is seen most clearly in the highly commodified Irish housing market where society is increasingly dependent on the market to meet their basic housing needs, leaving it highly vulnerable as demonstrated in the 2007 housing crash, banking crisis and economic crash, and consequent high numbers in need of social housing or homeless. More recently, the facilitation of international investment funds was managed through government policies and tax exemptions for Real Estate Investment Trusts (REITs), special purpose vehicles for global financial capital (Ó Riain, 2014; Hearne, 2017), with spiralling negative impacts including increased evictions and homelessness (Lima et al, 2022). These impacts are experienced elsewhere in the world as Irish investment plays its part in financialised global processes that contribute to social destruction. Aspects of Irish welfare are also highly commodified including health, housing, third level education and pensions. Commodification of child and elder care is discussed in Chapter 6.

Taxation in a financialised political economy

Base erosion and profit sharing (BEPS) are taxation instruments used by corporations to reduce their global tax bill to negligible amounts, sometimes to zero. Ireland's BEPS tools have played a significant role in attracting American multinationals to set up a base in the jurisdiction. These tools included the notorious, and now defunct, *double-Irish* which facilitated multinational corporations in shielding hundreds of billions of dollars in global profits from being taxed, anywhere. The Irish tool alone facilitated the avoidance of tax on €100 billion in global, multinational corporate profits in 2015. A case study of Malawi illustrates how the interaction of Ireland's debt and tax policies creates a complex and potentially devastating fiscal burden for countries in the Global South (Killian, 2015).

The practice of tax avoidance was so popular among American multinationals that, in 2016–2017, these corporations employed one-quarter of the country's private workers, paid 80% per cent of corporation and business taxes (over €8 billion) and made up 25 of the top 50 Irish companies by revenue in 2017. The American Irish Chamber of Commerce estimated that US investment in the country in 2018 was €334 billion, more than Irish GDP of €291 billion in 2016. It is in this context that the controversial Apple tax ruling came about in 2016. The European Commission issued a ruling that 'Ireland granted undue tax benefits up to €13 billion to Apple'.[3] The Commission ordered Apple to pay unpaid taxes between 2004–2014 of €13 billion plus interest to the Irish State, the largest corporate tax fine in history. However, Ireland, captured by corporatism, decided to appeal the ruling, rejecting what would amount to around 10% of Irish GDP. Apple joined the Irish government in its appeal and the General Court of the European Union reversed the Commission's decision. The case has been appealed to the Court of Justice of the European Union but, at the time of writing, the appeal is pending.[4] The case demonstrates the lengths to which the Irish political system and political elite will go to protect the interests of huge corporations over and above those of its citizens and the global community, particularly the Global South.

Contrary to this example, Irish expressions of neoliberalism and neoliberal policy preferences have more often been 'concealed, piecemeal, serendipitous, pragmatic and consensual' (Kitchin et al, 2012, p 1306) and are hued with visible manifestations of patriarchy. Political rhetoric is often subtle, making it more difficult to identify and agree the actual influence of neoliberalism on Irish policymaking, but it is present as an ideology, a project and a policy in defining Ireland's political economy. Marketisation and public–private partnerships are a well-documented part of the commodified welfare state (Murphy et al, 2020), while corporate welfare, fiscalisation and procurement are features of neoliberalism in the Irish welfare state (Murphy and Dukelow, 2016). The overall cost of tax expenditures has, for example, been described as 'a little explored policy wilderness' (Collins and Walsh, 2011, p 6) while the maldistribution of the €15.8 billion tax credits has significant gender and class regressive impacts, with only those earning high incomes able to afford the type of investment that enables them to benefit from such tax credits and from this highly commodified political economy.

2

From unsustainable environmental outcomes to a post-growth world

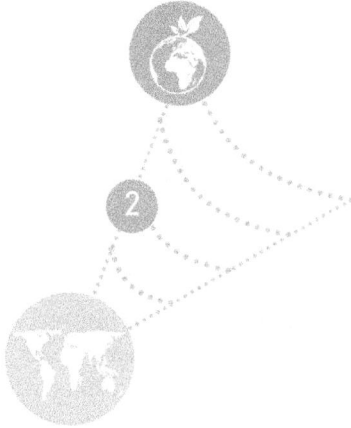

Chapters 2 and 3 are different sides of the same coin. They demonstrate the impact of the highly financialised and commodified global regime on the environment and the damages associated with dysfunctional treatment of animals, mindless travel and excessive consumption. This chapter explores the impact of this regime on the planet, and the following chapter examines the impact on society; the interrelated problems in both chapters require cojoined solutions. The collective impacts on both the planet's eco system and society cannot be overstated. We are approaching planetary tipping points which may be irreversible; global warming is triggering devastating impacts such as major ice melts and disrupted wind and ocean currents. Mitigating these effects will require radical transformation. Recent reports of the Intergovernmental Panel on Climate Change (IPCC) conclude that unprecedented transformation and implementation is required within this decade, and that a system change is now required (IPCC, 2022a). The cost of climate transition is already being felt more by those who can least afford and who least contributed to the problem (Gough, 2017), hence the need for transitional justice and welfare state intervention at a global level. Neither technological adjustments nor price mechanisms will achieve such transformation, whereas a post-growth orientation offers a potential pathway to decommodification (Hickel, 2021; Jackson, 2021). The chapter concludes by reflecting on how Ireland's political economy impacts negatively on local and global ecological sustainability and biodiversity.

How bad is environmental degradation?

Climate change refers to a range of complex issues and is integrally related to the concern with conserving and protecting our biodiversity and avoiding ever increasing species loss. More specifically, social environmentalists understand contemporary climate change as rapid global warming caused by humans emitting greenhouse gases (GHGs) and carbon dioxide (CO_2) into the atmosphere and oceans. Major concerns now encapsulated within climate change became dominant over the last 50 years, particularly since Rachel Carson's 1960's book and film, *The Silent Spring* (Carson, 1962). Following the publication in 1972 of the *Limits to Growth* report (Meadows et al, 1972), sustainability became a growing concern leading to the establishment of the Brundtland Commission by the United Nations and its 1987 landmark report (Brundtland, 1987). The issue of global warming began to gain some prominence in the early 1990s and, through various UN summits, began to dominate climate change discourse, accompanied by a focus on our dependency on fossil fuels (and awareness of reaching Peak Oil in the early 2000s). The concept of limits, while not universally popular, has been repopularised as a way of understanding planetary boundaries and human impacts on nature including oceans, nitrogen cycle and land use. There is now a better understanding of our individual and common ecological and carbon footprints. Globally we are consuming the equivalent of one-and-a-half planets to feed our insatiable greed, while we would need five planets if we all consumed the per capita consumption of America. Such consumption and damage are not equally generated, nor are its burdens equally shared (Gough, 2017, 2022). While this book focuses on climate change, there are other forms of environmental degradation across nine planetary boundaries. An ecosocial welfare system can also safeguard these other crucial bio-physical processes (Rockstrom et al, 2009; Raworth, 2017).

The World Health Organization (WHO) estimate that 24 per cent of global deaths are linked to environmental damage, with eight million deaths caused by air pollution annually. As the former UN Special Rapporteur on Extreme Poverty and Human Rights, Philip Alston, put it, this is an 'unconscionable assault on the poor' (2020). Inequalities underpinning these statistics are worsening over time. The concept of 'atmospheric commons' is used to measure who contributes to and who suffers the impact of climate change.[1] Countries representing 19 per cent of the global population create 91 per cent of carbon emissions and ecological damage: the USA (40 per cent), the EU (29 per cent), Russia and the rest of Europe (13 per cent), Japan (5 per cent), Canada (3 per cent), Australia (1 per cent). The Global

South suffers most of the impact of 'atmospheric colonialisation', bearing 82 per cent of the total costs of climate breakdown, estimated to rise to 92 per cent by 2030, and accounting for 99 per cent of the 530,000 annual deaths that will be caused by drought and disease as a result of climate change (Hickel, 2021).

Unequal causes of ecological degradation

It is a stark reality that climate change will impact most harshly between the tropics. The IPCC (2021) found that various climate and biodiversity thresholds are at tipping points or have already been surpassed. It was harrowing in its assessment: the harm that humans have caused to our habitat is 'unequivocal' and 'unprecedented'. Various visual aids illustrate such damage. Carbon 'footprints' and 'shadows' demonstrate the extent to which we collectively overreach sustainability and the degree to which the contribution to the global carbon footprint is so unequal between the Global North and the Global South: 81 per cent of growth since 1990 is generated by rich nations with impacts everywhere. Carbon Brief[2] analyses data from 70 peer-reviewed climate studies to show how global warming is projected to affect the world and its regions. By capturing the impact of climate change of 1.5°C, 2°C and 3°C (above preindustrial levels) on various aspects of nature or life sources, they highlight the inequality and unequal distribution of climate change impacts. Those with least responsibility, more often in the Global South, will suffer most, while those with the highest carbon footprints and who bear most of the responsibility, the Global North, will suffer least.

The Kim Stanley Robinson novel, *The Ministry of the Future*, opens with a description of a region in India that has suffered 20 million heat wave deaths in a two-week period due to extreme heat in the year 2050. In March 2022, fiction met reality when India recorded its hottest temperature since records began. Scientists affirmed that the record temperatures were caused mainly by human-induced climate change. Other causal factors included changes in land use, concretisation and deforestation. In the summer of 2022, it was impossible to work in many parts of India after 10am. Temperatures have been rising in India for decades and March, traditionally a spring month, now has temperatures as hot as mid-summer. Heatwave days (defined as above 40°C) have increased from 413 in the 10-year period 1981–1990 to 600 in 2011–2020 (an increase of almost 50% and representing 60 days, or two months of above 40°C temperature days per year). The extreme weather conditions disproportionately affect poor and marginalised groups who often work in labour-intensive jobs that require long periods of work outside. Workers in Dehli were forced to change working hours, working only before

> 10am in the morning and resuming in the evening when temperatures became more bearable. This causes a loss of hours and income. The vulnerability of India's workforce to increased temperatures cannot be overstated. Indeed, half of India's working population are farm workers and the second largest employer is the construction industry, both of which require long hours of labour outdoors.

Little surprise that the IPCC (2021, 2022a) escalated our understanding of the problem with the image of 'zone red' and declared a 'state of emergency'. It is unequivocal that climate change is caused by human activity and is already disrupting human and natural systems. This includes more frequent and intense extreme events beyond natural climate variability. A high proportion of species is vulnerable to climate change, and current unsustainable development patterns are increasing exposure of ecosystems and people to climate hazards. Reaching 1.5°C in the near-term, as we are forecast to do, will cause unavoidable increases in climate hazards and present multiple, existential risks to ecosystems and humans (Rassouk, 2022, p 5). Climate change impacts and risks are becoming increasingly complex and more difficult to manage as hazards occur simultaneously and interact with each other and with non-climatic risks, cascading across sectors and regions. Some impacts will be irreversible, even if global warming is reduced. Up to the 2022 COP 27, there was little progress in reparation. There has, however, been some progress in adaptation planning and implementation, but this is unevenly distributed, and the effectiveness decreases with increasing warming. This leads to lock-ins of vulnerability, exposure and risks that are difficult and expensive to change and exacerbate existing inequalities. Safeguarding biodiversity and ecosystems is fundamental to climate resilient development. This depends on effective and equitable conservation of approximately 30 to 50 per cent of Earth's land, freshwater and ocean areas, including currently near-natural ecosystems (IPCC, 2022b).

What needs to be done

It is clear to most that we are in a climate emergency. The real debate, about what to do and how to do it, has been rehearsed in recent COP meetings in Glasgow (2021) and Cairo (2022). These meetings are informed by alarming data and while they are not short of creative proposals, they lack real urgency. The Paris COP (2015) targets to keep warming to well below 2°C while aiming for 1.5°C continues to lack the political mechanisms to translate this urgent global target into action. The IPCC (2018, 17) reinforced the need for unprecedented transformation at a global level beyond technological solutions or carbon pricing mechanisms. In 2022, the Paris agreement rule book for implementation, action, and frontline adaption was advanced at COP 27 through adoption of a 'loss and damage' fund but this is not a full compensation mechanism.

The IPCC (2021) has begun to make their reports and its framing of the problem more accessible to both media and citizens, which, alongside increased political consciousness and global collective action of environmentalists, youth and faith groups, assisted in the unprecedented level of interest in and reporting of recent COPs. The bottom line is, despite acceptance that global emissions seem likely to rise by 16 per cent by 2030, there remains no collective agreement on how to limit global warming to less than 2.4°C, a potentially catastrophic level, particularly for the Global South.

However, it is important to recognise, and build upon, progress. The COP 26 Glasgow Climate Pact requires States to 'respect, promote and consider their obligations on human rights when taking action to address climate change' and notes the need to consult with indigenous peoples, local communities and other vulnerable groups including migrants, people with disabilities and young people. There is more articulation of 'system change' and 'climate justice', and awareness of exclusion, and gender and generation gaps in the democratic deficit concerning climate change. COP 26 also saw progress on stopping afforestation, cutting methane, phasing out coal, backing hydrogen fuel and more clarity about the functioning of carbon markets, while COP 27 brokered a loss and damage fund.

What would success look like?

The COP tends to be an exclusive and inaccessible process with insufficient respect for diverse voices (including indigenous peoples) and an inadequate focus on human rights. Avaaz (2021) observe progress in some states and find hope in local actions that are progressive, quick and agile. However, success, it argues, calls upon meaningful 'immediate, drastic, annual emission reductions unlike anything the world has ever seen'. This requires an end to all fossil fuel investments, subsidies and new projects, and an immediate ban on all new exploration and extraction. It also means an end to 'creative' carbon accounting and the publication of total emissions for all consumption indices, supply chains, international aviation and shipping and the burning of biomass. Success will also include delivery of the US$100 billion promised to the most vulnerable countries, additional funds for climate disasters and just transition, an enactment of climate policies to protect workers and the most vulnerable, a reduction in all forms of inequality and a commitment to including and respecting indigenous voices. This would amount to system change.

Situating arguments within the politics of economic growth

Returning to the focus on commodification and decommodification in the previous chapter, this book advances a vision of reducing the role of markets and money as a way to living within ecological limits while meeting human needs. Arguments for an alternative way to measure progress have been a mainstay of feminist and other civil rights movements for 50 years. New Zealand activist and Nobel prize nominee Marylin Waring long argued that unpaid work (usually performed by women) should be better recognised while activities that may be environmentally and socially detrimental should not be deemed productive. Bednar (2023, p 8) argues: 'we are both self-interested and prosocial, but we currently construct lives, families and meaning in a system that prizes maximising GDP, that elevates self-interest over collective and common interest'. While many echo such arguments and have been part of processes generating alternative, more comprehensive, indicators, the focus on GDP as the primary metric is still obvious. Little wonder that Raworth (2017, p 40) echoed Meadows' 1970s words: 'growth is one of the stupidest words ever invented by any culture ... we've got to have an enough'.

Gross National Product, the measurement for economic growth, no matter how much critiqued as an emperor with no clothes, remains the main driver of political ambition, with governments careful to reassure markets they are committed to economic growth. However, continuous growth has not trickled down to the poor. In fact, the opposite is the case, as global and intersectional inequalities increase. Growth, on which all capitalist models depend, is quickly reaching the limits of finite resources, particularly of oil, while growth's byproduct, greenhouse gas emissions, is threatening the habitat of both human species and biodiversity. Acknowledging such threats, 'green growth' is the dominant strategy at both the EU and the global level. This hegemonic strategy is based on technological hope. Governments and corporations pragmatically insist that they can achieve what is needed to address global warming through eco-efficient technological methods, that capitalism can innovate the type of technological change that can reduce emissions while increasing production and growth (Obersteiner et al, 2001). These technologies have not yet been invented.

Post-growth rather than technology as the answer

The 2018 report of the European Academies Science Advisory Council warns society to stop speculating about technological fantasies and get serious about deep and aggressive cuts to emissions. However, 'techno-optimism' is deeply embedded as an alternative to a post-growth world, and has found its way into global climate change policy (IPCC, 2014; Bregman, 2017). Technology will inevitably have an important, but limited, role in mitigating climate change (Gough, 2017, p 132). But technological solutions will not be enough and cannot replace a central focus on the objectives of equity, justice and ecological wellbeing. Placing these at the centre leads to questioning the compatibility of growth, over-production and over-consumption. Post-growth, as an alternative paradigm, leaves aside economic growth as a policy objective and focuses on ecological and human wellbeing, prioritising basic needs and reducing inequality (Hickel, 2021; Jackson, 2021). It pours cold water on techno-optimism and insists that green growth is not possible and, in some forms, not desirable (Hueseman et al, 2011; Hickel, 2021; Kirby, 2021).

Bednar encourages us to 'look beyond GDP as the North Star, and instead embrace the constellation that comprises social flourishing' (2023, p 12). Raworth's (2017) doughnut (Figure 2.1), described 'as a 21st century compass', offers 'a way of achieving balance and a world in which every person can lead their life with dignity, opportunity and community – and where we can all do so within the means of our life-giving planet' (Raworth, 2017, p 43). The concept of 'donut economics' outlines a safe and sustainable space for humanity by illustrating the nine spheres that together comprise our nine planetary boundaries[3] and the 12 domains of our social foundation which meet our social needs. This concept of balance is also reflected in the 17 United Nations Sustainable Development Goals (SDGs) agreed by 193 member countries in 2015. These common goals for humanity are to be achieved by 2030, with little progress yet evident.

There is debate about whether post-growth can be achieved within capitalism. Some call for 'open, creative, and diverse engagement' and are agnostic about whether ecosocial transformation requires the abolition of capitalism; as Fitzpatrick puts it, 'no one has the correct song' (2014, p 13). For others, post-growth is an ultimate destination, but much can be done to focus on meeting human needs even in the present capitalist economic model (Gough, 2017, p 87). Others insist that the focus should be on meeting needs and respecting 'limits' and are relatively agnostic about growth per se (Raworth, 2017). The latter approach is useful as it frames the core challenge of meeting needs within planetary limits. Regardless of the nuance, all agree that emergency action is required at a global level to meet needs within planetary limits (see Chapter 8 discussion on language and framing).

A post-growth paradigm requires definition of consumption levels that enable the Global North to stay within ecological limits. It must enable adaptation and mitigation, and provide adequate compensation for the Global South. This link between distribution and sustainability requires a political mechanism capable of delivering a global equity framework (a requirement

Figure 2.1: Raworth's doughnut

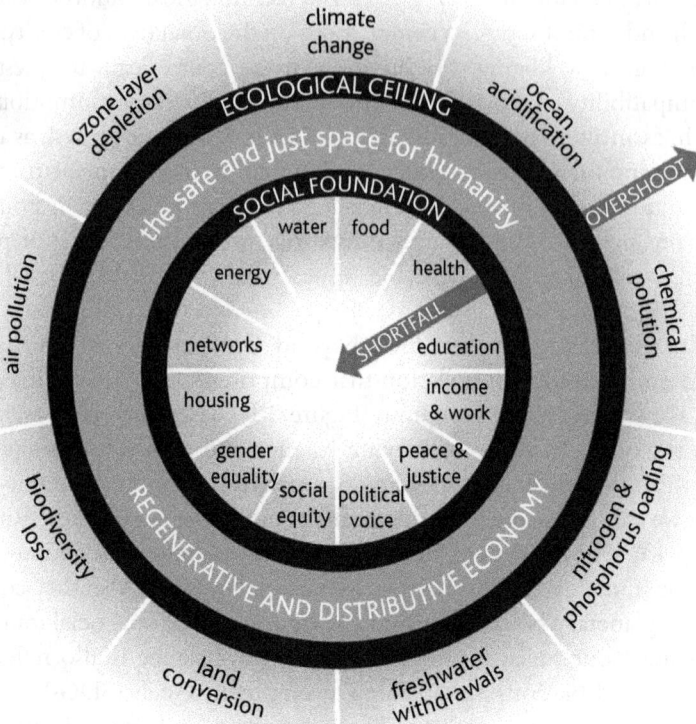

climate change
ozone layer depletion
ECOLOGICAL CEILING
ocean acidification
the safe and just space for humanity
SOCIAL FOUNDATION
OVERSHOOT
water food
energy health
air pollution
SHORTFALL
networks education
income & work
housing
gender equality peace & justice
social equity political voice
REGENERATIVE AND DISTRIBUTIVE ECONOMY
chemical pollution
nitrogen & phosphorus loading
biodiversity loss
land conversion
freshwater withdrawals

Source: Raworth, 2017

beyond the remit of this book). Gough argues these global mechanisms should focus on basic needs satisfaction, arguing needs are satiable and more likely to lead to lower emissions than policies that facilitate consumer preferences (2017, p 93). Policies will also need to enhance the eco-efficiency of production and address the sustainability and composition of consumption and demand in rich countries, with implications for global equity and for the duties, responsibilities and obligations of different nations (Gough, 2017, p 99). Equity and welfare sustainability must, therefore, be at the heart of climate change policy.

Equality: the other side of the coin

Tackling climate change through a post-growth lens offers the opportunity to address wider economic injustices that already exist, hence the calls for 'system change not climate change' (Klein, 2017). Such a transition would radically reform the taxation system, by, for example, shifting the burden from economic goods (such as incomes) to ecological bads (such as pollution). It would stimulate local economies, supplying as much of their needs from their own resources as possible, and develop strong public systems of transport and alternative forms of locally-based health care. Examples of institutional mutual aid and social provisioning arrangements are visible in studies of the past (Graeber and Wengrow, 2021), while many contours of a post-growth world are hiding in plain sight in contemporary welfare and public policy, for example, in universal pensions (Stamm et al, 2020; Murphy and Dukelow, 2021). Other policies are being prefigured in various political projects such as *The Future is Public* (Kishimoto et al, 2020). Remunicipalisation and local democracy is central to low carbon transition and energy democracy (Kirby, 2020), discussed in Part II and III).

COP 26 amplified the need to address inequality. The challenge is immense, requiring no less than radical transformation and environmental justice. Some recent responses to crisis (financial, pandemic, war, cost of living) offer some glimpse into temporary transformation towards a future scenario, some dystopian based on austerity and autocracy, others more democratic and inclusive. The challenge of climate change requires permanent adjustment, and we need to be sober in our assessment of opportunity for just transformation (see Chapter 7). Crisis tends to reinforce existing inequalities, exacerbating the central challenge in cutting global emissions while meeting basic needs for all, and underscoring the importance of being ready and organised for transformation, and the urgency of now.

Moving towards environmental justice

The IPCC (2022a) assert that the rise in weather and climate extremes has already led to irreversible impacts as natural and human systems are pushed beyond their ability to adapt. Approximately 3.5 billion people live in contexts that are highly vulnerable to climate change with the most vulnerable people, regions and systems disproportionately affected. Integrated, multi-sectoral solutions that address social inequities require differentiated responses based on climate risk (IPCC, 2022a). Addressing inequality is key. Concepts such as 'climate justice' and 'just transition' were clearly on the agenda of recent COPs. The just transition movement originated from the US trade union movement which argued that given polluting industries must change completely, transition to an environmentally sustainable economy should be just, and should address the livelihoods and wellbeing of workers in polluting industries. Just transition revolves around three core features: collaboration and trusting working relationships between national and regional governments, local authorities, workers, unions, employers and other stakeholders; local processes that recognise that each context is unique to the local or regional transitional goal; and proper funding and power are essential to enabling local affected communities to genuinely shape what happens.

Many argue that the concept of just transition has been co-opted by government and the fossil fuel industry as part of a process of green-washing (Rassouk, 2022). At the same time others have expanded the concept beyond workers' transition as a unifying concept inclusive of community and environmental justice that includes existing inequalities and moves beyond the provision of a narrow compensation package for workers displaced by transition (Mandelli, 2022) effectively reframing the role of welfare (Galgóczi, 2022, p 349).

The *Just Transition Alliance* adopts a wide concept of Just Transition as 'a vision-led, unifying and place-based set of principles, processes and practices that build economic and political power to shift from an extractive economy to a regenerative economy', requiring production and consumption to be waste free. Central to the wider environmental justice movement is a concern for environmental racism where communities of colour and low-income communities are disproportionately exposed to, and negatively impacted by, hazardous pollution and industrial practices. This is consistent with the principle of intersectional political economy described in Chapter 1 of this book. This approach stresses the need for bottom up organising, centred on the voices of those most impacted, and shared community leadership. The focus is not only on workers but on whole communities and strategies to build thriving economies that provide dignified, productive and ecologically sustainable livelihoods, democratic governance and ecological resilience.

For the international *Climate Justice Alliance*, 'transition is inevitable, justice is not'. Their 'Just Transition Principles' moves us towards Buen Vivir where we live well without living better at the expense of others. This wider vision creates meaningful work centred on the development of human potential and upholds self-determination and the right to participate in decisions that impact one's life. Equitable redistribution of resources and power leads to new systems that are good for all people and regenerative ecological economics that are economically and ecologically sustainable. This wider vision of Just Transition retains an inclusionary culture and tradition which makes reparations for land that has been stolen and/or destroyed by capitalism, colonialism, patriarchy, genocide and slavery. It embodies local, regional, national and international solidarity and is liberatory, transformative and interconnected. Such a vision has gained traction with the Canadian LEAP project and in many US cities (Klein, 2017) but has yet to become embedded on a global level.

Ireland's record on the environment

The University of Leeds project, 'A good Life for all within Planetary Boundaries', has charted country pathways of social achievement and ecological sustainability from 1990 to 2018 (O'Neill et al, 2018). Its assessment of Ireland shows that six of the seven biospherical boundaries measured have already overshot safe limits (CO_2 emissions, material and ecological footprints, land use change and phosphorus and nitrogen). This has significant adverse impacts on nature and biodiversity. For example, many species of terrestrial birds are at risk of extinction, including farmland birds. Less than 2.5 per cent of marine waters are protected, with sustainability of the huge wealth of marine biodiversity in Ireland now under threat.

Ireland's Climate Action Plan

Like the rest of the EU, Ireland is captured by a dominant technocrat green growth ideology consistent with financialised capitalism, the key driver of which is economic growth (Mercier et al, 2020). Until recently, Ireland repeatedly ranked among the worst in the European Union Climate Change Performance Index (Torney, 2020). Mitigation and adaptation face 'socio-cultural, governance, institutional, resource and physical barriers and resistance' (Sweeney, 2020, p 29). Dismal Kyoto Protocol emissions reduction targets were not met, while two decades of political divisions on carbon tax led to the issue being shelved with, until recently, no development of alternative policy instruments (Little, 2020). An absence of proactive policies left Ireland resorting to emissions trading mechanisms including purchasing emissions credit, a significant sign of policy failure. Little wonder Torney's (2019) analysis found Ireland 'a climate change laggard'.

Following pressure from the Irish environmental movement and citizen mobilisation, the government convened the 2017 Citizens' Assembly, entitled 'How the State can make Ireland a Leader in tackling Climate Change', and later declared a climate emergency. A 2020 Draft Climate Action Bill was weak on definitions, targets, carbon budgets, IPCC commitments, compliance and goals relating to biodiversity and environmental sustainability. Since then, a significant political shift demonstrated more ambitious national emissions reduction objectives in the Climate Action and Low Carbon Development (Amendment) Act 2021. Targets are to achieve a 51 per cent emissions reduction by 2030 compared to 2018 and a carbon neutral economy by the end of 2050. Legislative carbon budgets support Ireland's climate ambition with sectoral emission ceilings adopted in 2022. Ireland's Environmental

Protection Agency (EPA) is charged with monitoring the Climate Action Plan targets for environmental sustainability and in June 2022 it published its first set of projections related to the Climate Act's 51 per cent target. The report concluded that full implementation of all existing climate plans and policies, plus further new measures, are needed to put the country on track for carbon neutrality by 2050, and that there is a considerable 'gap' between all scenario projections and the 51 per cent target (EPA, 2022). Three key sectors consistently have the largest share of emissions: Agriculture, Transport and Energy Industries. Agriculture, and the agri-food industry, present the most serious challenges.

Agricultural emissions

The agricultural sector accounts for over 38 per cent of Ireland's emissions and appears underprepared in the context of the challenges of food insecurity, biodiversity loss and climate change (Oxfam and Trócaire, 2021). While emissions are projected to remain static in the sector, agriculture is projected to account for over 43 per cent of Ireland's emissions by 2030 (driven by reductions elsewhere in the economy). Agriculture sector emissions include methane emissions from livestock, manure management and soil treatment using nitrogen and urea, as well as fuel combustion from agriculture, forestry and fishing. While the national herd overall is projected to decrease by 6 per cent in the period 2020–2030, driven by a reduction in beef cow numbers of 30.1 per cent, methane emissions in particular will remain static due to an increase of 13.3 per cent in the numbers of dairy cows, which produce more methane, in the same period. This is driven by higher levels of profits per hectare in dairy farming, the increasing price of milk-related products, and the interests of the agri-food sector. Dairy farming also uses more nitrogen fertiliser, which is estimated to contribute to a 7.3 per cent increase in its 2030 use relative to 2020. Agricultural sector practices have already resulted in over 1,000 rivers becoming polluted by nitrates and, increasingly, by ammonia. Compounding the harms associated with agriculture and food production are increased use of carcinogenic weed killers and the unsustainable practice of importing cattle feed. While awareness is increasing of how our food production system contributes to greenhouse gas emissions, there is less awareness or consensus of how to reduce these emissions without negatively impacting on farm incomes. Given Ireland has little in the way of fossil fuel industry, the real challenge for Ireland in achieving a just transition lies in reducing agricultural-related emissions while also ameliorating impacts on farm incomes and rural communities (Mercier et al, 2020).

Weak enforcement of EU policy

The EPA reports significant barriers in the stringency and enforcement of environmental regulation in Ireland and raises concerns relating to water stress, wastewater treatment, carbon concentration and changes in forest cover. Ireland is the only EU country yet to fully transpose the 2014 Environmental Impact Assessment Directive. While a higher level of compliance with EU and national law would reduce objections based on environmental grounds, the Irish Office of Public Works consistently fails to do robust assessments or provide sustainable designs. Moreover, Ireland has been criticised by the EU for the penal and uncertain costs associated with environmental litigation (the most expensive country to do so in the EU) and the related aggressive targeting and threats to cut the funding of critical environmental NGOs (O'Sullivan, 2022).

Ireland is also the only EU country yet to fully transpose the EU Water Framework Directive. In 2022, the EU criticised Ireland's record on water across several grounds: water leakage rates in Ireland are one of the highest in the EU; 50 per cent of Irish urban waste waters are not collected and treated in compliance with the Urban Wastewater Directive; and domestic drinking water is not fully compliant. Furthermore, Ireland has 3,000 communities, 90 coastal areas and 7,000 kilometres of river that are designated as a 'flood risk' but there is no legislative imperative or funding to decommission these areas. Instead, post-flood rebuilding is permitted, with expectation of disaster relief contributing to lack of flood risk preparations.

The EU's approach to the circular economy prioritises production in a hierarchy with prevention followed by reuse, recycle, recover and disposal as a last resort. Ireland launched its first Whole of Government Circular Economy Strategy in December 2021, but, again, implementation and convincing the public of its merits may be challenging. Ireland only began to engage with a deposit return scheme for plastic and glass bottles in 2022.

Fossil fuel and energy industries

Major commercial emitters, as defined under the EU's Emissions Trading System, account for 25 per cent of Ireland's emissions. The sustainable business organisation, Business in the Community Ireland, in its Low Carbon Pledge, commits to achieving net zero emissions in the business sector by 2050 in line with government commitments. However, so called 'green washing' is a major barrier to accountable and transparent corporate investment strategies in Ireland and elsewhere. Assessment of the energy extraction policy and practice in Ireland's political economy model of the Corrib gas field highlighted the generosity of Ireland towards the multinational fossil fuel industry. Ireland not only made no demand for state shareholding in, or royalty payments for, any natural resources found, it also lightly taxed profit arising from the sale of natural resources, while facilitating access to both public and private land, policing and other resources (Afri, 2012; Slevin, 2016).

Ireland remains among the largest consumers of plastic and petro chemicals, by-products of the fuel industry and among the biggest global environmental challenges. It has the highest per capita plastic consumption rate in Europe with 35 per cent of all waste shipped out of Ireland for energy recovery elsewhere and 3 per cent (9 m of 300 m tonnes annually) ending up polluting the marine environment. The 2021 Wind Energy Ireland report, 'Endgame: A zero carbon electricity plan for Ireland', demonstrates that plans to eliminate fossil fuel from Irish electricity are achievable and that, when available, 100 per cent renewable energy is possible. However, this requires the political will to plan and invest in new grid infrastructure including a north–south interconnector and the implementation of Eirgrid's DS3 programme, Ireland's electricity grid operator's multi-year programme to reach EU renewable energy targets.

Optimism and despair

There are parallel reasons for optimism and despair. Some associate the Irish green movement with urban elites and assume it to be antagonistic towards rural Ireland. It has been associated with a pursuit of technocratic expertise and policy without any attempt to curb hegemonic power of industry (JCFC, 2020). Yet, reflecting on COP 26, O'Sullivan (2021) describes Ireland as a leader, with Irish Aid amplifying the voice of those most vulnerable and supporting adaptation and climate security. Torney (2020) also finds increased policy ambition. A 2022 Citizens' Assembly on Biodiversity recommendation for a constitutional amendment to protect biodiversity and for a range of protections to deliver 'substantive and procedural environmental rights for both people and nature' has potential to reframe this issue in the public imagination (Citizens' Assembly, 2022).

It is important to acknowledge progress and recent momentum (Torney, 2020). However, Ireland still lags behind international best practice and while there is more salient consensus on some of the policy responses to climate change, it is not yet regarded as a priority for voters or politicians (Little, 2020). Contemporary Irish capitalism relies on growth as a legitimating narrative. The challenge is to contest our entrapment in consumption and the growth myth (JCFC, 2020). This requires a political imagination that integrates the cojoined demands for justice and sustainability as the basis for a rejuvenated society. Our entire political imagination must undergo an ever deeper ecological conversion (JCFC, 2020, p 48).

3

From an unequal society to ecosocial welfare

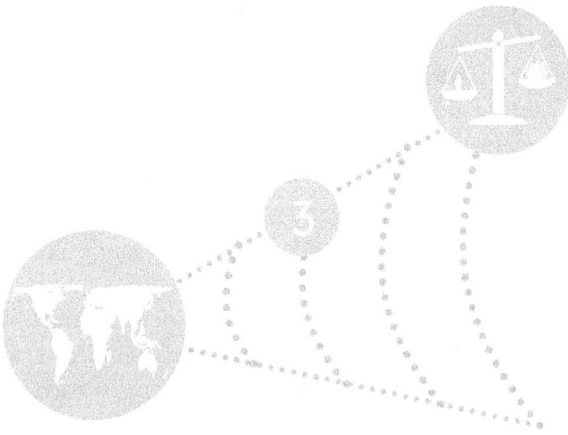

The contemporary global model of financialised capital not only leads to environmental destruction, loss of biodiversity and global warming but also, without doubt, leads to greater inequality (Piketty, 2014). The first part of this chapter focuses on inequality, itself unequally experienced across different groups in society and between nations. It explores how inequality intersects with the ecological crisis, increasing wants and fuelling consumption in the Global North, while leaving countries and people in the Global South vulnerable to poverty and ill-equipped to meet the challenges that climate change is already presenting. This is particularly true for women and girls who bear the worst impacts of both inequality and climate change. The second part of the chapter discusses tensions at the heart of welfare policy in the Global North. A less conditional and more enabling and flourishing form of careful social policy is needed to resource the scale of active citizenship required in an ecosocial state. The challenge is to redistribute and support work, income, time and democratic participation in a post-growth society and economy. The chapter concludes by reviewing the state of inequality and wellbeing in Irish society.

Social inequality

Inequality

The Oxfam Inequality Report is launched annually to coincide with the opening of the World Economic Forum summit in Davos, Switzerland, an annual gathering of the rich and influential. The contrast works. The Inequality Reports have become an important annual statement. Sobering statistics and memorable frames and images are used to illustrate the degree to which wealth is increasingly concentrated. The 2022 report highlighted how a new billionaire emerged every 30 hours during the COVID-19 pandemic, the same time it took nearly a million to fall into extreme poverty. There were 573 more billionaires in the world by March 2022 than in 2020, while a million people every 33 hours were pushed into extreme levels of poverty, 263 million people in 2022, because of the pandemic, growing global inequality and rising food and energy prices that have been exacerbated by the war in Ukraine. These Oxfam reports work as an excellent example of framing, discussed in Chapter 8.

Over a decade ago the book, *The Spirit Level*, demonstrated the corrosive impact of economic inequality. In more unequal countries, social impact outcomes are structurally worse for almost everyone in areas such as public health, education and social mobility. The level of inequality correlates much more clearly with social problems than either the overall wealth or the level of poverty in a country. *The Spirit Level*'s 2018 successor, *The Inner Level*, focuses on how inequality and one's place in the income hierarchy impacts on individuals and correlates unequal status with stress, anxiety, depression, addiction, unnecessary spending and ruinous gambling as well as physical symptoms of ill health associated with physical stresses. By contrast, people in more equal societies are more confident of their status, less vulnerable to advertising and less motivated by status purchasing. The market economy and economic growth in rich countries is part of the problem; once basic needs are met, increasing material wealth does not increase wellbeing. Reducing inequality can decrease consumption and directly contribute to emission reduction targets in a more egalitarian society that will contribute to climate sustainability (Wilkinson and Pickett, 2009, 2018).

Inequality is a core aspect of the ecological crisis. Greed and the pursuit of profit drives the neoliberal economic system. Concentration of capital creates powerful interests that, despite the clear knowledge that it drives carbon emissions, maintain a focus on the goal of economic growth. In 2015, 3.75 billion people lived on less than US$5.50 per day and 2.1 billion people lived in relative poverty, while in 2020, 735m people lived in extreme poverty with many more highly vulnerable with no defense against ill-health, or a failed harvest, drought, or flooding (World Bank, 2015; Oxfam,

2021). The extreme global inequality in wealth means the world's richest 1 per cent have more than twice as much wealth as almost half of humanity. Trillions of dollars of wealth are concentrated in the hands of a very small group of predominantly men. Billionaires, of which there were just 2,668 in the world in 2022 according to Forbes, have more wealth than 60 per cent (4.6 billion people) of the world's population. This level of wealth inequality creates extreme levels of power inequality (Oxfam, 2021, 2022, 2023) with clear class, gender, race and other status dimensions. The eight richest men in the world are all part of global media corporations with capacity to influence our ideas, democracies and daily lives. Their business model, based on the commodification of our attention, is driven by corporate greed and growth in consumption. Increasingly, algorithmic forms of advertising through social media drive humanity to consume insatiably beyond need and planetary limits.

Impacts of inequalities

The basic rights to a decent education or access to health care or housing has become a luxury to be purchased and remains unaffordable for many. This has profound implications, reinforcing intersectional inequalities across generations and regions, within and between countries. The pandemic demonstrated how extreme economic and racial inequality exposed vulnerable populations to an unequal threat from COVID-19, with severe impacts on their wellbeing and on their lives. The 2021 pandemic images of people desperate to buy oxygen canisters in India offered a real-time example of the cruel link between climate change, capitalism, commodification, poverty and inequality.

Poor people have lower life expectancy, dying 10–20 years earlier than people in wealthier areas, while the mental health fall-out of the chaos and instability associated with climate change includes psychological distress, climate depression, environmental grief, mood disorder and anxiety, as well as suicide. Post-traumatic stress disorder is directly associated with fire, flooding and extreme weather events such as hurricanes, particularly among the young, and extends to those suffering second hand, for example, those observing, studying or researching climate change (Wallace Wells, 2019, p 136). Climate change-related agricultural decline often electrifies political fault lines and causes forced migration, and political and social instability. By 2050, it is estimated that 200 million people will be displaced, rising from 70 million in 2017. Those left behind may fare even worse (Wallace Wells, 2019, p 127). The 2018 UN Global Compact on Safe, Orderly and Regular Migration links the adverse impacts of climate change and environmental degradation (natural disasters, desertification and loss of drinking water, degradation, flooding, drought, and rising sea level) with forced migration and lack of security where climate change can exacerbate existing tensions and conflicts. The Centre for Climate and Security fears that climate change will be the spark that ignites conflict in many vulnerable states.

The climate and care crisis and intersectional inequality

This merge of capitalist, colonial and patriarchal values results in a deeply unequal intersectional political economy (Folbre, 2021). We live in a global patriarchy where men own 50 per cent more of the world's wealth than women. The 22 richest men in the world have more wealth than all the women in Africa. Yet women's unpaid work is worth an estimated US$11 trillion a year, more than double that of the tech industry. As well as inadequate public services, there has also been a shift to outsourcing the delivery of public services to private companies, thus commodifying public goods and making them unaffordable to the poorest people, often women. This intersectional political economy is not only sexist but also racist and ableist. Low-paid female frontline workers are economically vulnerable and experience structural inequality. Commodification of care and welfare has amplified the care crises and intensified the scale of care penalties experienced by women in raced and classed terms (Folbre, 2021). Globally, women account for 70 per cent of frontline workers in the health and social care systems and carry out most of the unpaid care work in the home and in communities. Women were highly vulnerable to infection during the COVID-19 pandemic when intensification of women's unpaid care work was a 'driver of inequality' across wages, income, education and health (UN, 2020). A care crisis in Europe has negative implications for quality, accessibility, affordability and further widens inequality (Barry, 2021).

> Climate change is a manmade problem that requires a feminist solution. (Mary Robinson, in Harvey, 2018)

Eco-feminism has, since the 1970s, sought to develop awareness of the relationship between gender inequality, patriarchy and the destruction of nature. Over decades, feminist environmentalists shifted focus towards the Global South and non-western analysis and feminist political ecology made the links between states, markets and power more explicit. Women and girls' vulnerability is frighteningly pervasive. Buckingham (2020) draws our attention to the Bangladeshi floods in the 1991 Cyclone where 90 per cent of the over 140,000 deaths were women and children, explained by greater exposure to poverty, less value being placed on girls' and women's lives and to cultural norms, in this case women not being taught to swim.

Successfully engaging with addressing climate change also requires us to challenge existing social gender norms. Reimagining work, care and time can only happen by engaging with issues of power, voice, representation, alliances and coalition-building. This requires the inclusion of everyone experiencing exclusion, including queer and trans people, Black minority women, indigenous women and disabled women. Yet, reality is demonstrated in exclusive processes like the Glasgow COP in November 2021 which was memorably described by Greta Thunberg as 'male, pale and stale'. The ecosocial state needs a shecosocial foundation.

In 1984, while living and working in London, I participated in the Greenham Common Women's Peace Camp, a series of activist camps established to protest nuclear weapons being placed at a Royal Air Force Base in Berkshire, England. The camp began in September 1981 after a Welsh group, Women for Life on Earth, marched to Greenham to protest the decision of the British government to allow nuclear cruise missiles to be stored there. Remaining there to continue their protest, they began a camp that was active for 19 years, and which only disbanded in 2000. There is now a memorial to the creative, inspired, determined, energetic women who used collective actions, human chains, fence cutting, posters, art and songs to inspire global action against nuclear missiles. 1984 was also the year of the UK miner's strike. It was the confluence of these that taught me the importance of joining the dots when miners' wives came to Greenham Peace Camp to distribute food donations left over from the miners' protests. Class and gender intersected with colour, ability, race and sexuality. The images in this book are inspired by a spider's web symbolising the fragility and perseverance of the Greenham women and the importance of a shecosocial analysis.

Reimagining social protection as ecosocial welfare

A new social settlement: reimagining welfare in a post-growth world

Since the late 1800s, the Global North's welfare regimes have mitigated the damage of capitalism, and the worst excesses of poverty and inequality, often treating the symptoms but not the cause of these social ills. Originally an instrument to address the immediate causes of absolute and relative poverty, the late 1940s post-war settlements are associated with more contemporary redistributive welfare states and were oriented to decommodifying citizens, making them less dependent on the market (Coote, 2015; Button and Coote, 2021). While national welfare regimes focused to different degrees on policy objectives of stability, poverty reduction and equality, all had some decommodification functions. Since the shift to neoliberalism in the late 1970s, the function of welfare has shifted from decommodification to recommodification. Most welfare states are now on the defensive and it is clear to many long-standing promoters of welfare policy that it is time to reimagine welfare (Pierson, 2021).

This is not to throw the baby out with the bath water. Undoubtably, the welfare state is still needed to perform crucial roles in meeting need or social provisioning and to provide 'income security, income buffers, social services and social investment' (Gough, 2017). In the context of ageing societies, the changing nature of work and automation, as well as the challenges of climate change, a new model of the welfare state needs to focus on addressing inequality by (re)distribution (Pierson, 2021). Welfare policy must enable populations to survive new social risks, including automation and particularly climate change and transition to a post-growth world. The theme of ecosocial policy is rarely discussed in social policy and the study of welfare states rarely engages with issues of sustainability, except to focus narrowly on how objectives of equality and redistribution of resources can be balanced with fiscal sustainability (Matthies, 2017; Bohnenberger, 2020; Coote and Percy, 2020; Stamm et al, 2020). As Hirvilammi and Koch (2020) argue, the contemporary welfare settlement, based on a supply-oriented growth strategy, has, to date, failed to consider the urgency of the environmental crisis. The wider discipline is at best relatively silent or more often validates economic growth as the primary mechanism to redistribute resources.

Share the wealth

The Share Our Wealth movement began in the US in 1934, during the Great Depression. Huey Long, a left-wing governor from Louisiana, made a national 'Share Our Wealth' speech on radio, calling for massive federal spending, a wealth tax and wealth distribution. Millions mobilised, joining local Share Our Wealth clubs and influenced the content of Roosevelt's Second New Deal. While it is not clear where they got their inspiration, in November 1998 a Share the Wealth rally was organised in Ireland by seven national networks engaged in combatting poverty: the Irish National Organisation of the Unemployed, Irish Rural Link, One Parent Exchange and Network, the Irish Traveller Movement, the Community Workers Co-operative, the European Anti-Poverty Network and the Forum of People with Disabilities. They protested about the national disgrace of poverty in the midst of a booming economy, and to demand basic rights, and a decent and just society. It is ironic that just 20 years ago speakers at that Dublin rally had to learn how many zeros were in a billion. There are nine zeros in a billion. Twenty years later, wealth is counted in trillions, there are 12 zeros in a trillion.

Ecosocial policy unpinned by capability approach and values

Ecosocial welfare focuses on the intersection of social policy, welfare states and environmental issues, questioning the centrality of growth, employment and state control over individuals. The focus 'needs to be on satisfaction of basic needs for all humans now and in the future', and the 'integration of social and environmental policy implementation with a focus not only on carbon emission but on redistribution of work, time, income, and wealth' (Hirvilammi and Koch, 2020, p 3). With exceptions, social policy and related disciplines have long neglected their disciplines' reinforcement of economic growth. Ecosocial transition implies a radical transformative process of society's role in a sustainable future. This requires engagement of academics, civil society and policy makers (Matthies, 2017, p 22).

Capability approach

A normative framework underpins all welfare settlements, and is found in mixes of liberalism, equality, human rights, capability and other development theories. The capabilities approach (CA) (Sen, 1999) informed the understanding of structure and agency that contributes to this book's approach to power (Chapter 7) and is underpinned by valuing human autonomy and democratic participation. CA develops the human rights approach and argues that human development requires consideration of not only what resources are available to people, but also what are people actually able to do, and to be, in a given social, political and economic context.

Capabilities are defined as 'the real freedom to lead the kind of life people have reasons to value' (Sen, 1999). To achieve wellbeing, capabilities need the input of resources (materials such as income, goods and services), conversion factors (skills) and social conversion factors (social norms and institutions). This draws attention to aspects of the social and political system, including participation and democracy. Socio-economic vulnerability can therefore be the result of a lack of resources, constraining conversion factors and/or lack of free choice.

The classic example is that even if one has a resource, such as a bicycle, this is only useful if one has the conversion factor (the skill to cycle), or the social conversion factor (someone to teach you how to ride the bike, or a paved pathway to cycle safely).

Directly linking rights and capabilities, Nussbaum's (2005) ten 'central capabilities' are fundamental human entitlements inherent in the very idea of minimum social justice, including participation and imagination, discussed in Part III of this book. The IPCC (2022a) stress the importance of enabling conditions as key to transition and include political commitment and follow-through, institutional frameworks, policies and instruments with clear goals and priorities, enhanced knowledge on impacts and solutions, mobilisation of, and access to, adequate financial resources, monitoring and evaluation, and inclusive governance processes.

Needs and values

Sustainable welfare, informed by the understanding of sustainability in the 1987 Brundtland Report as 'development that ... meets the needs of the present without compromising the ability of future generations to meet their own needs', incorporates both limitations and needs. The degree to which our needs and wants differ is clouded by the degree to which capitalism through culture, media and advertising has successfully extended commodification into a realm of previously unknown 'wants' such as high-status branded goods, fashion, leisure, social networks and social media, and even non-fungible assets including ownership of digital artwork and avatars. This produces new markets with capacity to create new forms of social damage, alienation, social anxiety and ill health.

Life does not need to be like this. Many non-capitalist societies have lived according to the principles of sustainability, consciously meeting needs and ensuring that what they produce or generate is sufficient but not excessive (Graeber and Wengrow, 2021). Basic psychological needs for a flourishing life include autonomy, belonging and competence; these correlate with basic values (Lelkes, 2021). Without an underlying sense of safety and security that such needs will be met, people will find it hard to reach into their inner capability to take personal risks, to adapt and to transform. Welfare policy is in this sense vital and central to enabling individual and systemic transformation (Lelkes, 2021, p 174). Such needs are objective, plural and non-substitutable. They are satiable, cross-generational and offer a basis for building sustainability targets for public policy. We have an ethical obligation to use needs as a moral compass so that 'needs satisfiers have priority over surplus goods that meet our wants or preferences' (Gough, 2017, p 47).

In the late 1990s and early 2000s, I represented a national antipoverty organisation in national policy committees examining social protection policy. One high-powered committee began with an overview of the purpose of the committee and its terms of reference. One civil servant argued forcibly that we should park any discussion of values and simply retrofit a statement on values into the final report. Having failed to convince the committee of this approach, the committee spent time ensuring the statement of values informing its work would be consistent with values affirming the status quo; equity or fairness was always preferable to equality, while simplicity, transparency and value for money were standard tropes informing many such deliberations. Such values ensured no disruption of the status quo, which served those benefiting from the present welfare settlement. We need to talk about the values that people really believe in.

A focus on needs and values can inform which institutions and capabilities are needed to underpin a new social contract. Fundamental system change is needed to shift norms and tackle the centrality of contemporary 'wants' that traps us in an 'iron cage of consumerism' giving rise to discontentment and materialism as a way of life (Jackson, 2021, p 91). An ecosocial settlement can capacitate society to adjust consumption patterns and adopt new policies on work, care and time (Hirvilammi and Koch, 2020). The content or contours of an ecosocial settlement are informed by the values that might unpin a new welfare settlement. Schwartz theorises that humans are open to a balance of change (novelty), conservation (tradition), self-enhancement (self) and self-transcendence (other) (Raworth, 2017, p 108; Jackson, 2021, p 96; Lelkes, 2021). The challenge is to accommodate such creative tensions and maintain balance. Higgins (2021, p 280) argues for the relevance of moral sentiments such as care, trust and friendship and the centrality of principles of mutuality, reciprocity, redistribution and cooperation in the flourishing of our economic and social life. The doughnut in the previous chapter (Figure 2.1) is a model that promotes balance, as opposed to growth.[1]

First steps

The concept of ecosocial transition refers to the efforts of policy makers, activists and researchers towards creating sustainable changes both practically and conceptually (Matthies, 2017). However, 'research on welfare states has mostly been carried out at a rather abstract and conceptual level while more nuanced questions about alternative welfare systems remain underdeveloped' (Bohnenberger, 2020). Cautioning against overly specific policy prescriptions or institutional solutions is logical – the speed, scale and uncertainty of change means attempting to prescribe policy is 'fool hardy'. The alternative is to develop the future through experimentation and discovery to figure out what works in an environment of constant change (Raworth, 2017, p 30). While accepting this logic, it makes sense to elucidate at least the contours of and first steps towards an ecosocial welfare settlement.

We can define and discern ecosocial policies either in light of their intentions or their impacts (Mandelli, 2022). Both require a recognition that integrating social and ecological objectives reduces the welfare systems reliance on economic growth. Four primary ecosocial or sustainable strategies are identified as: prevention; economic equality; meeting basic needs; and green employment. These also generate co-benefits including gender equality, work-life balance, community building and reduced material impact (Bohnenberger and Fritz, 2020, p 3). While the specific focus of this book is on two ecosocial welfare instruments and policies, services (Chapter 5) and income support (Chapter 6), these are only two of multiple ecosocial tools relating to many welfare dimensions (see, for example, Table 4.1 in Chapter 4). Schoyen et al (2022) and Galgóczi and Pochet (2022) recently published innovative ecosocial welfare reflections.

The contemporary political, economic and social settlement is associated with temporal and spatial derivation and controls on our collective space and time – an 'ecosocial account of poverty' must address these aspects of life (Fitzpatrick, 2014, p 88). Building from the previous chapters, the 'Policy ingredients for a post-growth ecosocial world' box captures a non-exhaustive but wide range of policies, including, but wider than, ecosocial policies that could form the basis of a post-growth world (Gough, 2017; Hickel, 2021, pp 210–25). We need more time for living what are likely to be more locally-focused lives (Schoyen et al, 2022). The vignette on page 54 attempts to illustrate daily life in an ecosocial world, a life that is strangely familiar, but perhaps easier and more inclusive. Seeking to avoid overly prescriptive blueprints but offering compass points and first steps, Part II of this book focuses on enabling institutions, Universal Basic Services and Participation Income (the bold content of the box). The fiscal and political feasibility of such reform is discussed in Chapters 4 and 9.

Policy ingredients for a post-growth ecosocial world

- Maximum individual and national carbon budget thresholds.
- Minimum and maximum incomes, pay and income ratios.
- Reorientate from 'growth' and exchange value to use value within ecological boundaries.
- End intentional or planned obsolescence; extended warranties on products, right to repair, lease models to include modular upgrades by industry.
- Bans on advertising and excessive marketing, liberating minds to think and imagine.
- Shift from ownership to usership, promoting a sharing economy.
- End food waste.
- Scale down ecologically destructive industries, end fossil fuels.
- Public job guarantees and living wage for socially useful work; reduce working hours; triple dividend increased quality of life; reduced unemployment and reduced ecological pressure.
- Reduce inequality, introduce living wages.

• Tackle wealth inequality and fund commons through a solidarity wealth tax and high tax on breaches of consumption thresholds.
• Promote equal care work both for each other and the planet, the right to care for to be cared for.
• Nurture institutions that support people and communities to live sustainable and valued lives.
• Support participation by valuing and rewarding socially useful work and participation.
• Collective consumption through sustainable welfare and universal basic services.
• Decommodify public goods and expand the commons; improving the welfare purchasing power of incomes; end dependence on needing higher incomes to access the things needed to live well.
• End temporal and spatial deprivation and controls on where and when people work (conditionalities, remote working, four-day weeks, right to work part time).
• Debt cancellation for the Global South.
• A new money system, for exchange not commodity speculation, ending compound interest.
Sources: Hickel, 2012, pp 210–225; Fitzpatrick, 2014, p 88; Gough, 2017; author

Social inequality in Ireland

Building on the earlier discussion in this chapter, this section seeks to understand the nature of Ireland's welfare state and the societal challenges of this rich but unequal country in the Global North. The 2020 KOF Globalisation Index, which measures the economic, social and political dimensions of globalisation, ranked Ireland as the fourth most globalised economy in the world. Chapters 1 and 2 rehearsed Ireland's open financialised global political economy. Here we examine the welfare state as part of that political economy and the social impacts of it.

Poverty and inequality in Ireland

The Irish welfare state (discussed in more detail in Chapter 4, and in the Appendix) is predominantly liberal in character but mitigates significant levels of market-related inequality. Social welfare payments and the statutory minimum wage fall short of a minimum essential standard of living. Light-touch employment regulations combined with the lowest market wages in the OECD means up to one-third of the workforce are low paid, with many also experiencing precarious working conditions. This market inequality is levelled up quite considerably by an effective tax and transfer system so that net inequality is close to the EU norm. According to the 2020 Survey on Income and Living Conditions (SILC), 13.2 per cent of the population were living below the 60 per cent poverty line (at risk of poverty) of €14,402 per annum. Consistent poverty (those both at risk of poverty and who experience material deprivation) was at 4.7 per cent of the population, while those experiencing material deprivation (unable to afford at least two of the 11 goods or services considered essential for a basic standard of living) reached 14.3 per cent. Ireland has also embraced a policy of labour market activation in which welfare claimants are pressured into low-paid employment. Despite near 'full employment' Ireland's overall employment participation is low, particularly for people living with disability. The labour market is unequal and highly gendered and racialised with significant intersectional inequalities particularly for women of colour, disabled women, migrant women, indigenous Traveller women and other ethnic minoritised women. Spatial and socio-economic discrimination, and class, contributes to an increased likelihood of experiencing poverty and inequality, even for those in employment.

> Emer and her school friends, Ana and Tori, as teenagers visiting France were intrigued by the statement of values displayed over every school gate and public building. Reflecting on the clarity with which the state affirmed foundational values of liberty, fraternity and equality they wondered what corresponding Irish values might be and where they might be found. The Irish constitution provides a statement of values but with significant ambiguity. Irish conceptions of equality, freedom and democracy are often mediated through the lens of patriarchal family, private property and theocratic power. Recent referendums have focused on asserting the value of children's rights, marriage equality and reproductive rights. Future referendums have been called for to value care, homes, water and nature.

The Irish welfare state was and is traditionally oriented around Church provision of all forms of health and social care, primary- and second-level education, and other social services, with largely family-based but gendered provision of non-institutional care. Social conservatism around distributional politics alongside the state's ideological commitment to social disinvestment embedded a low income tax effort per capita. This meant that there was insufficient revenue for investment in the welfare state, while revenue raised was used disproportionately to pay for income supports. This low income tax per capita policy was embedded in the political economy and reinforced historically poor public service provisioning. A form of 'vicious cycle' emerged with pressure on income in the form of wages and transfers as citizens needed income to purchase in the private market the gaps left by the absence of public services (Hearne, 2017). The inability to capture tax revenue pressured existing public services such as social housing which, since the 1980s, is increasingly met through the market. The significant tax and transfer redistributive welfare policy brings net inequality down to the average in the EU and the OCED but this costly welfare system combined with a low-income tax effort means there is little revenue remaining to invest in public services. The long-term underdevelopment of public services leads to a combination of costly subsidies and tax reliefs to enable the purchase of private market services (in pensions, care, housing, education and health).

Inadequate public services

The highly intense use of taxes and transfers to mitigate market inequality translates into a lack of means to invest in public services, leading to commodification of, and often unaffordable, eldercare and childcare. The absence of public investment in all kinds of child, elder and social care has profound gendered impacts. Women are among the groups most likely to be living in consistent poverty (including single parent households, predominantly headed by women). Lack of access to key public services including housing, education, health and public transport tends to reinforce inequalities. These fault lines were fully exposed throughout the pandemic, particularly in relation to care, health and gender inequalities. House prices are unaffordable for many while private sector rents are increasing beyond the reach of poorer people, and this has translated into record levels of homelessness of both adults and children in 2022. Women, Travellers, lower income groups and people with poorer health status were most likely to have an unmet need for health care.

The basic reality of poverty, inequality and absence of any meaningful provision of public services leaves many feeling insecure as they face the possibility of just transition that is simply unaffordable. Climate change policies including retrofitting of accommodation and shifting from petrol/diesel to hybrid/electric cars are out of reach for many, and are unrealistic policy goals. In practical terms, many low- to middle-income households feel disempowered and lack capability to make any kind of climate transition. These dynamics are intensified in 2022 by the biggest rise in inflation rates in decades. It is in this context we must understand the challenge of just transition for Irish society. The National Economic and Social Council (NESC, 2020a) describe just transition as a powerful idea, aiming to leave nobody behind. Those most impacted, or most vulnerable, must be supported to embrace the transformation. Just transition means using the principles of justice, fairness, equality and equity to act as a lever and guide to shape policies and practices. Despite this positive framing, just transition in Ireland is relatively narrowly interpreted, less associated with climate justice themes, and often focuses on the concerns of the labour movement and upgrading skills for workers in high carbon–emitting sectors. The wider social consequences of poverty and inequality are less considered, particularly from a gendered and intersectional perspective or from the perspective of those most vulnerable and already left behind.

Environmental (in)justice in Ireland

A recent report, commissioned by the Irish NGO, Community Law and Mediation, examined environmental justice in Ireland, defined as 'the extent to which the physical and economic burdens of pollution and degradation ... are equitably distributed across society ... and the degree to which [the most vulnerable communities] can access and participate in relevant decision-making processes' (O'Neill, 2022). Applying this lens highlights the differentiated experiences of the burdens of climate change, pollution and energy poverty across different socio-economic groups, and shows that lower socio-economic groups face distinct vulnerabilities to the effects of environmental degradation and the policies implemented to address it. A central aspect of environmental justice is that all those affected by a decision should be involved in the decision-making process. However, low-income, migrant and Traveller participants in the study reported that they were largely excluded from these important decisions (this has also been reported in studies related to political processes more generally (Cullen and Gough, 2022)). These communities are particularly vulnerable to energy poverty which needs to be addressed in inclusive ways that support low-income households in private, rented and social housing settings. Retrofitting is also crucial but, while there are provisions in legislation to accelerate this process, it will take Dublin City Council 12 years to retrofit its stock of social housing at current funding levels. Marginalised communities are also disproportionately affected by flood risk and air pollution, estimated to account for over 1,300 deaths in Ireland per year. Access to public services like transport and environmental amenities such as trees, litter control and parks is also unevenly distributed with some communities particularly affected by 'transport poverty'. Women, migrants and Travellers experience exclusion and discrimination on grounds of gender, race, ethnicity, language and residency status but these are not yet seen as environmental justice issues and these groups often find themselves excluded from key decisions as a result.

Morning to evening in an ecosocial state

Ruth starts her day cycling through her local town, noticing that the pothole near her house has been repaired by the local authority. Her 22-year-old son went to the local sports project earlier where he supports local children, funded by his Participation Income, and her 24-year-old daughter went to her four-day week job in the local authority-delivered public crèche. Ruth then visits her elderly father who lives in the community-managed nursing home. After a swim and a workout in the public recreation centre, she attends a local authority consultation on plans for environmental protection and waste management and water. In the afternoon she goes to her own job in the local primary school where she works in special education and engages with other public services in social psychiatry. Part of her work that day is to make a submission to the National Consultation on Social Services. She is interested in economic democracy and wants her union to have more regulatory, supply and fiscal responsibility. She thinks this will improve her life as a worker and as a citizen who might need social services.

After her part-time work, she attends a free local class on preventative health and finds out more about her local services for care and rehabilitation, home care and treatment of alcohol and drug abuse. She is interested in career progression training. In the evening, she volunteers teaching English in the local authority-run service for integration of refugees. She hopes to bring the refugee she is working with to the local museum and other local tourist and cultural attractions, including the local art collective where participants are supported by Participation Income. On the way home, she has a pint with a friend and makes a plan to get tickets to see their favourite band. Home and tired, she remembers to sort her different recycling bins for the weekly co-op collection. Late at night she reflects on how lucky she is to have the security of her long-lease cost-rental home and hopes at least one of her children will choose to move out but stay local. She feeds the dog, Fred, and heads to bed.

PART II

Building an ecosocial imaginary

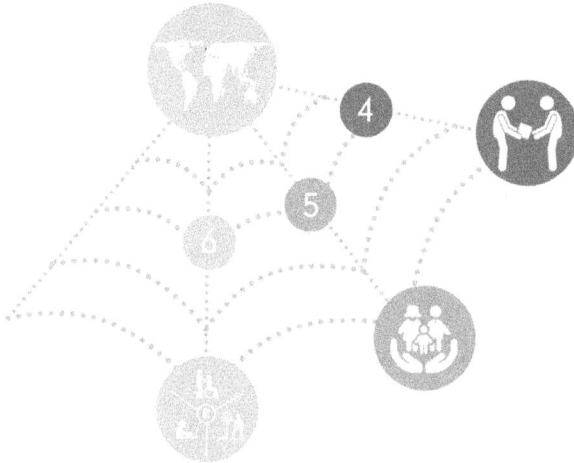

Part I of this book argued that the contemporary capitalist political economy's destructive impacts on both environmental sustainability and society underpins the urgent and compelling need for transformation. The case for an ecosocial state is manifold, from the obvious perspective of climate change, but also from the wider perspective of systemic change. Our political economy models and our related worlds of welfare capitalism are deficient, failing to secure gender and other equalities, socio-economic justice, health and wellbeing, social reproduction, democratic participation as well as sustainable ecologies. The case for change is altogether stronger from these multiple perspectives and demands a comprehensive politics of transformation embracing recognition, redistribution, representation and sustainability (Fraser, 2013).

Part II attempts to apply the theory to practice and link welfare reform with the urgent need to decarbonise the economy and pursue other environmental goals including biodiversity. While a variety of policies are needed, as illustrated in the 'Policy ingredients for a post-growth ecosocial world' box in Chapter 3, the focus here is on three core options:

- An enabling institutional infrastructure to enhance the eco-system of people's lives and limit our collective dependance on the market to deliver core services and supports.
- A foundational economy as a network of provisioning systems for satisfying basic and essential needs and a way of meeting our collective needs through a system of Universal Basic Services.
- A Minimum Income Guarantee, a form of Participation Income, to enable participation in socially useful activity and life choices consistent with a post-growth world that values and supports care, reciprocity, mutual interdependence and democracy.

4

Reciprocity and interdependence: enabling institutions

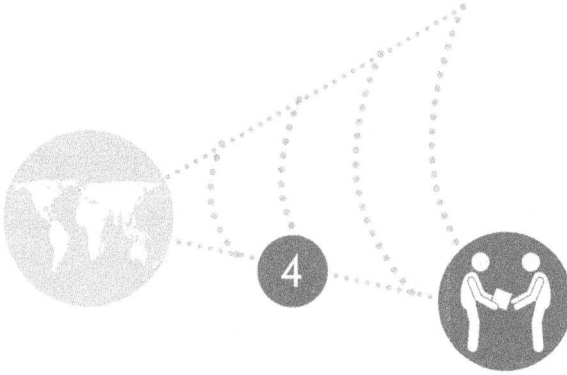

There is an interdependence between people's agency 'to do and be' and the societal, culture and structural institutions that mediate their lives (see Chapter 7). An anthropological view of humanity illuminates how survival and flourishing are generated through three functions: distribution/ production (the market economy); redistribution (the state); and reciprocity (society, community, kin). A reimagined welfare system needs to address these three roles. While market production and purchase are the primary vehicle of survival in capitalism, reciprocity and redistribution remain embedded features of contemporary societies and imaginative reform can draw on mechanisms to integrate welfare into the tissue of social interdependence.

'We cannot save the world by playing by the rules, because the rules have to be changed' (Thunberg, 2019). Institutions are 'the formal and informal rules, norms, precedents, and organisational factors that structure behaviour' (Pomey et al, 2010). As humanly-devised constraints and enablers, they structure our political, economic and social interactions (Folbre, 2021, p 23). They influence our opportunities to be and do what we value, while also enabling and constraining our agency, and unequally impacting on different social groups often exacerbating social divisiveness. A new ecosocial paradigm needs to resituate freedom and liberty and generate substantive equality through collective reciprocity and mutual aid. New institutions need capacity to promote new norms, or revive old ones, that can counter behaviours and beliefs that maintain myths of individualism, competition, consumption and selfishness (Folbre, 2021; Jackson, 2021).

This chapter establishes the need for a balanced ecosocial settlement (Button and Coote, 2021). The first part focuses on how institutions might creatively balance reciprocity, freedom and our collective interdependence. The second part discusses how particularly local institutions need to reimagine work and care, enable or facilitate autonomy, and work collaboratively through a culture of co-production, collaboration and participation. This rebalancing requires a rethinking of activation policy as a tool for just transition. Enabling institutions are needed to facilitate socially useful and environmentally sustainable work, enabling social inclusion policy and employment in the care and social economies (Dukelow, 2022). This theme is explored in the Irish case study in the third section of this chapter.

Values, welfare institutions; reciprocity, collective freedoms

Capitalist and for-profit market institutions emphasise material incentives and pit our egoist and social selves against one another, shaping negative perceptions of others as competitors (Bednar, 2023, p 10). Privilege and disadvantage are deeply coded in structures and social institutions (such as public services or legislation). These organise and internalise norms of behaviour and socialise how we perceive the world, socially engineering both cooperation and competition (Folbre, 2021, pp 33, 84).

What social institutions are needed to generate the norms and values that would underpin a post-growth ecosocial world? The political settlement and practical design of welfare states has always had to grapple with whether or how the rights associated with state welfare provision could or should be tempered with responsibilities or obligations, and how this tension can be reconciled with objectives of equality, freedom and reciprocity. This has also been and remains a central tension in non-capitalist societies (Graeber and Wengrow, 2021). Institutions and networks that support innovation and transformation should be 'highly connected, flexible, porous, cultural and creative infrastructure' and should be building blocks for nurturing values (Leicester, 2020, p 108).

Freedom

Freedom is creatively understood as both an individual and collective concept that includes three freedoms: to move or relocate; to disobey; and to reshape our social reality (Graeber and Wengrow, 2021, p 503). Freedom is often conceptualised in the context of personal autonomy but the assumption of autonomy may be a false one that undervalues our mutual interdependence (Knijn and Kramer, 1997). A useful perspective on freedom is to understand it in relation to the market (Konczal, 2021). Too many important policies are democratically regulated to enable the free market to determine our lives, effectively forcing us to live in market societies (Kirby, 2020). Arguing against over-dependance on markets, Konczal (2021, pp 7–10) argues market distribution does not enable society to match what is needed to live lives that are valued. Freedom can be understood as what society chooses to keep free from the control of the market, or to keep free of the market. People have always sought limits on markets as a way of preserving and extending freedom and sought to decommodify land, labour, time, care and income as a way of creating a free society (Konczal, 2021, p 179). Regulatory rules can be rewritten to restrict market dominance of or decommodify these key areas of life (Stiglitz et al, 2015).

The contemporary welfare state reaches deep into the social order, influencing the organisation of everyday life and, within that, gender relations through care work and welfare or social security and public services. It permeates all resources and power, both micro and macro, personal and political. Patterns of control and relations of authority link the design of the payment or programmes and micro-level behaviours and outcomes (Daly and Rake, 2002, p 167). Chapter 1 discussed how the early development of capitalism was associated with the destruction of communal welfare institutions including the commons, and an enforcement of a new form of work, not to meet needs (based on use value), but to enable the extractive profit (based on exchange value).

A core question for freedom is what do people need to live flourishing lives across time, health, housing, transport, care, pensions, education, water, utilities and other services and infrastructure (Konczal, 2021).

Reciprocity

A core norm associated with human sociability is reciprocity. Reciprocity implies humanity would freely care for each other, even when strangers (Graeber and Wengrow, 2021, p 516). Human relationships flourish when people give as much as they receive. Many of us already thrive in reciprocal lives, doing things, including care, freely (Solnit, 2016, p xv; Hickel, 2021). Formally through citizenship, taxation and welfare redistribution, and informally through reciprocal relationships, our open-ended mutual obligations can join us together to sustain the social order (Kirby, 2021, p 124).

Differing ideological positions stress the role of reciprocity or mutual aid as a positive underlying feature of welfare policy. For some, reciprocity is an essential norm for legitimating welfare and taxation; people are required to contribute productively to the common good as far as they can (Lister, 2020). Corresponding obligations to make a productive contribution to the community in return for support require the obligation to contribute to be scaled to ability (Hillamo, 2022, drawing on Kenworthy and

Bothstein). Such reciprocity norms are only valid in societies which are just, for example, significant poverty, insecurity or domination limits the legitimacy of obligations (Hillamo, 2022). White (2010) offers the concept of 'fair reciprocity' as a guiding principle for policy, not only in the case of conditions for welfare eligibility but also against accumulation of wealth and as a justification for a tax on inheritance, land value and wealth. He justifies the principle of contribution arguing as long as expectations to contribute are reasonable, reciprocity is consistent with social rights. In this context, contributions are interpreted widely and include unpaid work including care work. Others understand humans as strong reciprocators and inclined to large-scale cooperation, but with diverse cultural norms of reciprocity depending on the structure of the state, market and society (Raworth, 2017). Promoting reciprocity as mutual aid and a form of solidarity means embedding it as a value in institutions (tax, welfare, family codes, local government), but also allows for promoting some forms of competition alongside collaboration and cooperation (Jackson, 2021, p 171).

Pre-capitalist indigenous American communities,[1] with diverse forms of political economy, experienced little tension between ensuring significant personal autonomy, liberty, freedom, and collective well-being. Their institutional arrangements enabled mutual aid, communal provision and a range of forms of collective ownership. The key for guaranteeing autonomy was to ensure sufficient mutual aid such that no one was subordinated to another, so that mutual aid or reciprocity supports individual freedom. Rather than the 'possessive individualism' associated with the narrow legal definition of property we understand today, in non-capitalist society, private property or ownership, both collective and individual, also brought with it caring obligations, meaning care for each other and nature, or non-productive modes of production, were built into the political economy (Graeber and Wengrow, 2021, pp 161, 189).

Reimagining work and freedom

Capitalism broke the link between reciprocity, freedom and work. An early feature of capitalism was new legislation forcing people to work in the emerging labour market. The first Vagabond Act in 1531 introduced the earliest and cruellest form of workfare, under which King Henry VIII sentenced 72,000 people to death. In 1547, King Edward VI branded vagabonds with a 'V' stigma and sentenced them to two years of forced labour. Second offences were punished by executions and applied to 400 people annually in the 1570s. Over time, this enforcement stripped work of meaning, pleasure, talent and mastery, and paid work based on exchange value became a 'natural' part of life (Hickel, 2021, p 75).

Five hundred years later the redistributive nature of the post–World War II welfare state is under sustained challenge from neoliberal ideologies, manifested in marketised welfare and narrow but substantive conditional obligations and sanctions that systemically reduce individual and societal agency, and effectively commodify welfare (McGann, 2021). Micro welfare conditionalities exert unreasonable conditions and dominate our experience of 'mutual or reciprocal obligations', curtailing our freedom to choose decently paid work or other forms of socially useful work including care. Governments since the 1980s have placed emphasis on forms of work conditionality including workfare (requiring that all welfare claimants work for their payment) and activation (requiring that claimants engage in activity to enhance capacity to access paid employment). The English word 'free' is derived from a root meaning friend (Graeber and Wengrow, 2021, p 187). Freedom and reciprocity are relational and deeply intertwined even if these ties are weakened in contemporary welfare states where policy forces competition between the two. These experiences of work conditionality and commodification lead people, quite understandably, to reject principles of mutual obligations and seek more freedom in contemporary welfare policy.[2]

To eliminate employment conditionality we need to reconceptualise the type of work we value. Policy currently values and obliges productivist paid employment (the many critiques of this we will not rehearse here). A post-growth ecosocial welfare state promotes a wider understanding of work as a valued and diverse, necessary human activity. In *The Human Condition* (1958), Arendt distinguishes between labour, work and action. By 'labour' she means the daily natural sphere of human activity: what we do to consume enough energy to stay alive. By 'work' she means the domain of artificial activity, our construction of durable artefacts beyond nature, the construction of which require craft and skill. By 'action' she means how we communicate and make sense of ourselves as relational or political beings, how we express and 'authorise' our lives. One can reject a narrow vision of conditional paid employment while seeing 'work' as an integral part of the post-growth world, a position Dukelow (2022) argues is consistent across a range of authors who validate 'good' work. Care work is both paid and unpaid and arguably more of such work should be renumerated as paid employment. The 'right to work' or our commodification may still offer freedom from unpaid work, familial entrapment and dependency on family or kin (this is discussed further in Chapter 5).

Reciprocity and collective freedom

Identifying how policy can better support our interdependent lives requires a focus on our collective rather than individual freedoms. Unpacking the relationship between reciprocity and collective freedom illuminates a false polarity between 'structure and freedom'; both are needed and we should creatively navigate tensions between the two goals (Leicester, 2020). Conditional workfare and narrow productivist activation should not be part of ecosocial welfare but thinking about the tension between freedom and reciprocity in a less binary and less individualistic way helps us to understand real freedom. Freedom in this context can be understood as our ability to enhance collective wellbeing, this understanding of freedom relates to both reciprocity and solidarity (Kirby, 2021). Thus, an ecosocial settlement should be social in nature and help fulfil 'claims to freedom' in a complex society 'through being and doing, rather than having and controlling' (Fitzpatrick, 2014, p 6). It can also mean freedom from the market (Konczal, 2021). Prioritising collective solidarity over individual freedom allows us to approach social and climate justice as a collective endeavour based on our mutual interdependence. Reciprocity, understood this way, is not a burden but a necessary enabling function which helps us to live the best life that we can. The pandemic demonstrated how our lives are still very much dominated by our reciprocal relationships and we value community, solidarity, reciprocity and participation for our social reproduction. Many of us value, want to, and do, live our lives in reciprocal relationships achieving positive forms of freedom and life. Policy needs to affirm and support this value.

There is, understandably, fear associated with any form of continued mutual obligations, particularly ones attached to income support on which the poor are more reliant. Mutual interdependence is counterintuitive for many who have fought and continue to fight against corrosive welfare conditionality. At the same time, commitment to the care of others and our ecology has never been entirely voluntary and institutions have been historically necessary to nurture reciprocity and cooperation (Folbre, 2021, p 163). The argument here, to use the 'baby in the bathtub' metaphor, is that in throwing out the water (welfare conditionality), we should not throw out the baby (reciprocity).

Building institutions

As the world has dealt with societal challenges and various crises associated with war, pandemics, economic crashes and natural disasters, we have seen some experimentation with collective post-growth policies that give some insight into how we might flourish in a finite world. More turbulence can be expected in the context of the fourth industrial revolution – digitalisation and automation – as well as demographic, migration and climate change-related transitions. In such acute uncertainty we need flexible and adaptable institutions as well as a society that has freedom, autonomy and capacity to act and adapt. Any combination of working-age ecosocial policies can be part of an ecosocial state that facilitates autonomy and democratic control, supports the classic functions of welfare, redistribution, social consumption and social investment and reimagines the relationship between work, welfare, time and care (more policies are necessary to meet child and elder needs, and wellbeing). The working age range of ecosocial policy possibilities are captured in a non-exhaustive way in Table 4.1. Two core building blocks of an ecosocial regime are discussed in the following chapters on Universal Basic Services (Chapter 5) and Participation Income (Chapter 6).

Table 4.1: Diversity of working-age policies in an ecosocial welfare regime

Promoting autonomy and democratic control	Redistribution	Social consumption	Social investment		
Enabling Institutions	Cash Income	Consumption services	Distribution of paid employment	Distribution of non-paid work (care, ecological, democratic)	Active labour market policy
Capacity building and integrated delivery	Universal Basic Income; Transition Income; Participation Income	State services including care	Minimum/ Maximum incomes	Childcare infrastructure	Enabling Public Employment Services
Navigational agency	Social insurance and income tested income support	Free consumption goods	Paid work equality policies	Taxation policy and carbon budgets	Capacitating education and training
Community innovation, initiatives, institutions	Taxation (income, wealth, consumption and environmental)	New forms of public innovation and ownership	Four-day week and reduced working time	Time equality parental care policies	Ecological and other sustainability projects
Local government/ local democracy	Quasi-currency vouchers	Needs vouchers	Regulated decent part time/ remote/ flexible work	Shift vouchers	Decent work, employment protection regime

Source: Murphy and Dukelow (2022, p 515)

There are many ways to build a welfare state (Konczal, 2021, p 112). The following section explores aligning state and social institutions, recognising and valuing the ambivalent tensions and dilemmas between the two. It is crucial to leave room for conflict in that relationship while also striving for symbiotic innovation in enabling just transition (Leicester, 2020). Underlying institutional principles of an ecosocial regime include strong local democracy, enabling institutions and navigational agency, support for social reproduction and gender equality and collaborative and coproduced policy.

A strong local democratic state

An ecosocial state facilitates and enables an active society without rolling back on the fundamental role of the state as a provider of last resort and a guarantor of human rights. The relationship between government and democracy, and the balance between individual and collective freedoms is crucial. Such institutions must be accountable, transparent and trusted by people. Strong local democratic institutions and local and municipal government or governance are supported by strong local capacity including taxation and legislative autonomy which foster trust, participation and equality. We expect a creative tension between local representation and informal and formal spaces and places, fostering local deliberation and participation. Theories of municipalisation and communalism stress the primacy and immediacy of local provisioning of need, while theories of subsidiarity (which holds that decisions should be taken as close to the individual as possible – local, national or supranational) are a strong feature of EU policy. Assessment of the strength of local government across Europe demonstrates the wide variability in local government powers and functions. For most European states, strengthening the power of local government is a key aspect of building the architecture of a facilitative ecosocial regime (Ladner et al, 2015).

Navigational agency

Welfare can never be reduced to money (and in-kind services) but also requires solidarity, opportunity and empowerment. A focus on reciprocity also means promoting capabilities to broaden educational and economic opportunity as well as institutional innovations to enable people to participate in achieving their own wellbeing, while also contributing to others. Central to this are institutions like Active Labour Market Programmes and Further Education and Training which can enhance social inclusion, navigational agency (Claasen, 2018) and participation in socially useful or valued activity through support for local communities, cooperatives and civil society (Dukelow, 2022). Such institutions are often 'hiding in plain sight' (Stamm et al, 2020, p 51) as policies with potential ecosocial and inclusion value, and include job-guarantee and other mechanisms that connect welfare and local grassroots economic activities and blur the lines between heteronomous and autonomous work. Adult and community education can lead approaches linked to emancipation, active citizenship and autonomous agency as well as personal and community development that can also deepen and widen democracy. Local education is particularly emancipatory for key oppressed groups and can enhance conscious raising and building of intersectional solidarity across different issues and peoples.

Social reproduction and care

Debates about the welfare state have always had a reproductive subtext (Folbre, 2021, p 159). If people have direct responsibility for one another then every able-bodied person has a place in the caring economy. Policy should reward and distribute paid and unpaid care work equally between women and men, and intergenerationally (through different mechanisms including, for example, paid paternity leave and four-day working weeks). Ideologies of maternalism permeate welfare institutions where some women (spouses and partners) have only derived rights to benefits via their husband's entitlements. Welfare policies sought to preserve and perpetuate the nuclear family, an institution that, in delivering unpaid social reproduction, served industrial capitalism well. Feminists emphasise gendered moral rationality as an alternative to individualism and arguments for a traditional 'moral economy of the poor' do likewise (Higgins, 2021). Gender equality must be coded into institutions, policy and practice.

A 'careful' project of state-building is best guided by feminist theories of leadership. This ensures equal participation across various statuses (for example, gender, ethnicity, age and sexuality), and ensure feminist values and an ethic of care are embedded in institutional processes. Moral rationality understands care as constituted by relationships and connections between givers and receivers of care. When relational assumptions guide policy there is a focus on 'connective tissue' to better understand the interdependent nature of our lives and how welfare is not just a set of services but a set of ideas about society, including social reproduction and family life (Cullen, 2021; Barry, 2021; Folbre, 2021). An ecosocial welfare regime makes care and equality a guiding principle for policy and practice, and promotes principles of autonomy and economic independence for women. Individualism is a normative principle often associated with neoliberalism, commodification and a market society but is different to the normative principle of individualisation which seeks to free women from familial traps associated with male breadwinner welfare. Individual rights to income and services are not a celebration of individualism but are promoted in the interests of gender equality (see the vision of ecosocial care that follows).

Co-production and collaboration

Encouraging deliberation and wider forms of democratic participation such as co-production and collaborative governance processes involving citizens, workers and service users are found in a 'high-energy democracy' with high levels of mobilisation of diverse forms of participation (Unger, 2009; see Chapter 9). An ecosocial state enables and maximises the capacity of society to actively and collectively co-produce policy and practice. The validation of different forms of knowledge, including experiential knowledge of workers and service users, is found when a state proactively values citizens as active contributors with agency to think, act, judge and participate. Co-production affirms citizens' agency in creating public value from the programmes they participate in and depends not just on the interactions between service users and frontline professionals but wider social systems in which they are embedded (Larruffa et al, 2021). This state respects that citizens' voice and participation can enhance service quality and efficiency, allowing problems to be understood in more nuanced ways and promoting trust and ownership. An enabling approach fosters institutional norms whereby workers in public institutions (particularly local and municipal government) are positively rewarded for facilitating such participation and where local network governance arrangements facilitate robust partnerships between public providers and community-based organisations (Larruffa et al, 2021), as found in Danish municipalities as well as in Scotland, Netherlands, Finland and Ireland. What follows in the 'Principles for collaborative governance' box is a list of the principles for collaborative governance developed by the Community Platform in Ireland (Community Platform, 2022).

Principles for collaborative governance

- Leadership, with a real willingness to engage and a belief that the process will lead to better outcomes.
- Early trust building and processes to support dialogue and deliberation.
- Identifying power differentials and transparent motivation for engagement from all participants.
- Collaboration with relevant stakeholders, and innovation in supporting different forms of participation.
- Co-design and shared decision-making.
- Informed and deliberative approaches and processes valuing relevant expertise and lived experience.
- Flexibility and innovation and linking mechanisms to the issue specific purpose they are required to serve.
- Willingness to adequately resource collaborative processes.

- Commitment to early planning, transparent, accountable implementation & monitoring mechanisms.

Source: Tools for Collaborative Governance; Community Platform Discussion Paper, 2022, Dublin

The feasibility of ecosocial welfare: fiscal and political

Rejecting dominant values of rationalism, individualism, consumption and competition is not simple. The dilemma is well captured by Streeck's assertion that

> a central issue of political conflict is precisely how far efficiency may be allowed to govern social life and where the zone of social protection begins, in which social relations are to be governed by obligations rather than by contract, by responsibilities to others rather than to self, by collective duty rather than individual voluntarism, or by respect for the sacred as opposed to the maximisation of individual utility. (2017, p 208)

Reimagination of welfare towards greater decommodification requires adjustments in norms, behaviours and attitudes,[3] and a fundamental rethink of care, work, income and services (Hillamo, 2022). The process of decommodification, prioritising society over the market, offers opportunity for changes in how we understand our relationships and interdependence, and offers new subjectivities making transition more possible. Enabling institutions can also be a source of enabling subjectivities, working to reaffirm or reinforce solidarity, mutual aid, collaboration and cooperation, and facilitating more equal and caring societies that offer opportunity to redistribute work, care and time between and across gender, ethnic and other marginalised groups.

Taxation policy is located within power and political choices, and reflects the nature of the social contract between the state and citizens. Central to the challenge of reimagining the welfare state is to imagine funding welfare without an underpinning assumption that economic growth will increase revenue and facilitate greater expenditure. Human rights-based approaches lay emphasis on the definition of the state as a duty-bearer with obligations to maximise resources to progressively realise human rights. Human rights principles observe both 'obligations of conduct', such as maximising available resources, and 'obligations of result', such as progressively realising human rights. This relates governments' fiscal policy and taxation choices to the world of equality and human rights, both domestically and internationally.

While challenging, funding ecosocial welfare is affordable and realistic, particularly if we tax wealth and related high value consumption and limit corporate tax evasion. Oxfam (2023) calculates that a wealth tax of 2 percent on the world's millionaires, 3 percent on those with wealth above $50m, and 5 percent on the world's billionaires would raise $1.7 trillion dollars annually and, amongst other outcomes, lift 2 billion people out of poverty.

Wealth, in all its forms, also remains a source of inherited inequality (Pierson, 2021). Global inequality in wealth and power is both reinforced and hidden by elaborate tax evasion and avoidance strategies, some legal, some illegal, but all immoral and unethical. Governments, fearing capital flight, leave wealth untaxed, with only 4 per cent of tax revenues originating from taxes on wealth. While recent OECD and EU policy processes have agreed a global minimum corporate tax rate of 15 per cent, more can be done to eliminate significant loopholes and accounting practices that enable corporate tax avoidance. Challenging extreme wealth inequality requires taxes on wealth in its most obvious forms: property ownership and luxury consumption. Wealth taxation can be both a mechanism for (re)distribution but also for revenue, replacing the taxes on labour that may be lost in the context of a shift to a post-growth economy and society (Fitzpatrick, 2014; Picketty, 2018; Pierson, 2021). See the discussion in Chapter 9 on money supply and quantitative easing.

Shifting the focus of welfare to equality and sustainability requires political imagination and courage (Pierson, 2021, p 134). However, we already have many of the tools that we need to effect this ecosocial future. These are as diverse as carbon taxes, political apparatuses, new agricultural practices, capacity for public investment in green energy and carbon capture, wealth taxes and ecosocial policy (Wallace Wells, 2019, p 226). Increases in life expectancy in the Global North require social care to be revalued and centred in the welfare state, while the changing nature of work requires the 'disarticulation of a whole complex of income – work, security, housing, pension – that binds contemporary welfare states together' (Pierson, 2021). There is likely to be generational, gendered and other forms of contestation, with winners and losers and political consequences: 'losses of privilege are always more keenly felt than rather generalised increases in well-being' (Pierson, 2021, p 134). Contestation is not easy when agency is stifled by structure. In the Global North, marketised welfare policy is systemically reducing societal agency and potential for political contestation or a 'double movement', while the absence of safety nets in the Global South undermines capacity to respond to societal inequality and social risks (Polanyi, 1944; Kirby, 2021) but we are in a climate emergency (Hirvilammi et al, 2023). There is much to lose, but there is more to gain.

Seeds of the future: Ireland's welfare institutions

National institutions and politics matter in explaining welfare trajectories. Some variables such as globalisation, regionalisation and marketisation are experienced in different ways in smaller, more vulnerable political economies, and social security is an important automatic stabiliser in the context of volatility and crisis. Ireland's welfare institutions are often described as a hybrid version of a liberal regime as opposed to the UK's more classic liberal version (see Appendix). Historical breaks in path dependency (for example, an expansionary trajectory in the early 2000s) demonstrate that transformative change is possible (Murphy and Dukelow, 2016).

Ireland is a small, highly centralised sovereign state, where policy implementation is challenged by weak local government. Ironically, this has led Ireland to experiment with potentially transformative local processes of networked governance. The consensus-oriented proportional electoral institutions both constrain and mitigate neoliberalism, balancing elements of coercive commodification with a social democratic hue. The tendency towards corporate power-sharing embedded in national policy analysis processes like the National Economic and Social Council has facilitated moments of macro reflection and welfare imagination with potential for transformation. The challenges for developing facilitative institutions and practice – structural, cultural and practical – are significant but there are 'pockets of the future in the present' (Leicester, 2020, p 41) and seeds for transformation embedded in the Irish welfare system – some historical, some new – that provide a way forward.

Irish values and welfare institutions

Ireland has been described as a *passive-aggressive* welfare state which often appears somewhat of a paradox in contemporary times. The impacts of the welfare state are mixed, with Ireland enjoying high placement in many international non-economic league tables on key aspects of human development like the United Nations Human Development Index, yet at the same time flirting with the bottom of league tables for tax effort and investment in public services. Despite considerable wealth, many of Ireland's citizens and residents cannot exercise basic rights to housing, health or care services and are forced to depend on market provision of services while experiencing significant commodification and financialisation of everyday life. Contemporary levels of trust in the institutions of the state are relatively high in the European context. This is evident in, for example, the very high levels of vaccination against

COVID-19 with over 95 per cent of the over 12s fully vaccinated in 2022. A November 2021 IPSOS Global Trends survey, which included Ireland for the first time, illuminates some interesting trends. A relative absence of nostalgia means less of a sense of loss than elsewhere, and less sense of reactionary populism. Yet this is tempered by the realisation of urgent problems including of inequality, climate change and dangers of overpowerful social media companies.

So, while like elsewhere, political parties in Ireland are the least trusted political institution (Edelman, 2022), Ireland, while increasingly vulnerable, has not yet succumbed to far-right populism. The proportion of people who say they are very proud of their country (82 per cent) has grown over the last few decades (in contrast with Britain's stagnant 58 per cent). In 1991, foreign-born residents amounted to 7 per cent of the Irish population. The figure for 2022 has doubled – 13.8%. Being an immigrant society, with a fluid type of emigration and a historical and contemporary familiarity with travel and living abroad might explain why two-thirds of people appear comfortable with migration and globalisation. However, consistent with other European societies, a sizeable one-third of people express anti-immigrant sentiments and the far right are actively mobilising anti-migrant sentiment. Ireland's young population (with an average age of 38 and the youngest population in the EU) have over the past decade led Ireland towards social change that, even 15 years ago, seemed unimaginable. It is in this context that arguments for a new welfare imaginary for Ireland need to be understood. If hope is a political position, despite all the challenges explored in this book, Ireland, a relatively young and increasingly diverse society, often feels a hopeful place.

> Reflecting its theocratic and patriarchal origin, Ireland's welfare state was historically a strong version of a male breadwinner state, or a largely careless welfare state (Cullen and Murphy, 2017). Pressure associated with 1970s feminist mobilisation combined with reforms required for European Community membership to modify the male breadwinner system led to a range of gender equality-oriented reforms. However, significant male breadwinner legacies remain in the Irish tax and welfare system. A 'careless' form of male breadwinner activation requires availability for full-time work and, in 2014, activation for lone parents was introduced. Women, young people and migrant workers dominate essential low-paid sectors and experience flex-insecurity. With a weak care infrastructure, care is sourced from private or familial rather than public spheres, leaving lone parents, 86.4 per cent of whom are female, experiencing a very high risk of poverty in both regimes. Welfare policy has slowly modernised but has yet to individualise more fully.

Transformative change?

Substantive developmental change throughout the 1970s and early 1980s was arrested during the protracted 1980s recession, but the Celtic Tiger decade of growth over 1996–2006 was a period of social investment and catch-up. This was abruptly interrupted in 2008 by the financial crisis and subsequent austerity regime. A recent glimpse of transformation is seen in Ireland's income support response to the early onset of the pandemic where Ireland's consensus-oriented political culture innovated a generous income support – an individualised €350 PUP – for those who lost work because of pandemic-related restrictions. This compared to the core social welfare rate of €203 per week. This more generous rate was administrated ex post with a suspension of activation requirements. The pandemic experience highlights how, in the context of an emergency, new approaches can be designed and implemented quickly. Such rapid innovation suggests that disruptive or innovative forms of policy change are a feasible feature of public sector reform in welfare regimes (Hick and Murphy, 2021).

Seeds of the future found in the present

Crucial welfare state institutions that bridge society (people) with state (welfare) and market (work) include Public Employment Services (PES), Active Labour Market Programmes (ALMP) and Further Education and Training (FET). All need to be reoriented from their functional labour market roles to a wider developmental role that includes career navigation and facilitating navigational agency to open new forms of participation enabling individual and community level transitions. Enabling participation in new forms of work and valorising different forms of agency and activity requires, for example, that we rethink how concepts like activation may have post-growth application (Dukelow, 2022; Johnston, 2022).

Ireland has had some innovative experimental policy and practice. Its ALMP, the Community Employment programme, for example, is an outlier in Europe given the degree to which it is embedded in local not-for-profit organisations and focused on social inclusion (Dukelow, 2021), while senior citizens are universally entitled to a range of free public services including a medical card, public transport and a household benefits package that includes a winter fuel allowance and a TV license.

Present reflection on future challenges to the sustainability and capacity of Ireland's welfare regime focuses on the changing nature of work in the context of both the digital economy and climate justice. This will require disruptive transition, adaptation and carbon reduction and mitigation policies. New forms of work, including new forms of remote work, and particularly digital work, blur distinctions between paid and unpaid work, bringing with it new social risks but also possibilities for supporting and valuing new and existing forms of participation outside the formal paid labour market, while using social security income to support such participation.

Rethinking activation away from its role as a route to productivist, commodified, paid employment and towards an institution that facilitates social inclusion through socially useful activity was discussed as a Participation Income by the National Economic and Social Council (NESC) in 2020 and influenced the text of the National Climate Action Plan (Government of Ireland, 2021, p 44) which, while limited in its overall vision for ecosocial or sustainable welfare, does argue that employment activation policy will play a key role in providing opportunities for people at the margins to be part of Ireland's transition to a greener economy. 'Developing additional community-based projects and supported employment places in green sectors will provide opportunities for individuals to contribute and develop new skills and experience.' Action 17 commits to 'Create additional community workplaces and supported workplaces in green sectors for people who are economically inactive, long-term unemployed, and/or with severe needs.'

5

Universal Basic Services

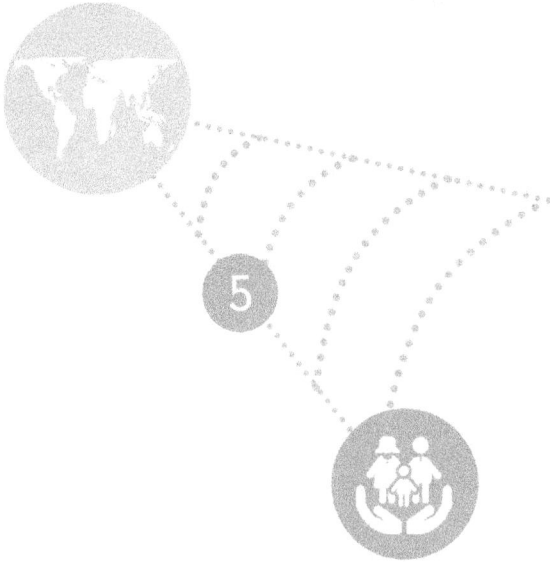

Building on Chapters 3 and 4, this chapter examines how to best meet people's basic non-substitutable needs, and to do so in ways that enable ecological and societal wellbeing. Some needs, clothing, for example, can likely appropriately be met within the scope of the market, but many needs are best provided through state, social or collective mechanisms. Reducing collective consumption offers the best potential to reduce emissions and safeguard natural resources, while also being key to more equal outcomes (Gough, 2017). The chapter draws heavily on the concept of Universal Basic Services (UBS) (Coote and Percy, 2020; Coote, 2022) which are key to reducing reliance on the market to satisfy essential needs and are a central building block of a more decommodified ecosocial state. The first section of the chapter argues for the importance of collective needs and against market provision, it makes the case for reciprocity, and state, society and economic democracy, all of which can be promoted through UBS. The second section of the chapter further clarifies the concept of UBS, unpacks the functions of the state and uses care services to ground the discussion of UBS. The Irish case study offers a blueprint for UBS and universal care in Ireland.

Arguments for UBS

Satisfying collective needs

An ecosocial welfare state has two broad, mutually reinforcing objectives: ecological sustainability and reducing all forms of societal inequalities (Coote, 2022). Previous chapters outlined how the post-war welfare settlement embodied and enhanced social solidarity by pooling resources, sharing risks and collectively providing essential services according to need and not ability to pay. This was underpinned by a deep value: the principle of reciprocity that underpinned rights and obligations (Hiilamo, 2022). Previous chapters discussed how neoliberalism undermined this value and was associated with an attack on comprehensive welfare, leading to poverty and insecurity, inequalities and related breakdown of trust in democratic institutions. Chapter 2 established the relationship between neoliberal capitalism and ecological catastrophe (Coote and Percy, 2020).

Tackling all of this requires a restoration of the principle of reciprocity and a recognition of mutual interdependence. This can be positively practiced in the concept of the commons or collective provisioning. Social security as social insurance works through pooling resources and drawing on collective resources in times of need. By only drawing from collective consumption when needed there is opportunity to make more effective use of limited resources which, in turn, can limit individual and collective consumption and so reduce emissions and safeguard natural resources. A new ecosocial system, therefore, combines universal provision of need with sufficiency and sustainability (Coote and Percy, 2020).

Chapters 2 and 3 discussed the concept of basic needs upon which people's wellbeing and flourishing depends and outlined why such needs are both non-substitutable and satiable (Lelkes, 2021). These needs are universal but will manifest in different ways across time and space, and cultures and generations. There are generic categories of universal 'intermediate needs' that are well-recognised including water, nutrition, shelter, secure and non-threatening work, education, healthcare, security in childhood, significant primary relationships, physical and economic security and a safe environment. Those have informed the development of human rights and the SDGs. New needs emerge over time, they can evolve slowly or be established quickly in the case of digital media or advances in healthcare, or in the context of crisis when all children needed access to digital media for basic education during pandemic-related restrictions.

Basic human needs, unlike wants or preferences, cannot be substituted for one another. In this sense they are expansive and untradeable, but each basic need is satiable and can be satisfied (Gough, 2017). Wants, on the other hand, can vary across people and culture and are both infinite and unsatiable, they can multiply exponentially and never be fully satisfied. So central to meeting universal needs is the concept of *sufficiency*, where going beyond sufficiency (for example, over-heating) can be harmful individually, collectively, as well as socially and environmentally (Coote and Percy, 2020). Chapter 2, Figure 2.1 illustrated the doughnut, a schema that links the relationship between basic needs and planetary wellbeing. The inner space meets need and so provides a 'safe and just space for humanity' which can be provided without breaching planetary boundaries (Raworth, 2017). UBS can meet the inner circle of basic needs in a manner that also satisfies conditions for planetary wellbeing. Gough (2017) delegates the task of defining needs thresholds to local citizens' assemblies, hence making sure that needs and luxuries are defined democratically. Reference group methodologies for defining consensus-based minimum essential living standards can also identify real needs.

The case against market provision

Arguing against over-dependance on markets, Konczal (2021, pp 7–10) contends market distribution does not enable society to match what is needed to live lives that are valued, is an unreliable provider of essential goods, is a site of domination and power, does not reward work that is socially valuable, is related to state power and not necessarily democratically controlled. Over time, as neoliberalism progresses through marketisation and privatisation, needs are increasingly met through commodified market processes, and through individual rather than collective consumption. Chapter 1 discussed how commodification led to a market society with negative consequences for individual, collective and planetary wellbeing. Neoliberalism means more and more land, labour and money (or nature, bodies and finance) are marketised. Some needs, particularly those requiring economies of scale and significant infrastructural investment, were traditionally funded by the state but have been increasingly marketised and delivered through public-private partnerships (PPPs). This includes energy utilities and infrastructure but also welfare provisions such as housing, health and education. Market mechanisms are increasingly embedded into the management of public services and the procurement and delivery of state-funded services. New models of commissioning and procurement have replaced traditional charity models of funding and provision. Market principles have also shaped state funding models, leaving provision of essential services with charities or third sector organisations, but forcing them to adapt to quasi-market norms and rules (Rees, 2014). There is nothing natural about such market provision (Konzcal, 2021).

The case for reciprocity

The reciprocity at the heart of a social contract that meets basic human needs fosters a sense of our mutual obligations, interdependence and responsibility towards each other (see Chapter 3). Collective provision can offer better results than market transactions in terms of equity, efficiency, solidarity and sustainability (Coote and Percy, 2020). Such services can be delivered through citizen participation, local control and diverse models of ownership that can enhance economic democracy (Cumbers 2018). This can include less market and more societal provision, but the state remains crucial as a regulator and primary funder. A caveat here is that the role of civil society should not be reduced to merely service provision. Statutory funding to deliver services should enhance rather than hinder the independence of civil society and its capacity to conflict with the state or to act as a public sphere. Feminist analyses understands the welfare state as not just a set of services but a set of ideas about society, including social reproduction and family life (Barry, 2021). The shared provision of services to meet collective needs requires us to consciously avoid individual provisioning through the market, reserving it for use only when it is the most efficient and sustainable way of meeting needs.

Mark Boyle (2013) in *The Moneyless Man* points to the essence of reciprocity as our common humanity and membership of reciprocal communities and argues such reciprocity is our greatest source of both security and sustainability. Creating a world where we trust in each other to meet our basic needs means we have less motivation to draw on scarce resources that we do not need. It also means legitimating strong institutions needed to enable collective provision, including taxation. However, collective welfare must also meet the need for sustainability, broadly understood, to be at the heart of any renewed welfare project.

Often collective provisioning can draw on our reciprocal and mutual interdependence, meeting needs through our social relationships, including local community, family and kin networks. At the same time, we know that reciprocity, no matter how voluntary, is the source of deeply embedded gender inequality. Hence the requirement for some needs to be met through public or collective forms of provision, where those providing the service, for example care, are paid at least the living wage and where decent working conditions are regulated. Services and entitlements, no matter who delivers them, should be universal as much as possible to foster a sense of inclusion and equality; means tested and targeted services in contrast foster differentiation and fragmentation. The very act of using common and universal services gives us points of connection to each other, from which a sense of common need is fostered. They are a basis for interdependence, solidarity and social citizenship.

Balancing state, market and society

UBS acknowledges the need for less 'market' and more 'state' and 'society' in the provision of essential services. The contrast between state, society and market actors is, of necessity, exaggerated but this exaggeration can underplay the diversity within each broad sector and the different positive and negative experiences of service delivery associated with each.

The most fundamental argument against market delivery is the excessive motivation to extract surplus profit from investment intended to meet the needs of society. Without excessive profit-making underlying the rationale for market activity, there is less reason to differentiate who might deliver UBS. However, without a potential profit, many market actors will not be interested in delivering UBS, hence the assumption that it will be primarily state and not-for-profit social actors with occasional market provision. There are, for example, many historical and contemporary examples of private sector investment in and delivery of essential services including housing, transport, childcare and health services to workers, families and local communities. Profit is rarely a direct motivation in these services. Needs will always be diverse, and some needs, such as clothing or digital communication devices, are always likely to be provided through market mechanisms which is acceptable only when markets are effectively regulated.

Many different roles are played by non-profit or civic society actors and there is huge variation in terms of motive, intention and working method. There are many wonderful examples of effective provision. But there are also examples around the world where societal organisations, including, but not only, religious orders, were responsible for the most egregious harms to people, particularly the most vulnerable. There are other examples of corruption, inefficiencies and ineffective civil society service delivery. Similarly, the state has played different roles over time in provision of services, acting to directly deliver, commission and regulate services, and often establishing agencies to separate the role of delivery from government. The state withdrew from direct services over the last few decades, sometimes because of ideology but also because there were real weaknesses in state provision, or because of political or bureaucratic blame-avoidance strategies. Proffering an enhanced role for civil society and the state risks returning to previous forms of poor/unaccountable services, albeit the emphasis on new forms of co-production and democratic accountability are a bulwark against this possibility.

While there may be a role for the market, it is clear, nonetheless, that environmentally and in terms of equality, most services are best provided through state or social mechanisms. UBS offers an opportunity to reimagine how new forms of socially valued participation (discussed in Chapter 4) can help deliver basic needs. This requires an openness to the ways in which such services can be delivered, including mutuals, communities, cooperatives, not-for-profits and limited profit-led commercial companies (Coote and Percy, 2020). The state or public sector – local, regional and national – can be a delivery mechanism. More importantly, a state-led model facilitates people to be central in the development of and delivery of collective services that meet core needs.

Where the state does deliver UBS it is important that the principle of subsidiarity informs where the services are located and how they are delivered. One exciting mechanism enabling local service delivery has been the process of 'remunicipalisation' reversing decades of privatisation, outsourcing, competitive procurement, PPPs and/or Private Finance Initiatives (PFI) by returning public functions to local government or municipalities. In the 'Preston Model' 'anchor institutions' – large-scale city-based public institutions with a central role such as colleges and healthcare bodies – are big enough to intervene in procurement practices so that services are contracted from local, socially responsible, suppliers in an integrated local model. New institutions like 'social licensing' can play an innovative role in creating new vehicles for public ownership (Coote, 2022).

We can find inspiration in the 2020 TNI report, *The Future is Public* (Kishimoto et al, 2020), which charted how social movements and governments across the world are quietly building a different future based on meeting needs through principles of solidarity, equality, sustainability and radical democracy. Remunicipalisation refers to a global trend since 2000 of cities taking formerly privatised assets, infrastructure and services back into public ownership (Pierson, 2021). In almost 1,500 examples of 'remunicipalisation' in 58 different countries, services were restored to local public ownership as processes of privatisation and profit maximisation were reversed (Kishimoto et al, 2020). Initiatives to restore provision of public services to public ownership were driven by different logics including principles of democratic ownership, quality services, workers' rights, accessibility and affordability. Public ownership plays a critical and strategic role as the starting point in enabling new processes of democratic public ownership, or partnerships between public institutions and citizens as forms of co-ownership, co-governance and co-financing, all vital instruments of democratising public ownership that can unlock local knowledge and empower citizens. The projects to reverse privatisation have included a wide range of services as diverse as water, pharmacies, refuse collection and recycling services, data, gender-based violence prevention services, nurseries and kindergartens, dental services, funeral services, electricity grids and retailing.

Economic democracy

Responding to the climate emergency requires public alternatives that reorientate the economy and society towards social and environmental justice. TNI's collaborative work with the global trade union Public Services International (PSI) leads the way in demonstrating how to build on theory and emerging practice to imagine different ways in which democratic and public ownership in different spheres can be introduced and structurally developed in different urban and rural contexts. The 2021 TNI report, 'Democratic and collective ownership of public goods and services: Exploring public-community collaboration', illustrates new mechanisms to enable local government and citizens to provide essential services while also enhancing economic democracy (Cumbers, 2018). In innovative approaches, public institutions and collective citizen organisations co-produce ideas and policies and jointly deliver these public goods and services. The co-production approach, elaborated upon in Chapter 4, is an essential characteristic of public-community collaborations, and underpins many inspiring collaborations in food, care, climate, energy, water, housing and urban development.

One of the central attractions of 'new municipalism' or 'mutual communalism' (Bookchin, 1991) is its potential to organise a radical politics based on participatory democratic control as opposed to concentrating state power in the hands of 'experts' or 'bureaucrats'. Cat Hobbs of the pro-public campaign group 'We Own It' proposed that if we want a model of public ownership so successful it cannot again be dismantled, then it must be thoroughly democratised so that citizens and workers have veto power (Hall and Hobbs, 2017). The concept and language of 'the commons' is used to depict processes through which people take power by collectively governing resources or services. 'Commoning' – the creation and regeneration of commons – emerges through autonomous (or semi-autonomous) citizens' organisations such as cooperatives and community-based non-profit organisations. The state can also participate in public-commons partnerships, or public-public partnerships, in which public administration is enhanced and democratised through, for example, collaboration and/or co-ownership with workers and residents (Kishimoto et al, 2020, p 10).

'Communing' occurs where local communities are stakeholders in the management of collective action problems. Cooperative community-based action offers innovative ways of managing commons, shared access and shared ownership that is often superior to top-down government. Local context, investment scale and local distribution of benefits to participating members means people might be more willing to accept consequences that might otherwise be seen as unacceptable 'sacrifices' (Ostrom, 2015). Cooperative community-based action offers ways of managing commons in the domains of community energy, agriculture and transport. 'Commoning' is understood as 'collective self-governance of any common good or resources by their co-producers and users' promoting shared use, collective governance and sustainable stewardship (Stone et al, 2022). Community land trusts are legal institutions that collectively manage purchased or gifted land, property, resources or assets, safeguarding them in perpetuity. Commoner-led projects are now a common feature in the UK spreading across energy infrastructure, farming, food, land, housing, post offices, local shops and pubs, with some promotion of supply chains between commons-led projects. Cumbers (2018) prefers the concept of public ownership to commons arguing it points to the potential of more diverse and pluralistic forms of ownership.

Universal Basic Services, the practice

UBS are a central building block of an ecosocial state (Coote, 2022; Gough, 2022). First articulated as a concept by the Institute for Global Prosperity, University College London, the idea was further developed in *The Case for Universal Basic Services* (Coote and Percy, 2020). UBS promotes the normative principles of agency and participation of both service users and workers. Their provision requires recalibration of the role for the state, a reduction in the role of (for-profit) markets and a greater focus on societal provision of services, while protecting civil society as a democratic public sphere. The concept of UBS is wide-ranging with potential to apply to, for example, housing, health, transport, energy, water as well as education, culture, leisure and libraries. The normative goal of UBS is to ensure that everyone has access to life's essentials – what every individual needs to participate in society and lead a life they value. UBS is based on several core principles (Gough, 2022) (see the 'Core principles of UBS' box that follows).

Core principles of UBS

- Access to life's essentials is a universal entitlement and should be based on need, not ability to pay.
- Power in deciding how needs are met must be devolved to the lowest appropriate level (subsidiarity).
- Services should be delivered by a range of organisations with different models of ownership and control, all of whom share a clear set of enforceable public interest obligations.
- Priority to collaboration and reinvestment over competition and profit extraction.

- Meaningful participation in planning and delivering services by residents and service users.
- Close partnership with professionals and service workers, reflecting the model of co-production.
- Service workers have fair pay, secure conditions and high-quality training and career development.
- Clear rules and procedures for establishing and enforcing entitlements.
- Services designed and delivered to promote and enable sufficiency within planetary boundaries.

Source: Coote and Percy, 2020

The role of the state as planner, funder, regulator and monitor

As discussed earlier, within this framework the state will directly provide some, but not all, services at national and local levels. In addition, the state has four essential functions that no other actor can perform: regulations, monitoring, planning, funding (Coote and Percy, 2020). While such functions may seem similar to existing roles of the state, they take on a new dimension in the context of UBS. The state must guarantee equality of access for individuals, between and within localities; set and enforce ethical and quality standards; collect and invest the necessary funds, distributing them to maximise inclusion and fairness; encourage and support diverse models of service provision; and coordinate activities across the different areas of need to achieve optimal results (Coote and Percy, 2020). Maximising the capacity of the local state in all four functions requires a recalibration of the role of the state and society and a reduction of for-profit markets.

Regulation

While power may be devolved beyond the state to collaboratively deliver services, the state has ultimate responsibility for regulation, legally determining who has the responsibility and power to deliver services, under what conditions and to what quality benchmarks. The question of regulation is complex. A recent focus on 'essential workers' has stirred critical reflexivity about the (lack of) capacity of markets to provide key services and to value essential work, and prompted appreciation of the importance of robust public services and our mutual interdependence on often precariously employed and low-paid frontline service workers. Regulation of quality services is an ongoing concern of the capitalist state while regulation of workers' terms and conditions is an essential function of the state. However, in this regulatory scenario, the state assumes new and innovative regulatory roles. Social licensing, for example, is a form of regulation which can make the right to trade dependent on providing a service and meeting wider community responsibility criteria (Coote, 2022, p 11).

Monitoring

Wilkinson and Pickett (2009) and the OECD (2014) demonstrate that poorer households benefit proportionately more from investment in public goods. The 2013 European Union Social Investment Package analysis pointed to the preventative value of such services, an important factor in generating not only more equal outcomes but also efficiency. Common accountancy-led evaluations of efficiency usually rely on static input/output models and cost-benefit analysis mechanisms that cannot capture the dynamic and longer-term benefits of investment in meeting human need. Alternative techniques based on social value analysis and social return on investment paint a different picture of efficiency and prove the benefits of social investment. Given the lack of compatibility between capitalism and care, UBS offers a mechanism to move humanity beyond a narrow capitalism–centric set of logics and values (Lynch, 2022).

Cost benefit analysis

From both equality and ecological perspectives, access to and participation in local renewable energy infrastructure may well become a basic need and a universal basic service. However, despite considerable state investment in its provision, in some countries access to such infrastructure is governed by market mechanisms. When cost-benefit analysis is used to analyse the return on investment of local citizen participation in renewable energy production, it is difficult to justify such public investment. A business case for investment cannot be demonstrated and those promoting this policy find it difficult to convince finance or public expenditure ministries to invest in such a policy. However, if other mechanisms are used to measure the return on such investment, the case for investment becomes obvious. The Irish Environmental Protection Agency correlate opportunity for citizens' production of renewable energy with increased political support for renewable energy policy. This leads to easier passage of relevant legislation and planning applications, and greater public support for related policy initiatives. Thus, what is hard to justify on economic grounds alone becomes a plausible investment when assessed across wider criteria.

Planning

Arguments for effective delivery of UBS requires an approach to identifying and meeting needs that is closely connected to the people who are delivering and consuming such services: citizens, residents and workers. Participation is central to human rights and democratic principles. The principles of citizen participation and local control filter through diverse models of ownership and delivery mechanisms. Not all forms of participation are positive; some forms including statutory consultation processes can be manipulative or at best tokenistic, but other forms of participation can be meaningful, leading to real power and input in decision-making (see Chapter 4 on collaboration and Chapter 9 on high-energy democracy).

Funding

Chapters 4 and 9 discuss the fiscal feasibility of the ecosocial state. The estimated cost of shifting to UBS will vary across countries but is estimated to be around 4.3 per cent of GDP, or less than 15 per cent of government spending in most OECD countries (Coote and Percy, 2020). Between revenue-raising, borrowing and reallocation, there is considerable fiscal space to accommodate this, especially in low-revenue liberal states. The role of the state extends to maximising tax-based revenue and borrowing to fund UBS which will have varying resourcing arrangements depending on the ownership and delivery model. For example, tax-based funding will be extended through grants, contracts and other service delivery agreements and forms of social licenses. UBS can, in some instances, be partly funded from philanthropic sources, financial contributions and co-funding. While sources of funding may vary, the service itself is an entitlement which the state as a duty-bearer has an obligation to ensure for rights-holders. This requires that central government supplement local funds, allowing for equitable distribution between localities (Coote and Percy, 2020, p 109).

Care

The concept of UBS has wide-ranging potential across all essential needs. Care services are discussed here as an example of UBS in the critical area of social reproduction. An ecosocial care perspective moves beyond the boundaries of public and private spheres, embracing the social totality of relations including human care relations and our ecological relationship with nature, and defines care as:

> a species activity that includes everything that we do to maintain, continue, and repair our world so that we can live in it as well as possible.

That world includes our bodies, ourselves, and our environment, all of which we seek to interweave in a complex, life sustaining web. (Fisher and Tronto, 1990, p 40)

For practical purposes the focus here is on child, adult and elder care and draws heavily on Coote's (2022) account of care as a UBS.

Social perceptions of gender, a most fundamental cleavage in contemporary life, informs norms, roles, life chances and power relations (Daly and Rake, 2002, p 178). As noted in Chapter 3, women account for 70 per cent of frontline workers in the health and social care system globally and carry out most of the unpaid care work in the home and in communities. Women, many of them workers as well as mothers and/or grandmothers, experience intersectional inequality in a gendered political economy. The key to equality in care services is a gender-neutral distribution across paid and unpaid care.

Childcare is also vital for an environmentally sustainable world, and its provision as a collective good enhances equality. It does this in several ways, for example, by overcoming childhood disadvantage and enabling poorer households to use scarce money to meet other basic needs. Security in childhood along with education are recognised as generic 'satisfiers' of basic early human needs, while access to decent work is an essential adult need and childcare is central to each of these needs (Coote, 2022). Childcare can also contribute to ecological sustainability enhancing relationships, and avoid damage to people's wellbeing that might otherwise require costly and often resource-intensive interventions (Coote, 2022).

Childcare is typically provided by a mix of for-profit, public and voluntary organisations, while systems of childcare vary across the globe depending on the degree to which childcare is accessible and affordable (Barry, 2021). Care penalties which impact on wage inequality, pay and pension gaps are common (Folbre, 2021, p 186). A range of inputs are required for quality childcare: appropriate buildings, investment in training and qualifications of staff, low ratios of children to staff, diversity of social and ethnic backgrounds, suitably warm, consistent relationships between children and staff, parental involvement in managing childcare centres, and opening times to suit parents' working lives (Coote, 2022). Quality is influenced by who the provider is. For-profit provision is associated with increased cost and decreased quality, and when combined with a demand-led, fee-paying system, there are issues of affordability and inequality of access (Penn and Lloyd, 2014, p 453). Norway is offered by Coote (2022) as a positive example of UBS in childcare with good practice in staffing, care ratios, infrastructure and continuity of care as well as 'a legal guarantee' of places and income-related subsidised fees. The Norwegian childcare infrastructure accommodates some private provision which the state regulates for quality. It funds 85 per cent of childcare costs, caps fees, implements systems for regulatory governance, directly limits profit and requires co-creation-oriented governance processes. This range of policies provides a coherent example of how the state can play an active role in accommodating a diverse eco-system to provide a UBS for childcare (Coote, 2022). These indicators of effective and quality UBS can equally be applied to adult, elder and social care, other prime candidates for UBS.

Social relations remain key. Provision for the care of children and the elderly cannot be either totally private nor totally public but is often rooted in reciprocal social relations, respectful of diverse family forms (Daly and Rake, 2002, p 168). It is crucial not to marginalise reciprocal care and the family, although there is a need to be aware of the quality of care in terms of the needs of care recipients. PI, the subject of the next chapter, can support socially valued care activity, including wider forms of social reproduction, and so complement UBS. A PI can decommodify care in a different way to UBS, freeing up time to enable people to engage in voluntarily caring for people. A post-growth ecosocial state interconnects UBS and PI, recognising that both can enhance the capacity of people to access and provide quality care that they value, while also enabling people to rebalance work, care and time. This can also contribute to a rebalancing of the distribution of care work with households and families, and ultimately greater gender equality. The Irish case study that follows illustrates how a care UBS might evolve in a national context.

Seeds of the future: Universal Basic Care Services in Ireland?

As discussed in Chapter 1, Ireland has followed a commodified route and made for-profit market delivery central to the provision of needs in many areas of welfare, including pensions, health, housing and care. This lack of balance and over-marketisation of care results in 70 per cent of childcare and 85 per cent of eldercare being delivered through the private, for-profit market. This is not an argument against private delivery, but an argument against policy that facilitates the generation of excessive profit from meeting people's basic care needs. Extracting profit from care relations requires that care is commodified and given a market value, a process that is not only costly but denies our relational ontology, humanity and interdependence. Little wonder Irish feminists and allies have framed care outside of marketised rationales and demanded income support outside of the male breadwinner welfare system. The account that follows problematises the negative consequences of Ireland's private care model, offers the framework of UBS as an alternative approach to childcare and comments on the politics of making this happen.

The problem: Ireland's marketised care model

In Ireland there is an imbalance in how care is delivered across state, market and society, and across paid and unpaid care. However, we must be realistic that an enhanced role for civil society and the state does not offer a 'silver bullet'. Focusing on the respective roles of state, market and society (known in Ireland as community and voluntary sector (CVS) delivery) can underplay the diversity within each sector. While there are positive examples of good practice in every sector, there are also examples of poor practice and Irish women and children have experienced negative care in each sector, including historical and contemporary tragic institutional abuse of vulnerable people, young and old. Much has improved since such terrible controversies and the state has adopted a stronger regulatory role that is focused on compliance.

The private sector now dominates provision in both childcare and eldercare in Ireland. The government has incentivised private providers, promoting an economic model based on high fees and low wages with consequences for affordability, accessibility, standards, staff ratios and poor pay and working conditions for the predominantly female and often migrant staff. With one of the highest rates of low pay in the OECD, care workers, particularly women, migrants and young people, live in a condition of flex-insecurity with precarious jobs and without the cushion of a strong welfare state. Difficult and dangerous labour conditions in the long-term care sector are exacerbated by privatisation. Despite requirements for third level qualifications, the care sector and its 98 per cent female workers lack career structures. While Budget 2023 increased minimum wages beyond the living wage for all workers, it also limited graduate employment opportunities.

Ireland leans heavily on reciprocity – household, women, grandparents and informal community – to perform largely unpaid care work. Women's capacity to absorb care needs is seen as an infinite elastic resource. Ireland's male breadwinner gendered welfare and tax system familialises these women (assigning many women dependent status). At the same time, lone parents are pushed to seek full-time work with little exception for care responsibilities and in the context of poor public childcare provision. The fault lines in this care model were brutally exposed in the pandemic. The largely privatised care infrastructure was ill-equipped to meet societal needs which impacted on quality, with negative consequences for care recipients, women's participation in the labour force and low-paid care workers. These market and state failures are absorbed through the community and family and primarily by women.

A 'careful state': Universal Basic Care Services

Policy needs to be better balanced in relation to enabling a spectrum of care across the life cycle, with positive consequences for gender equality. The solution lies in a 'careful state' that rebalances care delivery across state, market and society, and values and practices care as a right, not in a binary of givers and receivers, but as a universal phenomenon where we can all care and we are all cared for (Cullen, 2021). The key is socially valuing care work, including self-care, so that it has status and so that care entitlement can be accessed through collaborative collective processes, rather than competitive for-profit markets. Ireland could adopt a two-pronged approach to advance care and gender equality through:

- a universal care service, a state-led model of universal care services with mixed provision that approaches care provision from the perspective of those caring and those being cared for; and
- a complementary income support, PI, that values and enables provision of a less formal type of care associated with reciprocity and our mutual interdependence (discussed in the following chapter).

Care can be delivered across a variety of actors, with the state as the regulator of pay, conditions, fees, governance and quality, and as funder, planner and monitor of child and eldercare. A public universal care service assumes that the state is a duty-bearer and must ensure provision of social rights across all those giving and receiving care and ensure all care provision is underpinned by quality care and decent work.

A key step, planting seeds for the future, was recently achieved through the Big Start campaign. This was led by Ireland's largest trade union, SIPTU, which represents, among others, early years educators and managers, which fought for better pay, recognition and increased government investment in the Early Childhood Care and Education (ECCE) scheme to improve the sector's quality and accessibility to children, affordability for parents and value placed on educators. Recent Budgets provided evidence that the campaign paid dividends. ECCE was a political priority with government funding to support an historic pay deal for early years educators and to underpin negotiations in a newly-established Joint Labour Committee where wages and conditions are negotiated and are now above the living wage. This is an important step on the road to state regulating and funding of professional pay and conditions, and, ideally, to the provision of a Universal Basic Care Service.

The regulatory role of the state needs to extend beyond quality provision and workers' pay and conditions. A further key step in a Universal Basic Care Service requires state regulation that limits profit-making in the care sector and supports new models of ownership and control needed to transition from market-dominated to a public and social-dominated infrastructure. Regulation must also extend beyond standards and compliance to enabling, training and support. A mixed-delivery system oriented to social and public provision implies a 'ratcheting down' over time of for-profit private delivery and retention of market provision geared towards a reasonable return on investment which can be reinvested in quality, affordability and wages. A social licensing model can require social outcomes to be delivered by all providers (minimal levels of profit, controls on fees, wages, community engagement, and so on). Regardless of who the provider is, a key step is to reorientate procurement towards not-for-profit economic activity.

Feminist not feminised

How campaigns are framed is important in whether they promote feminist or feminised claims (Cullen and Murphy, 2017). Some anti-market or anti-privatisation campaigns can lose a gendered focus, while 'homogeneous universal claims can flatten racial, ethnic and other inequalities' (Cullen, 2021). The demand for a public universal care service in Ireland was supported by the 2021 Citizens' Assembly on Gender Equality (CAGE). The CAGE recommended that 1 per cent of GNP be invested in childcare and 'a care tax' to make the recommendations a reality. Government remains reluctant to commit to a universal state childcare system, believing that path-dependency of a commodified private sector means only a hybrid universal system is feasible or plausible. However, the model offered here, UBS and PI, is a mixed-delivery vehicle valuing very different forms of care and led by a state that, as duty-bearer, embraces a comprehensive role in regulating, funding, planning and monitoring care. UBS and PI are compass points in the direction of non-reformist reforms, and steppingstones towards constitutionally valuing care and gender equality in Ireland. The CAGE recommendation for a constitutional referendum to reframe Article 41.2 of the 1937 Irish Constitution (which ascribes to women a special role providing 'care in the home') offers a campaign vehicle for this state-funded Universal Basic Care Service. The CAGE demands were kept alive in the Oireachtas (Parliamentary) Committee on Gender Equality which in December 2022 published its final report recommending that such a referendum take place in 2023. This campaign offers an important vehicle to realise UBS and PI as policy vehicles to socially value care.

6

Participation Income

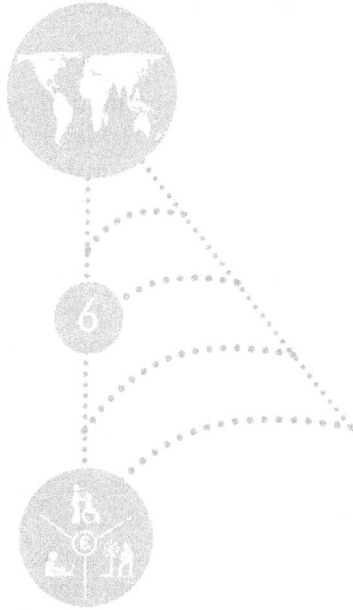

Transition of a sufficient scale towards an ecologically oriented social model demands a fundamental overhaul of existing welfare trajectories. This means shifting focus away from institutions and policies that 'commodify' labour and prioritise productivity growth and employment as the primary mechanism to social citizenship. This necessitates practical changes in supporting institutions (discussed in Chapter 4) and UBS (discussed in Chapter 5) but also to income supports, the focus of this chapter. Decommodification requires that policy and practice promote greater varieties of participation beyond the labour market and reciprocal interdependent care relationships throughout our life cycles.

The income support system needs to complement principles of an enabling and facilitating welfare system that primarily works through UBS to meet collective needs. The first section of this chapter explores a spectrum of income support options including Universal Basic Income (UBI), Minimum Income Guarantees (MIG) and Participation Income (PI). The mid-section of the chapter offers PI as an example of a state income support system that de-emphasises production, consumption and employment, and enables and values other forms of work, recovering time for activities that have social and ecological value such as providing care, democratic participation and sustaining the environment. The Irish case study offers a blueprint for income support reform towards a PI, in the form of the Pandemic Unemployment Payment (PUP) and a 2022 artist basic income pilot.

An income support to complement UBS

Options for income support

So far, this book has argued that a just transition demands a fundamental overhaul of existing welfare trajectories. However, the role of social policy in enabling sustainable transition remains marginal within the literature on decarbonisation (Bohnenberger, 2020). Recent literature argues that transitioning towards an 'ecosocial' welfare model requires re-anchoring welfare institutions in a 'post-productivist' architecture wherein income supports and public services are targeted at meeting essential needs rather than catalysing labour productivity and economic growth (Hirvilammi and Koch, 2020). While there is a growing consensus about the need for such an ecosocial policy agenda, there is far less agreement about what specific social policies might contribute to this reorientation.

Chapter 4 argued that institutional rules and norms play an important role in incentivising behaviour (Folbre, 2021, p 198). Altruism as a value requires institutional reinforcement in new forms of collective commitment to value and reward care for others. Commitment to the care of others cannot be entirely voluntary or reinforcing, especially in economic systems that encourage individual competition. Transfers can generate reciprocity with legal and social obligations that reinforce personal attachments (Folbre, 2021, pp 162–3). It is necessary to prompt, support, encourage or incentivise desired socially useful activity, for example, a greater sharing of care between men and women, more comprehensive engagement in democratic deliberation or direct environmental activity. Incentives can be generated in two ways: offering a social income (a wage, or an income support) to those who are willing to engage in socially useful activity and/or offering institutional mechanisms to enable such activity, for example, local government ecological programmes, civil society projects or social enterprises.

The case for less focus on income support

The previous chapter argued that any shift to a less commodified world requires a reorientation of policy towards collective provisioning of needs through UBS. Cash payments or 'money' inevitably reinforce consumerist pathways and lead to more commodified ways to meet needs. This individualises choices and moves us away from collective solidarity and reciprocity. There are interesting contemporary and historical accounts of living without money as a medium of exchange (Boyle, 2013; Graeber and Wengrow, 2021). While not going so far here, the focus is more on promoting collective provision as crucial to sustainability, new forms of care and solidarity. Individual income support must play a complementary role to the primary focus on UBS, a more preventative form of investment than cash payments. To avoid Arendt's fear that 'eventually no object of the world will be safe from consumption and annihilation through consumption', (1958, p 133) cash payments need to be seen as a less dominant form of welfare and income support must work in a complementary fashion to UBS (Button and Coote, 2021; Coote, 2022).

A spectrum of income supports

Forms of 'income supports' differ according to a number of criteria: eligibility (whether they are targeted or means tested); entitlement (who can access the payment: age, gender, disability); and conduct (the levels and types of conditions or behaviours) (Bohnenberger, 2020).

Comparing the options

1. Universal Basic Income (UBI): an expensive option, a specific unconditional and universal form of basic income, it has no conditions and is a permanent payment, not targeted or linked to clear eco objectives.
2. Minimum Income Guarantee (MIG): has only income conditions and is otherwise a specific unconditional but non-universal form of basic income with no reciprocal activity requirement. It may be temporary, and it is income targeted but not linked to a clear eco objective.
3. Participation Income (PI): a non-universal payment with broad reciprocal activity requirements and conditions. It is flexible and targeted, and linked to clear non-productivist eco objectives.
4. Job Seekers Allowance (JSA), or, in the UK, Universal Credit (UC): payments with strong multiple conditions, they are means-tested and the least expensive policy option with severe restrictions and sanctions. They are highly targeted provisions, and linked to narrow productivist objectives.

Assessing the four income support reform proposals across a range of criteria demonstrates the complexity of the debate, a complexity beyond the scope of this book. It is clear from the above that contemporary approaches to social assistance are insufficient, targeted, conditional and productivist and are unable to meet ecosocial objectives. This leaves us with the other three possibilities: UBI, PI and MIG.

Universal Basic Income

We first discuss UBI using a Global North 'classic' formulation as 'an income that is at once unconditional and universal or paid to everyone based on their shared humanity' (Hiilamo, 2022). The case for an unconditional UBI is often overstated. A UBI may miss opportunities to target need, norms and behaviours, a valuable characteristic of income support. There are real fears that an adequate level of UBI would be fiscally unsustainable in terms of the level of tax required to fund it, while others fear a negative tradeoff between UBI expenditure and other desirable investment in public services. From a class perspective, some fear that a decommodfied UBI would lead to a demise of employment supports and reduced access to the labour market and leave people struggling to compete for livelihoods in a still highly unequal world, and with income below the poverty line (Coote and Yazici, 2019). Panitch (2011) challenges the claim that UBI has substantial de-commodifying effects. Others concur, arguing that UBI may foster consumerism and unsustainable consumption (Pérez-Munoz, 2018; Swaton, 2018). Many feminists rightly fear that contemporary unequal gendered patterns of care may be reinforced by a UBI. Daly and Rake (2002, p 176) argue the potential of UBI for social transformation is limited, potentially reinforcing the gendered divide in labour. Presenting UBI as a panacea to the crises of work and care is thus overstated (Lombardozzi, 2020; Folbre, 2021), with a lack of clarity as to how UBI, as an unconditional payment, would interrupt 'traditional' gender roles.

Participation Income

We now examine the key difference between the two mid-range income tested proposals, MIG and PI. Neither of these payments are necessarily universal, both can be income tested. The key difference between them is the degree to which PI is linked to a broadly-defined activity requirement. PI is a policy idea first introduced by the British economist Anthony Atkinson (1996), 'where people are paid, not for doing nothing, but in exchange for an activity that is useful for the society'. PI is a 'green conditional basic income' which can be either permanent/long term or transitional/limited to a short-term period, but is neither universal nor unconditional (Bohnenberger, 2020, p 596).

This reform option has the merit of offering a partial or complete pathway to reform with significant potential for alliance and coalition-building. At the heart of such proposals is an argument that the problem with existing systems of income support is not their conditionality per se, but their presumption that only market participation is a legitimate contribution that might satisfy a principle of reciprocity or contribution (McGann and Murphy, 2021). PI essentially retains a commitment to the principle of reciprocity or obligation, but for a wider range of activities that affirm forms of reproductive and ecological labour. PI is, at least in the short to medium term, a *necessary* institution to encourage, incentivise *and* enable activity and forms of social reproduction. PI shifts the focus away from paid employment, enabling interdependence, widening participation requirements away from narrow conceptions of paid 'work'.

Minimum Income Guarantee

Coote (2022) argues that the provision of UBS is best presented as a 'social guarantee' that includes a form of complementary income support in the form of a MIG targeted at a high enough income threshold to ensure it can be delivered without stigma. This is only one version of what can be understood as a MIG. The Scottish MIG steering group,[1] which first reported in 2022, outlined a set of principles to inform a MIG that offers a dignified and quality life. The complex issues informing design include assessing what such a payment would replace, whether it is assessed on an individual or household basis and how it would be tapered. Further questions relate to political feasibility, cost, affordability and how it might be paid, as well as issues relating to sanctions and conditionalities.

Coote (2022) argues that any MIG should be administered without conditionality, thus shifting income support away from the productivist and punitive mentality of activation or workfare. She argues this can open the possibility of space and capability for social engagement and contribution in new diverse forms of civic agency or reciprocity supporting provision of UBS. While this is an attractive theoretical proposition, in practice the complete abolition of reciprocal obligations may be problematic for two reasons. First, the necessary project of a social guarantee may be less politically feasible. Second, it may mean a lost opportunity to promote, target or make more likely the very forms of reciprocity that Coote (2022) argues is an implicit objective embedded in a MIG.

Bringing Participation Income and Minimum Income Guarantees together

It can be argued that even if absence of any type of obligation is theoretically preferred for normative reasons, it may be useful as an interim, transitional or bridging measure to consider a way of encouraging or incentivising participation in democratically-defined, socially useful activity. This is politically justifiable in the context of sufficient support and safeguards against exploitation or stigmatisation. Enabling reciprocal mutual aid offers an opportunity for creating substantive social value as well as vehicles for social inclusion and solidarity. It may also add to the political feasibility of the ecosocial welfare reform in that reciprocal activity or participation requirements may ease fears of those who worry that people 'might get something for nothing' while also opening the possibility of incorporating more actors in pro-reform coalitions and movements. For this reason, PI is the most politically feasible option in the short term. It is also most likely to promote, facilitate and enable socially useful activity and may also be a potential 'generational or transitional bridge' to a future social guarantee of UBS/MIG (Button and Coote, 2021).

Seven arguments underpinning the case for Participation Income

Arguments for valuing care, socially useful work and reciprocity

Having made a broad argument for PI, this section attempts to grapple with some of the practicalities of its design and implementation, starting with the first question: what type of participation, activity or work should a PI enable? A fundamental aim of ecosocial policy should be to reorient our lives to maximise collective capacity to realise our wellbeing without impacting negatively on the planet. A primary objective then is to remove consumption as the primary way we meet our needs and make us less dependent on commodified market mechanisms.

What is socially valued participation?

The connection between care, work and gender equality is crucial, and the intention here is to promote a form of PI that does not reinforce but weakens existing care-related gender inequalities. An 'ethics of care' requires that income support appreciate the social and political value of caring as a human activity. The objectives are to a) move beyond a narrow concept of employment-promotion to promote freely chosen decent work, and b) enable and value other activities, such as care work and civic engagement, and forms of participation that enable us to care for the planet and ourselves. A feminist lens insists on a form of PI that supports reciprocal care obligations to be equally shared between men and women.

Recognising and valuing wider forms of participation is not a rejection of work, paid or unpaid. Widening our understanding of work does not devalue but reinforces 'work' as essential to the 'human condition' and for achieving prosperity and hope (Jackson, 2021). As rehearsed in Chapter 4, Arendt understands the 'vita activa' is key to our freedom, wellbeing and potential. Labour involves care and sustenance, much of what we understand as the foundational or essential economy (Jones and O'Donnell, 2018, p 249). Labour, work and action can mean 'more fun' amidst 'less stuff' and offers potential for extraordinary fulfilment in living better with less (Jackson, 2021, p 104). PI would substantially widen the range and variety of options that are recognised as valued contributions that aid a post-growth world (Pérez-Munoz, 2016, 2018; Swaton, 2018; McGann and Murphy, 2021):

- child, elder and social care;
- community development and active citizenship;
- neighbourhood clean-ups;
- environmental protection and gardening projects;
- educational programmes;
- volunteering in service provision for example homeless shelters;
- community projects such as renovating cultural heritage sites, promoting traditional crafts, setting-up walking trails;
- raising environmental awareness in schools;
- arts and cultural activity.

Such work will often be local in nature, associated with the commons and the type of work and outcomes generated in the third sector, social economy, cooperatives and through voluntary working (Fitzpatrick, 2004). PI can support work which contributes to emotional and ecological reproduction, incorporating democratic work that allows a more careful eco-system to be negotiated, nurtured and maintained for sustainable social reproduction. Much of this reproductive work, particularly care responsibilities, already happens in an unpaid context and the question is not so much how to make care work 'paid work', rather, how to find time to do it in one's personal life and also how to ensure such work is equitably shared not only between parents but across society (Craig, 2008). A PI enables a redistribution of care work which is a prerequisite for gender equality. A PI that enhances capacity to participate in and contribute to arts and culture also offers capacity to engage in generating the norms and values needed for and in a post-growth world. Volunteer-based organisations may fear that a PI could negatively impact on volunteering. The intention is to recognise, socially value and reward full time participation. Supports are also needed to nurture, maintain and value part time volunteering, not through PI, but through creative work-life balance policies and supports for civil society.

Justifications for reciprocal obligations

The second argument relates to justifications for reciprocal obligations, some of which were rehearsed in previous chapters (see also White, 2010). PI's point of departure from UBI or MIG on a reciprocal participation requirement is the most controversial difference between them. Behavioural conditionalities, or 'conditions of conduct', however broadly conceived, make many people nervous (Clasen and Clegg, 2007, p 167). The experience of conditional income support has been negative and trust in the state is low across most welfare states. Welfare regimes have always stigmatised claimants; poor people and minorities have had obligations imposed on their daily lives, while those with independent income have greater choice and freedom to determine how they might participate in society. However, as discussed in Chapter 3, access to income supports has always been restricted as part of the social contract built on interdependence. Retention of behavioural conditionality in PI can be viewed as a pragmatic or political tactic, helping to secure political support for a basic income (Atkinson, 1996, p 67).

Reciprocity is also pragmatically justified on the grounds that a PI is better aligned with targeted policy goals, particularly reward for and redistribution of care and ecological work (McGann and Murphy, 2021). Reciprocity or a requirement for participation, expansively defined, can also be defended upon normative grounds. It promotes social cooperation as opposed to the liberal concept of individual freedom reinforced by UBI (Swaton, 2018), and builds access to the capabilities underpinning equal citizenship. The normative defence of reciprocity requires that it supports forms of participation that contribute to human flourishing (Laruffa, 2020, p 6), that it promotes mutual interdependence and 'navigational agency' (Claassen, 2018), enhancing autonomy and decoupling social esteem and security from paid employment, thus contributing to Beck's (2000, p 58) concept of 'a multi-active' society. Above all, it supports a redistribution of care work between men and women, and greater gender equality.

Practical arguments for feasibility

The third argument relates to whether and how a PI might be targeted and implemented in a way that avoids stigma and enhances the personal autonomy and agency aspired to in ecosocial welfare. From an administrative and political perspective, there are complex delivery issues and costs. A poorly designed and implemented PI could lead to a confusing, invasive and stigmatising policy (De Wispelaere and Stirton, 2018). However, avoiding these challenges could mean PI merges more into a MIG or an unconditional UBI and loses its focus on reciprocity. The resolution lies in enabling citizens to be involved, through processes of co-production, in actively participating in co-creating the participation requirements of PI.

Larruffa et al (2021) demonstrate approaches to co-creation in some European income support programmes, including the Netherlands 2015 Participation Act, and pilots in Denmark and Scotland. A range of municipal-level experiments have also taken place across Finland where a Local Authority Employment experiment ran from 2021–2023. Swaton (2018) offers France as the site for imagining a more societal-oriented form of PI, an Ecological Transition Income (ETI) that seeks to promote environmental or social activity along with tailor-made support necessary for people to launch projects as part of a social economy united by citizens' movements where conditions enable a sense of inclusion and purpose, and less atomisation. All these suggest a non-stigmatised practice is possible and practical.

Who should be targeted?

The fourth argument relates to the issue of targeting and who should have the right to a PI? It seems the jury is out on what 'conditions of circumstance' (Clasen and Clegg, 2007, p 167) might determine who a PI is paid to. Debates about different forms of PI suggest a spectrum of possibilities ranging from Atkinson's (1996) proposal for a universal payment as a full substitute for means-testing to Murphy and McGann's (2021) proposal for a more targeted PI retaining a degree of income testing, to Hiilamo's (2022) idea for a 'revised PI', a partial PI which largely tops up existing welfare payments.

A universal PI would have no income eligibility conditions. Universality of access can avoid any possible stigma related to PI and reward socially useful work. Such universality in the provision of PI would require an associated redistributive policy of increased progressive income and wealth taxation. There would still, of course, be other forms of conditions relating to the principle of reciprocity or the requirement for socially useful participation.

If some level of income testing was the only politically viable way to negotiate the introduction of a PI then such income thresholds should not 'screen in' the neediest but 'screen out' the most affluent (McGann and Murphy, 2021), and be tapered in line with salary earnings at a high rather than low threshold. This is crucial if PI and socially useful and ecological work is not to be the sole imperative of the poor. One targeted approach might be to mirror a proposal adopted by the New Economics Foundation[2] for a MIG, which is not wholly universal but is pitched at a high income threshold. This is more expensive than the present system of means testing and politically challenging, but it avoids 'claims stigma' related to poor treatment (Coote, 2022), lack of privacy and ultimately low benefit take up (Baumberg, 2015, p 183).

Broader and near universal eligibility is not only desirable, but necessary, as the key mechanism through which equality is maintained, stigma avoided and wider social obligations encouraged. Administrative specificities will need to be determined in each national social security system. The pandemic offered a glimpse of how these can work. Ireland's PUP (discussed in the Irish case study at the end of this chapter) was assessed post-award and delivered without any behavioural requirements (Hick and Murphy, 2021), while Canada's Emergency Response Benefit (CERB), a similar temporary programme, was lauded as a bureaucratic miracle. Post-award assessment of eligibility conditions removes barriers to getting support to people who need it quickly, while also enhancing affordability and political feasibility.

Potential for gender equality

A fifth argument relates to gender equality, a central ambition for a PI. Atkinson (1996) originally argued that means-testing that applies at a household level penalises women. Individualisation should not be confused with individualism. Individualisation of payments is one essential feature that a PI shares with a UBI and is an essential prerequisite for economic independence for women. A PI must depart from the convention that welfare of women resides mainly in the family and is reliant on a male breadwinner, and it must offer spouses and partners a departure from derived rights to income to full entitlement.

Individualisation must inform the design of PI even in the explicit recognition of interdependence as a normative principle. There is a clear dilemma in pursing individualisation in the context of a targeted payment that assesses household income and family circumstances (Daly and Rake, 2002, p 176). Means-tested payments aggregate a couple's or a household's resources, making it difficult to determine or deliver an individualised payment. Splitting or separating the payments to ensure access to an independent income based on individual circumstances is not easy to do. It requires apportioning the income and any child additions between two partners and determining how income disregards, earnings, other income, sanctions or deductions should be allocated between partners (Howard, 2020). While Australia has experimented with a partial individualisation and Scotland is examining possible options, it remains the reality that a universal condition of entitlement is the best way to guarantee individual entitlement. This also facilitates recognition and valuing of a wide range of care activities and women's social reproduction work. A PI also needs to be paralleled by a range of other working time policy initiatives that promote and support paternal care work if PI is not to reinforce gender care inequalities.

Institutional capacity for implementation

The sixth argument relates to the institutional capacity for implementation of PI which requires an efficient system of income testing and effective integrated tax and transfer systems capable of adjustment of payments. Even more challenging is the capacity for processes of production and co-creation, capacity as observed earlier that is more likely in certain institutional and cultural contexts. A rich local and national eco-system is needed to drive the trust relationships that maximise the autonomy of PI recipients. The experiments in the previous discussion have in common rich institutional contexts provided by well-developed welfare states with strong municipal capacity (discussed in Chapter 4). The potentially extensive role for civil society is most likely to work in the presence of strong local network governance arrangements or partnerships between public providers, community-based organisations and other local stakeholders (Swaton, 2018; Stamm et al, 2020; Dukelow, 2022). Procured welfare services may be especially difficult to administer through co-productive processes.

Political feasibility of Participation Income

The seventh and final argument relates to the political feasibility of PI. As well as its normative feasibility, whereby citizens accept some terms of reciprocity, political feasibility also requires sufficient administrative feasibility to avoid being vetoed by bureaucratic assessments that implementation lacks practicality – 'the computer says no'. Public sector workers and trade unions may resist changing work practices toward a type of co-production, even one that limits stigma and maximises trust. Seeds of PI are evident in contemporary welfare policy. Some states are piloting forms of income support that mirror principles of PI, while others have protected some claimants from commodification and at least indirectly valued or recognised the validity of other forms of contribution, particularly care. The pandemic provides the strongest argument that most reforms are politically feasible and that when need for reform is acute, concerns of political or administrative feasibility can be overcome by political will and leadership.

While PI may seem a significant welfare reform, conditions associated with the provision of income support have constantly changed (for example, age criteria). Entitlement conditions over time shift backwards and forwards between a dominance of means-tested assistance, social assistance and universal payments. Eligibility has moved from complex and multiple categorisations to simpler all-encompassing eligibility categories, as was the case with the unsuccessful UC reform in the UK. Conduct or behavioural conditions have shifted to require more productivist conditions and parenting obligations regarding, for example, children's school attendance. Many variants of income support already contain the seeds of PI in that they facilitate some forms of non-productivist activity including care, education, community development and voluntary work. In this sense, as Dukelow (2022) and Stamm et al (2020) observe, the idea of a PI 'is hiding in plain sight' and we can build on 'pockets of the future in the present' to create transformative reforms (Leicester, 2020).

Seeds of the future: an Irish Participation Income

Is Participation Income hiding in plain sight in Irish income supports?

'What we dream of is already present in the world' (Solnit, 2016, p. xv). This Irish case study offers a blueprint for income support reform towards a PI. COVID-19 has fundamentally challenged society, the market and the state in Ireland (and, indeed, globally). From the first case in early 2020, the Irish government moved to immediately strengthen its safety nets and respond to the urgent need for immediate cashflow for those impacted by the pandemic. In mid-March 2020, a new emergency welfare payment, the PUP, was rapidly administered through a one-page application form with compliance monitored ex-post. The primary focus was on speed of response and the PUP was paid on an individualised basis with no household limits at €350 per week. This was considerably higher than the existing €203 core weekly welfare rate for single people and equivalent to the weekly jobseeker's payment paid to an adult claimant with a dependent partner/spouse and to 100 per cent of the average take-home pay in the low-paid sectors most affected by job loss. With no means test or contributions criteria, the administrative simplicity also meant little claimant sigma for the recipients who were considered 'no fault' unemployed. The one-size-fits-all design quickly came under scrutiny and payments were subsequently tapered to reflect previous earning levels. While the PUP was intended as a short-term measure, plans to phase out the payment and integrate it into the mainstream welfare system were abandoned as the pandemic endured. Integration only began in late 2021. The final payment under the scheme was made in May 2022. This experiment demonstrated the administrative and political feasibility of a compliance-light, unconditional, non-means-tested, individualised, ex-ante assessment and pay-related, relatively generous and non-stigmatising income support payment. It has sparked welfare imagination as to what is possible (Hick and Murphy, 2021).

This was a major adjustment in the 'productivist' footing of Ireland's welfare state, which had intensified in the period following the financial crisis (McGann, 2020). Those on jobseekers payments saw their mutual obligations almost indefinitely suspended, as activation was largely put on ice until late 2021. Some outsourced employment services such as JobPath and the Local Employment Services continued to operate at a social distance, although the threat of payment penalties was formally removed. Moreover, until October 2021, from an administrative and legal standpoint, the PUP was entirely outside the field of sanctions and conditionality.

Pandemic Unemployment Payment as an individual payment

The PUP is not offered as a blueprint for the future but to demonstrate that it is possible to imagine and administer an individual payment for all who need it and to point out initial steps that might need to be taken on such a journey. This individualised approach promotes equality where women and men are paid equally, while the higher level of support recognised that the existing level of welfare was inadequate to maintain a decent standard of living. One legacy of the PUP in Ireland is more openness to the concept of reforming income support (including restoration of pay related benefits for Job Seeker Benefit). Recent proposals for pilots, although coming from different origins, mean the politics of making a PI happen seems more than a theoretical pipedream. Crucially, the principle of requiring and/or enabling meaningful non-productivist participation is already embedded in a range of payments in Ireland that support social reproduction (for example, Lone Parents Allowances and Carer's Allowance) or for cultural activity (exemptions from job seeking for artists in receipt of job seeker payments), and in activation programmes like Community Employment which prioritise social inclusion over economic productivity (Dukelow, 2022). To some degree, the seeds are not only sown but are growing and feed into demand for new forms of income support as in the campaign for an artist's basic income, for UBI and for PI, all discussed later.

The policy reform agenda

The 2020 *Programme for Government* commitment to 'request the Low Pay Commission (LPC) to examine Universal Basic Income (UBI), informed by a review of previous international pilots, and resulting in a UBI pilot in the lifetime of the 2020–2025 government' was actioned in January 2021 (Johnston, 2022). In late 2021, the LPC defined UBI as an unconditional state payment that each citizen receives and set out the terms of reference for the required pilot. In a parallel but separate process, the NESC recommended supporting higher participation (Johnston, 2022) and proposed that a form of PI could help deal with the complexities of the changing world of work, such as atypical work, self-employment and platform work, and recommended that a tripartite group assess the type of reforms that would achieve flexibility and security for the greatest number. As well as a more inclusive public employment service, NESC argued that greater participation and potential progression could be supported through a PI where work which is currently unpaid but of societal value, such as voluntary or caring work, is recognised and facilitated, targeted at people not currently in employment but with the potential to contribute to their local community or society. This proposal was recently advanced as Action 17 of the 2021 Climate Action Plan (see Chapter 4).

Artist basic income pilot

The arts in Ireland have historically been shamefully underfunded. Prior to the pandemic, the social welfare scheme for professional artists allowed them to claim Jobseeker's Allowance (JA) but exempted them from labour market activation for one year to enable them to focus on their artistic work and to develop their portfolio. The pandemic laid the context for a focused campaign for an artist basic income and a subsequent commitment to a 'basic income guarantee' pilot scheme for artists, as part of the government's COVID recovery plan (Johnston, 2022). Budget 2021, announced in October 2020, allocated €130 million to the Arts Council and an additional €50 million for the commercial entertainment sector to fund a pilot scheme to guarantee an income of approximately €325 per week for thousands of artists and cultural workers who often otherwise rely on precarious and irregular payments. The artist's basic income pilot, a state income support guarantee, can be topped up through paid employment (Johnston, 2022). By May 2022, over 9,000 artists and cultural workers applied to be one of the 2,000 randomly chosen participants who will receive the €325 per week pilot income for three years. Those unsuccessful will be a control group for the pilot which will conclude in 2025.[3]

This sectoral pilot has prompted demands from other sectors and organisations, including national carers' groups, for similar supports. The UBI LPC pilot, the NESC PI proposal and the Artists Basic Income pilot reflect demand in Ireland for changes in income support that avoid means-testing and narrow conditionality while resourcing valid forms of individualisation, participation and contribution. The three reflect demand for a wider valorisation of socially useful activity, beyond a productivist paradigm. The pilots also give some insight into the politics of making it happen. Alongside the three Irish campaigns described, diverse actors have also used pre-budget submissions, webinars, social media and other forms of campaigning and lobbying to call for a PI. Their conscious decision to promote PI is consistent with their members' demands and assessment of the political feasibility vis-á-vis alternatives. Policy change can trigger mobilisation for more transformative change.

In this context Ireland offers an interesting laboratory for social security reform (Johnston, 2022). Social imaginary is a sociological concept referring to the set of values, institutions, laws and symbols through which people imagine their social whole. It can be argued that the PUP aided Ireland's collective 'welfare' imaginary and offers potential to reset values, institutions and laws to look towards the post-productivist lives we need to live in a post-growth epoch. The emerging alliances discussed here are further explored in Part III. As Folbre (2021) argues, necessity is the mother of not only invention but also coalition, the urgency of addressing emerging needs and just transition offers an opportunity to coalesce demand for this exciting ecosocial combination of UBS and PI as the basic architecture of a new sustainable welfare regime.

Imagining care in an ecosocial post-growth world

The Care Collective (2020) call on us to develop a care imaginary while the Commission on Care Centered Transition argue that care-centred societies are a holistic approach to address the multiple challenges of ecological breakdown and social pressures. Markets and states in a capitalist political economy overlook and undervalue care and the women who work to deliver care. However, care becomes more visible and central in an ecosocial post-growth world that understands its importance, provides for and supports it. Part II discussed how an ecosocial policy approach would incorporate enabling institutions that support reciprocity, UBS and PI. Combined, these three policy tools would promote smaller scale reciprocal or non-contractual care relationships and support new forms of care practices that do not exploit carers. This new approach to care must enhance the autonomy of those being cared for, embedding the right to give and receive care as a societal value (Gopnik, 2023).

Such a world would develop relationships of care that are local and adaptive, and enable people to react to coordination and collective action problems across the life cycle. Creative mechanisms can enable the integration of caregiving into a modern moral political economy. Gopnik (2023) offers the following creative ideas. Policy can create new, or extend existing, institutions (for example, marriage) to enable people who agree to contract with and to each other to provide reciprocal care (this could require rethinking tax, income and inheritance policies). Policy can change the rules to better support care, facilitating remote working and working from home to enable closer physical proximity to care and work. Policy can reimagine care in local settings with cojoined child and eldercare, where older people could be cared for but also provide care and transfer their valuable knowledge.

Working age policies and income support policy can enable care relationships by giving caregivers gender neutral options to cut down on paid work or forego it altogether in favour of child, elder or other care, enabling early care (as distinct from education) and a safe environment of childhood learning and flexibility. This could be done through direct payments such as the PI discussed in Chapter 6, or family, parental or paternal allowances and tax credits, ideally enabling a diversity of caring relationships that enable lives to be lived through creative combinations of private, public and paid care.

Different forms of care services and provision are still provided though social, state and market actors but in a UBS scenario the state regulates to minimise extractive profit, to provide decent jobs and affordable childcare. A system of social licensing is used to promote a diversity of provision and positive social outcomes, including state and private provision such as employment-based creches. However, such a future would also enable new forms of provision which incorporate other social goals and outcomes as, for example, The Great Care Co-op, Ireland's first carer-run and owned co-op and not-for-profit social enterprise. Established in 2020, the team of migrant women with decades of experience in home care strive for systemic change in home care. They not only offer local, qualified, vetted, insured, experienced care services, but aim to change how care is provided using a human rights and equality approach. They stress the value of care and the value of people being cared for, and the terms and conditions of those caring. The women members invest profit back into the co-op and are continually improving carers' employment terms and investing in training. They aim to get their voice heard and get a say in #HowCareShouldBe.

PART III

An ecosocial political imaginary

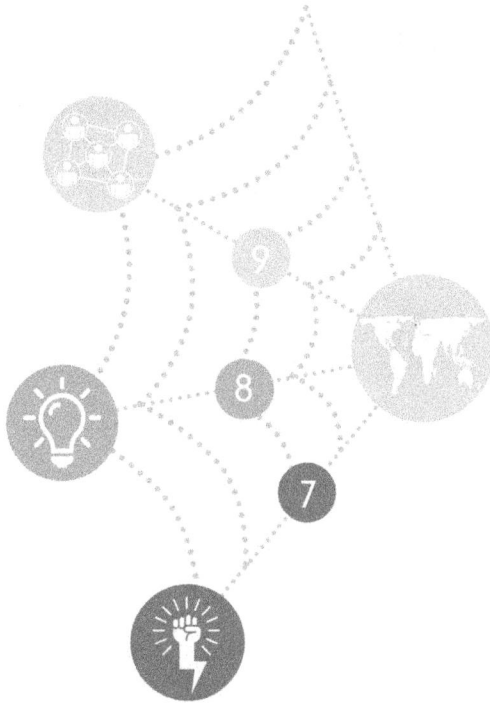

So far, a compelling argument has been made for system change to address the contemporary failure of our capitalist political economy and welfare system to promote environmental sustainability, societal wellbeing and equality. The case for an ecosocial state is manifold not only from the perspective of climate change, but also from the perspective of gender and other inequalities, socio-economic justice, health and wellbeing, social reproduction, democratic participation as well as sustainable ecologies. Part II outlined a case for ecosocial policy as an underlying feature of wider systemic change and explored the values needed to underpin enabling institutions that could enhance reciprocity and interdependence. It offered two anchoring institutions, Universal Basic Services and Participation Income, as core features of an ecosocial state.

Part III will discuss the democratic challenges of social transformation and mobilisation, the importance of imagination, ideas and language, and the significance of new forms of power, all in the context of what strategies might achieve the scale of transformation required for an ecosocial state. Theories of change and transformation translate into strategies for action. Our imagination and ideas influence what we think is possible and how we approach 'making it happen'. Democratic engagement of active citizens requires collective mobilisation across different interests and joining the dots across relevant political civil society campaigns and programmes. Ever mindful of the agency/structure dichotomy, agency needs to be of sufficient scale to thwart the obvious power of vested interests who gain from and so defend the status quo. This requires transforming political opportunity structures in democratic institutions and policy processes into a high-energy democracy. Each chapter concludes by discussing lessons from recent episodes of social transformation in Ireland.

7

Power and mobilisation

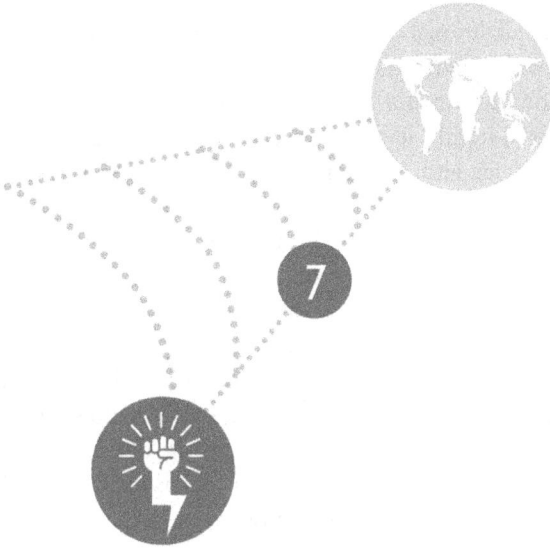

Part II of this book argued that a new model of social organisation, an ecosocial welfare regime, is required. If the old welfare state came about because of a post-war settlement, how might an ecosocial welfare state emerge? Polanyi (1944) understands that social protection emerges as the response of a double movement from society pressuring the state to re-regulate the disembedded economy to better serve the needs of society. How might various movements, including those seeking gender, climate and economic justice, coalesce to pressure for a new form of ecosocial welfare? Here we begin to tease out the politics of transformation and how the concept of ecosocial can offer a focus for a wider struggle for transformation.

This chapter is realistic about the strong structural power of those who benefit most from maintaining the status quo, and it is in this context that concepts of power and transformation are unpacked before discussing whether crisis might be an opportunity for change. The second part of the chapter explores civil society as a space for agency and mobilisation. Understanding strategic logics of transformation assists us in identifying barriers to effective transformation and inclusive participation in collective action. The Irish case study focuses on power and recent transformative moments in Ireland.

Power and transformation

Structure and agency

The chilling reality of the structural power of markets and corporations need not deny hope in collective agency. However, discussions about transformation need to be clear about the nature of power relationships and how structure and agency interact dialectically to shape change. Transformative coalitional strategies ultimately engage with dominant power found in democratic and governance institutions in the context of strong structural vetoes dominated by elite power.

This analysis is highly sensitive to the power of capital, vested interests, financialised power and the concentration of wealth and power in the hands of the few, often men, who also control social media and the production of knowledge that frames our individual experiences. The lobbying and advertising power of the fossil fuel industry is particularly ominous (Razzouk, 2022). This structural power cannot be denied and is underpinned by policies, the state and coercive power. Structure refers to these large-scale social institutions and the realities which frame our individual experience. It includes culture, society and static organisational patterns. Some ascribe structure with strong deterministic power that mitigates agency, predetermining the behaviour of individuals and communities. It is true that agentic power is, in part at least, determined by the position that the actor in question occupies in prevailing social structures (Callinicos, 2004).

Recognising the strength and power of structure does not, however, deny the possibility of agency, or the powers of independent individuals and societal actors who can benefit from social transformation. Sen's (1999) capability approach (CA), which informs this book, focuses on individual capability and recognises the potential and capacity of individuals to shape their worlds and make choices about the life they value. The analysis informing this book understands that individuals exist in a state of moral rationality embedded in community and society. Recognising asymmetrical power balances, the focus is on cooperation of individuals in collective power and interest group formation where informal social relations and structural or institutional contexts are bonded by culture (Jackson, 2005, p 18; Connor, 2011, p 104). This interdependent understanding of structure and agency is in keeping with Polanyi (1944) who rejects a strong version of historical determinism and understands agency as the power of society. This informs approaches to radical transformation and power analysis explored next in the Power Cube (visualised in Figure 7.1) and in the discussion in Chapter 9 of institutions to support a High-Energy Democracy.

Figure 7.1: The powercube

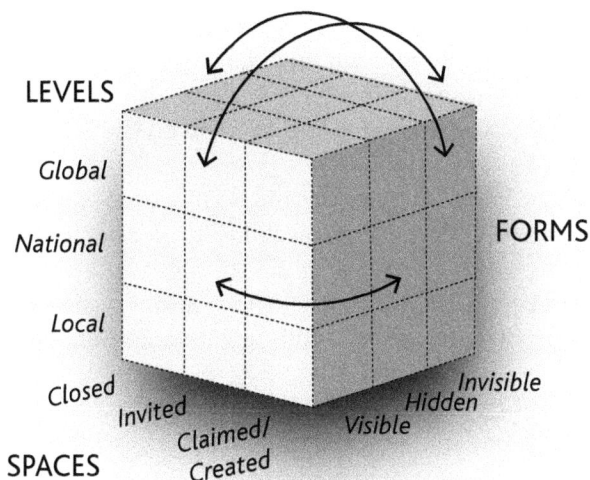

Source: Gaventa, 2006, p 25

Power and transformation

The Power Cube offers a concept or theory of power that seeks to make sense of social reality, structures, agency and/or social action (Gaventa and Petitt, 2010). It builds on the 'three faces' or 'dimensions' of power, a radical theory of power articulated by Stephen Lukes (2004) and developed by Gaventa (2006, 2021) who came to understand the three dimensions of power, decision-making, agenda-setting and ideological or discursive forms of power, as aspects of a single spectrum of power. The Power Cube[1] approach enables actors to visually map situations involving themselves, others, relationships and forces, and to explore possibilities for movement, mobilisation and change – allowing them to plan their advocacy and find entry points for action. The cube theorises that *power* manifests itself in visible, hidden and invisible forms. The *spaces* dimension 'refers to the potential arenas for participation and action, including closed, invited and claimed spaces'. The *levels* dimension refers to the differing layers of decision-making and authority held on a vertical scale, including the micro or household level as well as the local, national and global. It is in the interaction of these nested forms, spaces, and levels that we can locate effective strategies for change as work across all aspects of the cube (Gaventa, 2021, p 8). However, it is only through collective action that we can work across the spectrum of power.

Transformation is closely linked to the process of empowerment, experienced at a personal level of reflective and reflexive agency or a process of conscientisation, and at a structural level as collective action. The power cube traditionally worked through four dimensions of power: power *over*, *to*, *with* and *within* (Green, 2016, p 33). However, over time, a fifth concept of transformative power – power *for* – was added (Gaventa, 2021, p 114):

- Power *over*: the power of hierarchy and domination, as described earlier.
- Power *to*: effective choice, the capability to decide actions and carry them out.
- Power *within*: personal self-confidence and a sense of rights and entitlement.
- Power *with*: collective power, through organisation, solidarity, and joint action.
- Power *for*: motivational logic for sustained movement building for transformation.

While in practice more iterative, messy and non-linear, a unified approach to these interrelated forms of power is summarised as

> empowerment becomes a process through which relatively powerless groups develop a sense of power *within* and the capacity for power *with* others, in order to challenge power *over* their lives and gain the power *to* determine their own futures guided by a different vision of the world as in power *for*. (Gaventa, 2021, p 113)

In a similar vein, the 'power of domination' found in formal political systems and parties needs to be unified with the 'transformative power' of social movements. Wainright's (2018) vision of a 'new politics from the left' as a strategy for change is driven by the exercise of 'power as transformation' supported by an overlapping 'power of domination' exercised through political institutions. She concludes the creative tension between the different forms of power has to be underpinned by social relationships, new ecologies of ownership and tacit knowledge, agentic democratic participation and prefigurative alternatives (2018, pp 98–113).

Justice for the undocumented

After 11 years of campaigning by the Justice for the Undocumented Group, a scheme to regularise the status of people living in Ireland long-term without papers was announced on 3 December 2021. This huge step in realising the rights of undocumented people and progressive approach to immigration reform is an outcome of power from below. The policy shift can be attributed to the agency of a small group of migrants who courageously campaigned for rights and recognition. They are supported in this by the Migrants Rights Centre of Ireland. The regularisation scheme allows people who have been living undocumented in Ireland for four years or more (or three years or more if they have children) to apply to regularise their immigration status. International protection applicants are eligible once they have been in the process of regularisation for a minimum of two years. While not perfect, the scheme is relatively generous and comprehensive, and an outcome of power within, with, to and for.

Complexity

Defining power as 'capacity of one person or institution to command the resources, actions, or innermost thoughts of another', and using a 'power systems analyses', Green (2016, p 29) argues complexity is the defining property of human systems where multiple relationships and feedback loops make sense of the erratic behaviour of a complex system. Change results from the interplay of many diverse and apparently unrelated factors including thought and action, learning and adapting and developing multiple strategies. Change strategies require us to identify which elements are important and how they interact (Green, 2016). Unpredictability is a common feature in interaction between structures (such as state institutions), agency (such as communities and individuals) and the broader context (including shifts in technology, environment, demography, or norms). This requires iterative, collaborative and flexible approaches, or what Green (2016) describes as 'dancing rather than walking a single linear pathway'. Such an understanding of failure, iteration and adaptation offers hope in persistence and a long-term view (Leicester, 2020).

The scale and nature of such complex change is never inevitable but is mediated through three variables – *the three I's: ideas, institutions,* and *interests,* none of which are privileged over the others for their explanatory value or influence (Hay, 2004). The nature of the change is determined by the available ideas or alternatives, the interests that organise around these ideas and through the nature of the formal and informal institutional spaces where such ideas are processed, won and lost. These variables include formal and informal domestic and international institutions (rules of the game including processes, context and policy path dependence); interests (domestic and international actors, preferences and power resources); and ideas (domestic and international content, evidence, expert knowledge, framing, values and norms) (Shearer et al, 2016, p 1200).

My experience of the reproductive rights movement has stretched over 40 years. This political activism was not once-off or occasional or kept for emergencies. It became a part of, and even 'a pleasure of everyday life'(Solnit, 2017), with moments of intense frustration but also wonderful bursts of joy, deep friendships, solidarity, care, and compassion. It involved almost every form of political mobilisation: canvassing in referendums, lobbying, campaigning, postering, marching, shouting, crying and care. It included 8 years of direct action, volunteering for the Women's Information Network, a then-illegal underground telephone helpline providing vital access to information on abortion to women. Most recently, it involved accompanying a wonderful group of passionate younger activists, and some 'old timers' like myself, in the regional mobilisation tour of Together for Yes; a campaign for a yes vote in the 2018 referendum to remove a much-reviled constitutional ban on abortion in the state. Together we visited all 26 counties in the Republic of Ireland, hosting meetings, setting up information stalls, mobilising voters, convincing doubters. On the night of the result, I reunited with the elder lemons of the Women's Information Network, and we rejoiced at the change we were part of making, change we built together. After years on the outside, we were the new common sense.

Transformational and incremental change

Transformation can be best understood in the context of long-term transitions. The image of 'redesigning the plane while keeping it flying' captures the complexity involved in the requirement for three levels of innovation: sustaining, disruptive and transformative (Leicester, 2020, p 2). The latter works with purpose to transform the system towards 'an intentional vision of the future', sometimes building on the 'pockets of the future in the present' (Leicester, 2020, pp 11, 41). Action to transform towards this intentional future is already happening, but the cost of rebuilding the global infrastructure for energy, agriculture, transport, housing and other basic needs including care is inevitably contested (Folbre, 2021).

We can distinguish between first order (discrete, incremental) and second order (deeper, systemic) types of change. Incremental change tends to be piecemeal and fragmented, downplaying the need for changes in the patterns of distribution of assets and income that reproduce or intensify inequality. Such change can dilute or distort agendas and divert attention from the root causes of exclusionary and unsustainable development, thereby constraining transformative change. 'Instrumentalisation' occurs when powerful state or market institutions use social processes to advance their own specific goals, for example engaging in manipulative and cynical consultation processes. 'Isomorphism' occurs when alternative organisations assume behavioural features of the mainstream institutions with which they interact, for example when civil society attempts to justify a business case for equality (Utting, 2018).

Different interests are associated with transformative and incremental change. Often entrenched institutional cultures, interests and worldviews influence policy and strategy. Pragmatic governments and their bureaucracies, engaged in problem-solving, crisis management and compromise almost inevitably moderate their approach to social and institutional change. Positive change, when it happens, is often incremental, limiting the potential for significant transformative gains. However, transformative change is not necessarily positive, as has been the case with some populist and socialist regimes' transformative agendas. Change is positively transformative when it addresses the reorganisation of social reproduction, gender equality and more equitable power relations (Utting, 2018). This is what activists mean when they call for 'system change, not climate change'. Jones and O'Donnell (2018, p xv) wisely advise against assuming a reform/revolution dichotomy and are clear that incremental reforms can amount eventually to system change.

'Transformation' goes beyond addressing the symptoms of contemporary development problems to confronting their root causes, namely the structural conditions that reproduce inequality, vulnerability and social and environmental injustice. For Utting (2018) transformative outcomes should meet peoples' basic needs and promote environmental protection, decent work, the equitable distribution of resources and profits, and democratic forms of governance – consistent with the transformational vision of the SDGs. Transformative reforms can simultaneously make life better within the existing economic system and expand the potential for future advances of democratic power. Such 'non-reformist reform policies' require us to do things now which put us in the best position to do more later (Wright, 2013; Fraser, 2013, 2014). The objective is to work to create institutions and structures which increase, rather than decrease, the prospects of taking advantage of whatever historical opportunities emerge. But the task is more urgent than ever.

Reflecting on my work in the Irish National Organisation of the Unemployed it is striking how many short-term successes in policy negotiations with the state were incremental and might be classed as diversions from a more transformative agenda. In an apparent milestone victory, achieving a 20-year-old target for income adequacy in the Irish welfare system, the practical outcome amounted to the price of a chocolate bar a week for each adult claimant. That time might have been better spent campaigning for more transformative change. Yet income adequacy and benchmarking of income supports is a core feature of an equitable society and transformative in its own right. Unemployed people wanted this outcome. As Solnit (2016) observes many successes are incremental, these non-reformist reforms propel us towards the end goal.

Civil society

What really creates change is popular mobilisation and legislative changes to enforce new policy (Konzcal, 2021, p 124). Civil society is commonly understood as 'the arena, between family, government and market, where people voluntarily associate to advance common interests' (Crowley, 2022, p 14). It includes formal and informal groupings, positive and negative, peaceful and violent, that seek to advance or obstruct social progress. This autonomous space is a public sphere where people exercise their power and voice independent of, and often contesting or resisting, markets, states or both. A vital aspect of democracy, it is a political form of active citizenship and offers platforms for voices often ignored in mainstream politics.

This wide expanse of very diverse organisations is variegated in scale, style, values and type, however, often the study of civil society is of institutionalised forms of organisations (religions, trade unions, media, volunteering, women's groups, youth groups, and so on), many of which seek to shape change through relatively institutionalised routes and relationships with the state, or sometimes the market. In this scenario civil society is understood as a number of discrete sectors, functions or interests which compete with each other for resources and public attention. This siloing of 'civil society' leaves little space for discourse and action across civil society and limits capacity of civil society as a civil space or public sphere to grow purpose and ambition in relation to equality and environmental sustainability (Crowley, 2022).

Drawing out tensions within different traditions and strategies for mobilisation and collective action for emancipatory alternatives alerts us to how different understandings of change can also generate silos, tensions and differences between actors who fundamentally want similar end goals (Wright, 2013). As well as two foundational principles – egalitarian social justice and radical democratic empowerment – Wright (2013) identifies three strategic logics of transformation that characterise the history of struggle to transform capitalism:

- *ruptural* or revolutionary transformations envision creating new emancipatory institutions through a sharp break with existing institutions and social structures;
- *interstitial* transformations seek to prefabricate new forms of social empowerment in the niches, spaces and margins of capitalist society, potentially eroding constraints on the spaces themselves while ideologically and practically showcasing alternatives;
- *symbiotic* or more incremental transformations deepen the institutional forms of popular social empowerment while helping to solve certain practical problems, simultaneously make life better within the existing economic system while expanding the potential for future advances of democratic power.

This helps us differentiate four types of strategic logic in relation to civil society and capitalism (Kirby and Murphy, 2011):

- A neoliberal strand of organisations seeks reforms in society that are consistent with the dominant neoliberal model of development. They often perceive themselves as neutral while focusing on incremental change; however, they are often parasitic, accepting short-term solutions that contribute to longer-term structural problems.
- The social democratic strand of organisations that tends to seek a strong role for the state, seeking largely incremental policy change in the form of quality publicly owned services, equality and sustainable taxation to support a flourishing society.
- The ecological strand of organisations seeks social, economic, cultural and environmental change, often rooted in local ways of organising social and economic life and wellbeing.
- A ruptural strand that seeks revolutionary forms of transformation, more often found in small left political parties but also in anarchist social movements.

New communities of communities

These different modes of change operationalise different tactics and strategies, and different orientations to state-society relationships, differences that make it difficult for groups to work together, or to avoid 'getting in each other's way'. A narcissism of small differences can cause splits, fractures and tensions between actors, even as they all work towards similar transformative change. This can be dispiriting, causing many to turn away from such forms of organising. A search for new forms of working for change is evident in the break in intergenerational understandings of how digital communication has changed the nature of work and relationships, but also new understandings of power and contestation, and how knowledge is created, shared and consumed. There is a discernable shift from institutionalised forms of civil society to a less formal, less hierarchical and a more hyper-local, values-based form of activism, with consequences for strategising change. Often hyper-local in composition, this form of civil society taps into common values to establish common purpose and build from there, often prefiguring or prefabricating change in how they live their own collective lives as a way of influencing broader change. Jones and O'Donnell use the concept of the 'life world' to refer to new sets of non-hierarchical social relationships that are grounded in social bases (2018, p 246).

These new forms of civil society include contemporary movements like Black Lives Matter (BLM), #MeToo and Extinction Rebellion, all of which exhibit new energy. Their determination to be heard enhances capacity to animate and mobilise people, and to increase likelihood of contestation. This is also true of the 'new politics of the people' visible in new movements representing those made more vulnerable by contemporary capitalism, including new forms of trade unions representing precarious workers and renters' collectives fighting landlord power in the streets (Shenker, 2019). Bringing together these, often local, 'communities of communities' is key to organising human agency and overcoming barriers to consciousness-raising and joining the dots (Slevin et al, 2022). However, building from the bottom up is not necessarily loose, some communities, as places of belonging and central to the creation and maintenance of prosocial norms, are structured, while some are fleeting or ephemeral (Bednar, 2023, p 11). Decentralisation and supporting social infrastructure can enable society to build spaces where norms can emerge (Bednar, 2023, p 14). Most of these forces remain small and marginal, and even large and powerful movements like Occupy, Indignados, Extinction Rebellion, #MeToo and BLM struggle to stay relevant over time. Nonetheless, hope lies in the reality that no one ever knows when collective mobilisation will result in change (Klein, 2014).

Mobilisation as inclusive participation

'Sometimes silence can be a tool of oppression; when you are silenced … it is not simply that you do not speak but that you are barred from participation in a conversation which nevertheless involves you' (Ahmed, 2010, p xvi). Collective action or mobilisation is often a necessary catalyst for transformation, however, mass participation without meaningful empowerment is unlikely to lead to lasting transformation (Beresford, 2020, p 117). Meaningful participation should respect autonomy and self-determination of user-led organisations which define their own structure, agenda and language for collective action. Much participation, particularly of excluded groups, is local – poor people have less or no choice about where and how they get to participate and are often excluded from national organising (Crowley, 2022). Many interests struggle, particularly smaller collective actors working with or representing vulnerable communities, to meaningfully participate or to engage in consultation or policy processes, leading to 'consultationitis'. Negative experiences reinforce uneven power dynamics within society and between society and the state.

Power, consultation, participation, partnership and knowledge are all contested concepts. Some experiences of participation are negative, manipulative or at best tokenistic and conflate access and influence. Without redistribution of power, participation 'is an empty and frustrating process for the powerless. It allows the powerholders to claim that all sides were considered but makes it possible for only some of those sides to benefit' (Arnstein, 1969, p 216). It maintains the status quo. Truly participatory ideology is a rarity but is essential in developing empowering language that builds on experiential knowledge (Beresford, 2020, p 7). Knowledge is a source of power and ideas. It offers capacity to contest dominant understandings and framing of societal problems and to influence alternative ways to understand the range of potential policy responses. Being oppressed means having been through a process of 'colonialisation of the mind' and to be victims of epistemic injustice or violence associated with power and discrimination (Beresford, 2020, p 126). Inclusive participation needs to listen to and reclaim experiential knowledge and challenge assumptions.

'Who said "if I can't dance, I don't want to be in your revolution?"' was a common question in progressive pub quizzes throughout Ireland in the 1990s. The answer was Emma Goldman, the anarchist political activist and writer who wrote and campaigned in North America and Europe in the first half of the 20th century. While many of us, as activists, knew the answer, few of us ever investigated what she meant by the phrase, and we all developed our own nuanced interpretation. For my own part, I interpreted her words to mean what I wanted them to mean: that unless the ideology inspiring the revolution included me, talked to me, and made sense of my life, I did not want to be part of it. On these grounds, I ignored many calls to action from socialist, republican, nationalist and working-class causes that ignored and talked past women. The phrase has many meanings attributed to it, but I hear an objection to the exclusionary nature of prevailing political ideologies – and a call for activism to be fun, enjoyable and allow people to see and hear themselves in the 'dream'.

Barriers and enablers of inclusive participation

Assumptions of collective action also raise the challenge of how we 'do' participation. There are clear obstacles to coalition-building and weaknesses in organising and movement-building, including the level of fragmentation, short-termism and hierarchy in civil society (Crowley, 2022; Jessola and Mandelli, 2022, p 249). Much of civil society is spread thinly, forced to act as a public sphere while also depending for survival on their role as a service delivery agent of the welfare state. Civil society is challenged to reimagine not only siloed structures, but also its sometimes-exclusive processes and priorities. Current legislative, regulatory and governance regimes often lead civil society organisations to adopt forms of leadership and management styles that will comply with and protect funding regimes, rather than political leaders who aspire to coalition-building towards transformative change (Crowley, 2022). Obstacles include lack of clear leadership, fragmentation of the organised labour movement and the decline in significance of the national arenas of struggle, and the lack of desire to protect what, for many, is a negatively experienced welfare state which in contemporary times is stigmatising and limits personal freedom (Fraser, 2013, p 129).

Honest discussion is needed to unpack the real challenges in collectivity, inclusivity, organising and mobilisation. Developing ideas about how to promote equality and freedom should happen within inclusive societal claimed spaces and organisations. Meaningful processes of co-production that empower, recognise and validate various forms of knowledge for policy are largely localised and inclusive but national mobilisations are often less so. Often those seeking climate justice experience a common and profound sense of democratic and social injustice. This is prompted by increasing corporatisation of the state and the hollowing out of its democratic function (Szolucha, 2018), but similar processes are also evident in society. Shouting and retweeting will not save us (Bednar, 2023, p 14). We need to talk to each other. We need to listen to each other. We need deep listening.

We need to be open to opportunities to connect across civil and political society and to our moral obligation to listen. The key is to include those affected in imagining and creating their own future, and to acknowledge and respect their work on behalf of one another (Bednar, 2023, p 4). When we listen, we hear that to mobilise people about climate change it must be related in some way to their everyday life, to the bread-and-butter issues that dominate peoples' lives when they are poor, discriminated against or oppressed. We need to build on the political reality underpinning unequal experiences of oppression and vulnerability. This means avoiding false narratives that pit groups against one another for relative status and privilege and prioritises individual agency over structural barriers.

Inclusive movement-building

Much can be learned from environmental movements and activism, but also from other contemporary movements including pioneering welfare service-user movements, movements of people with disabilities, trans peoples' movements, migrants' rights and regularisation movements, feminist movements including #MeToo, class mobilisation, civil rights and race and ethnic justice movements including BLM (Perez et al, 2015; Beresford, 2016; Khan-Cullors and Bandele, 2017). As discussed, the focus of collective mobilisation is shifting, in some cases to connections based on lived experience rather than building movements based on siloed interests or 'mono' identities. Common experiences of oppression can be a uniting factor, enabling new forms of alliances and bringing together demands for care, ecology, inclusion and democratic participation and deliberation. These can be enabled within an ecosocial paradigm once movements are inclusive and generous, engaging with people who have shared goals but may have different language and traditions of organising. We need to reflectively and consciously avoid language that others find painful or divisive (Beresford, 2020, p 125). Cautioning against perfection, and advising we surrender 'purity' and let go of dividing tendencies of the left, the argument needs to be 'a better world yes, a perfect world never' (Solnit, 2016, pp 75–78, citing Richard White).

Difference is not necessarily oppositional, we need to see less 'sectarian righteousness' of binary left-right politics while 'puritan environmentalists' need to build a broader base towards a 'radical centre' (Solnit, 2016, pp 68, 88). An ecosocial vision can make sense of incremental goals linking them to a more transformative agenda and pathways for change. The key is focusing on what unites rather than what divides us, trying to see others' perspectives. Many of us can recount feelings of being caught in the 'narcissism of small differences', of feeling excluded from an emerging movement. Many of us have excluded people and ideas from our narrow perspective. We need to learn from and inspire each other to mobilise.

My personal experience of the Irish National Organisation of the Unemployed in the 1990s exposed for me the inherent tensions in organising around 'situations in life' rather than personal 'identity'. Mike Allen (1998) explored in his book, *The Bitter Word*, the challenge of organising on the grounds of a situation people want to be temporary (as in the case of unemployment or poverty), as distinct from more lifelong personal identities like gender, ethnicity, sexuality or disability, which people want to reclaim, celebrate, defend, and protect. In my early days of paid employment with the Irish National Organisation of the Unemployed, I was asked to wait outside while the membership debated whether employing me, not previously unemployed, fitted with the organisation's model of change and of empowerment and participation. After some intense debate they agreed to my involvement. It as a moment I will never forget.

Ireland: power and transformation

Power of money

Wealth inequality is a fundamental component of economic and power inequality. The distribution of wealth in Ireland is highly concentrated. Oxfam Ireland find that wealth creation in Ireland intensified over the last decade, with the richest 1 percent gaining 70 percent more than the bottom 10 percent of the population. The wealthiest 1 percent now owns more than one quarter of the country's wealth, an estimated €232 billion. Eight people are worth over €1 billion with the richest two worth over €15 billion between them, 50 percent more wealth than the poorest 50 percent of the population.[2] Distribution of financial assets is broadly similar to the distribution of net wealth, with over half of all financial assets held by the top 10 per cent, which also owns 82 per cent of all land.

These individuals (usually male) are also found in golden circles, overlapping on the corporate and financial boards of Ireland. Power is also located in corporations in Ireland. Corporation tax in Ireland has risen sharply to be Ireland's second largest tax base in 2022, giving companies that pay such tax even more disproportionate political power. Over half of all receipts from the business tax come from just ten large firms, including (in order of the largest payer) Apple, Microsoft, Google, Pfizer, MSD (Merck, Sharpe and Dohme), Johnson&Johnson, Facebook, Intel, Medtronic and Coca-Cola. These information technology, pharma, medical supplies and leisure companies are global actors, as are some smaller but strategic Irish-owned multinational actors including Glanbia and other agri-food businesses. All are disproportionately powerful in relation to the strategic role they play in the globalised Irish political economy, and all benefit from and will defend the neoliberal model that works for them so well. The civil society accounts of power and agency need to be understood in the context of such power.

Change strategies in Irish civil society

There is evidence in Ireland of civil society actors pursuing all four change strategies outlined: maintenance of the status quo as well as more transformative ruptural, interstitial and symbiotic strategies for change. Consensual political culture means that many civil society organisations work within a symbiotic or reformist theory of change seeking to influence politics and policy while maintaining neutrality across political parties. A relatively small proportion follow ruptural theories of change and strategies that are more revolutionary in intent. These include both civil and political society actors. Part of civil society tends to innovate by prefiguring the type of change they wish to see. While some interstitial actors focus on influencing policy and political society, others take more anarchist forms as 'societies against the state', while we also see a growing trend towards less institutional hyper-local values-based communities who prefigure the world they want to live in. The history of partition on the island has led to concepts of freedom being interpreted through the lens of nationalism, republicanism, sovereignty and civil liberties. At present, civil society spheres are relatively siloed, with significant fractures between them (Crowley, 2022; see Chapter 9). With some exceptions, there is also considerable distance between many civil society dynamics and political society, although this space is narrowing.

Insider strategies for change

The Irish mixed welfare regime incudes a relatively significant role for civil society or, in the Irish nomenclature, the CVS, comprised of small and large service delivery and other advocacy-oriented actors. The language of CVS reflects the important contributions of different traditions, ideologies and models of change over the history of the Irish state, differences still visible in the contemporary diversity and power struggles within civil society in Ireland. There are at least 29,000 non-profit organisations in Ireland (Crowley, 2020). Volunteering and service provision-type activities including sport, culture and charity dominate and often operate 'in the shadow of the state' (Kirby and Murphy, 2011, p 170). Key charities operate as the shadow welfare state, while the state advertises and promotes the use of such services. COVID-19 required many civil society actors to reimagine their role, services, processes and power. Many local community and voluntary groups, for example, worked in new relationships with local government and other actors to respond to local needs (Dekker, 2020; NESC, 2020b).

Social Partnership, an Irish model of corporatism or 'innovative form of networked governance' for business, trade union and agricultural interests had from the mid-1990s to 2008 given some actors in the CVS and the environmental justice sector greater 'access' to policy-influencing processes and institutions. While some see this as a positive form of deliberative democracy, or an extension and widening of participatory democracy, others see it as an unequal participation that effectively co-opts or smothers civil society in the embrace of the state. Civil society experiences an asymmetric power in social partnership (Larragy, 2016) and risks cooption for uncertain capacity to influence outcomes. At the same time, dual processes of austerity and marketisation have reinforced the service orientation of civil society in Ireland, reducing capacity for social documentation, while new political and legal clauses restrict the use of state and internationally sourced funding for campaigning purposes. Advocacy campaigns to influence government policy continue to place an 'emphasis on preferred insider consensual change strategies based on clear structures of engagement with government' (Acheson and Visser, 2019, p 1).

Outsider strategies for change

However, political or policy engagement is present in the shape of mobilisations which also conflict with the state, an historical pattern associated with partition that has extended over time into other themes of conflict including the environment. High points of organised resistance to state policy over the last decade include the Shell to Sea Movement which opposed the construction of a natural gas pipeline; a campaign against domestic water charges; and resistance to restrictions on domestic turf-cutting. Campaigns with environmental land use themes appear to generate a more conflictual and direct-action approach (Higgins, 2021), perhaps due to a cultural value associated with conflict about land ownership but also reflecting a deep-seated demand for democratic processes that reflect people's right to participate and to have their voice and local perspective heard (Garavan, 2007). There is also greater ideological contestation of inequality. Since the 1970s, EU-funded community development-oriented organisations working spatially and through communities of interest (for example, lone parents) have generated greater capacity for policy engagement and structural analysis of inequality, leading to more varied theories of change and action which conflict with state policy (Harvey, 2014).

There are also new and positive momentums. Social media and new horizontal forms of power and participation offer civil society new ways to engage in change and transformation. Legal and related human rights routes have been used by a range of social activists including migrants, asylum seekers, people with disabilities and Travellers. One such legal strategy was pursued by *Friends of the Irish Environment* (FIE) who sued the Irish government on the grounds that the 2018 National Mitigation Plan violated the 2015 Climate Act. This case is representative of a global strategy by environmental movements to use law, and in particular human rights law, to hold states accountable for environmental harms that threaten human health and lives. The Irish Supreme Court eventually agreed with FIE, an important legal outcome in its own right but one that also has impacts on political dialogue and policy (O'Neill and Alblas, 2020). Further evidence of these new approaches is the newly established Centre for Environmental Justice, a branch of the Community Law and Mediation civil society organisation (CSO) in a local working-class suburb in North Dublin. This centre aims to use law to ensure that communities are not disproportionately affected by climate change and that the states response is inclusive and fair.

New power momentums

These legal campaigns overlap with a period of 'New Politics' in Ireland which, since 2016, brought new political opportunity structures and innovative approaches to power and participation. These included deliberative processes like national-level Citizens' Assemblies and county-level Public Participation Networks (PPNs) as well as increased cross-party collaboration. These innovations facilitated shifts in political relationships within civil society and between civil society and the state. Irish civil society also experienced the international shift to new more horizontal forms of organising. There are more abundant opportunities to liaise with the political system, such as in parliamentary committees, to engage in setting agendas, framing narratives, collaborating and networking with more diverse actors (Connaughton, 2021).

The state will increasingly find that neither traditional and hierarchical forms of consultation nor partnership will meet the expectations of a flatter, less cohesive civil society. There is rich opportunity for lesson-learning in recent meaningful processes of co-creation that empower, recognise and validate various forms of knowledge. Recent successful civil society-led political campaigns have led to advancements in several progressive bio-political rights including divorce, abortion and marriage equality. Ireland became a less conservative and paternalistic country as a direct outcome of sustained people power and activism, particularly from groups experiencing intersectional inequality and oppression. These groups (women, LGBTI+ people, separated people, children's rights activists) have overcome structural violence and exclusion, stigma, micro-aggressions and coercive obstacles including, at times, potential imprisonment, personal debt, loss of employment, public and private acrimony to work individually and as groups, separately and together, to lead change in Ireland.

However, despite similar activism and leadership, and consistent with international observations (Klein, 2014), there has been less progress on socio-economic rights such as education for people with disabilities, and the rights to housing, water and care. This is consistent with historical experiences that structural distributional issues are harder to progress than issues of personal morality. Nonetheless, campaigns for legislative reform to advance and protect economic and social rights are alive in Ireland and include demands for constitutional recognition of economic and social rights including the rights to water, housing and care as well as the recognition of nature and the need to protect biodiversity. At the same time, however, practical policy becomes more coercive with greater welfare conditionality, commodification, and greater reliance on the market to deliver more (un)affordable housing, health and care.

8

Imaginaries and ideas

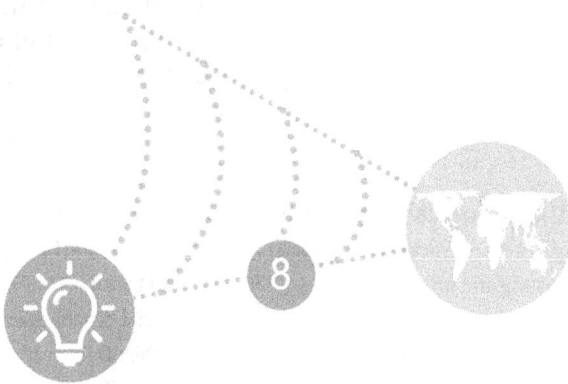

Graeber and Wengrow (2021, p 505) reflect on the possibility that we are stuck and unable to imagine or shape new social realities. The greatest poverty we should fear is poverty of our imagination, and many observe an intellectual vacuum when it comes to imaginative alternatives (Cumbers, 2018; Jones and O'Donnell, 2018). This is a chicken and egg conundrum: it is easier to mobilise people if they believe an alternative is possible, but without mobilisation it is difficult to generate alternatives (Meadowcroft, 2007). Alternatives need not be highly developed, nor do they need to be policy blueprints or detailed maps. Our social and political imagination provides direction or compass points, while our institutional or programmatic imagination can articulate the first steps of travel.

The first section of this chapter argues for policy imagination and for the need to articulate alternatives in the tradition of 'realist pragmatism' or 'real utopias' and assesses the role of ideas in orienting change during crisis (Wright, 2013; Fitzpatrick, 2014). The second section of the chapter examines the importance of framing alternatives in constructive, offensive rather than defensive, language capable of mobilising a wide range of actors, uniting rather than dividing society and offering hope in being 'for' rather than 'against'. This underscores the importance of who articulates alternatives and draws attention to the 'vocabularies of our imagination' (Massey, 2013). The Irish section reviews examples of framing transformative ideas in recent constitutional referendums that led to a level of transformation many middle-aged feminist activists (like me) could only dream would happen in their lifetime.

Imagination and ideas

Imagining how to live together

Many, in exploring the central organising principle of sustainable alternatives, draw on various visual images, myths and parables to demonstrate how ancient wisdoms of sustainable life collectively point towards 'balance' as a core principle or value (Green, 2016; Raworth, 2017; Leicester, 2020; Jackson, 2021). This orientation inspired the visual motif of this book, a symmetrical spider's web holding together and joining the dots between the book's themes.

An anthropological sense of political imagination

People 'give to' and 'receive from' society, but also 'judge' and have capacity for democracy and for political struggle (Bonvin and Larrufa, 2022). Society has always experimented with diverse forms of social organisation; many alternative and intentional communities still do this. Deliberating about how to live together is intrinsic to human capacity for self-creation and self-determination. The freedom to re-invent 'us', individually and collectively, is what makes us human. Graeber and Wengrow (2021, p 8) describe how anthropological possibilities for forms of social organisation include both collective, or communal, as well as authoritarian models of power and decision-making. As conscious political actors, societies were always aware of and found ways to limit the dangers of excessive authoritarian power or domination, limiting power to seasons, rotating between people or consciously avoiding excesses or forms of money that might be sources of inequality, subordination, and power.

Graeber and Wengrow (2021, pp 110–120), in their powerful book *The Dawn of Everything: A New History of Humanity*, describe how many remote forager ancestors were bold experimenters, breaking apart and reassembling societies at different scales in radically different forms with different value systems at one time of the year to another. While diverse, a common tendency was constant alteration and awareness of diverse social and political possibilities. With such institutional flexibility, no social order was fixed or immutable, all were designed to be dismantled. Societies could step outside the boundaries of an institutional structure and reflect about its role, purpose, and relevance – they could both make and unmake the political worlds in which they lived. There was often a seasonal variation in determining where on the political spectrum societies consciously decided to be, a possibility now openly discussed in the context of living with the seasonally endemic COVID-19 or seasonal impacts of global warming.

Role of arts and culture

At times it is difficult to imagine alternatives or identify cultural, social and political human possibilities, or to be politically self-consciousness about how we live. In centuries past, opportunity for individual and collective political imagination was a common feature of subversive popular festivals which acted as laboratories of social possibility – often 'turning the world upside down' with festivals that were 'a veritable encyclopaedia of possible political forms' (Graeber and Wengrow, 2021, p 118). Contemporary culture, including different genres of science fiction, social media, adult education and intentional communities, are spaces where political imagination can and does run riot. We need to mainstream this willingness to experiment with new flexible forms of social organisation. Wallace Wells (2019, p 145) reflects on literature, including poetry and fiction, that stoke such imagination. Classics like Attwood's trilogy, culminating in Maddaddam (2013), have explored potential alternatives, and the solarpunk art movement,[1] which emerged in the 2010s as a reaction to the prevalence of post-apocalyptic and dystopian media, focuses on hopeful alternatives. Much of this literature is considered a niche form of 'climate-fiction', however, Kim Stanley Robinson's novel, Ministry of the Future, demonstrates the potential impact of this genre. Increasingly, mainstream novels, such as Richard Power's Pulitzer Prize-winning Overstory, help us to make sense of climate change and think through the 'unthinkable'. They contribute to and reflect the growth in awareness of the reality of climate change and how we might deal with, or survive, nightmarish realities and catastrophic events. The treatment of the welfare state in film and literature has, on the other hand, been through the lens of social realism, shining a harsh light on the impact of capitalism and financialisation, but often offering little in the form of hopeful alternatives. Directors like Ken Loach create critically acclaimed work, such as I, Daniel Blake, but there is less in arts and culture speculating about the welfare state to guide our imagination. That said, there are local examples of participative art, poetry, music and theatre that engage critically with the lived experience of welfare and give voice to the views of welfare claimants and celebrate their spirit of resistance.

Ministry of the Future

Kim Stanley Robinson's book, Ministry for the Future, has been described as one of the most powerful and original books on climate change ever written. The fictional Ministry for the Future was established in 2025 by the United Nations to advocate for the world's future generations and to protect all living creatures, present and future. Set in 2050, the novel focuses on the account of the Ministry Director, Mary Murphy (my namesake and a tough Irish female politician known to drink, curse and practice unorthodox approaches to get the job done), who attempts to use United Nations institutional channels to avert environmental disaster, and along the way has to cope with the presence of environmental terrorism, corrupt power, techno optimism, new monetary systems, and more. Sharing a name (and some characteristics) with the novel's heroine, I had the pleasure of meeting KSR online to discuss the novel and its imaginative contribution; a vision of the relatively near future where hard collective work and constructive contestation, numerous strategies and conflict brings positive change.

A social imaginary

Social and political struggle requires social and political imagination that mixes hope and fear, anger and action. The concept of 'social imaginary' refers to the set of values, institutions, laws and symbols through which people imagine their social whole, and project their needs, aspirations, sense of participation and belonging. It includes 'the creative and symbolic dimension of the social world, the dimension through which human beings create their ways of living together and their ways of representing their collective life' (Thompson, 1984, p 6). This assumes multiple world views including those informed by indigenous knowledge, language and practices (Kimmerer, 2015). 'Political imaginary' refers to how our individual and collective understanding of, and experiences of, politics shapes, or constrains, our motivations and mobilisation for political and social change (Brown and Diehl, 2019). The dominant political imaginary reinforces the status quo of political engagement (Cullen and Gough, 2022).

There are clear links between freedom and capabilities and our individual and collective imagination. Democratic deliberation and political justification are crucial to defining which capabilities matter most, thus any list of central capabilities needs to be continuously 'contested and remade' (Nussbaum, 2005); *imagination* is a crucial capability. Leicester (2020, p 54) stresses the importance of imagination or 'future consciousness' as a societal capacity and argues against compromising to resolve creative tensions between what could appear as competing goals (for example, reciprocity and freedom, or agency and structure).

Crisis as opportunity?

Noting that inside the word 'emergency' is the word 'emerge', there is both danger and possibility in crisis (Solnit, 2016, p 13). Hope emerges when people seek to rebuild together in times of crisis, but this only occurs when people know what they want to rebuild together (Solnit, 2016). Examining why present-day shocks do not generate the scale of change that was seen in past eras of massive shocks (such as the New Deal following the Great Depression in the 1930s), Klein (2014) isolates two explanations: the absence of utopian imagination and the lack of the mass muscle of organised movements. She believes movements must predate any shocks, positively articulate 'what they are for' and use crises as an accelerant to 'leap toward transformation'. 'Mass muscle' is needed to identify common values and connect dots across disconnected and often competing silos. She attributes an absence of imaginative capacity to an absence of popular memory of alternative values and systems. While there are exceptions, including indigenous communities who have nurtured knowledge of other ways to live, many of us are caught in 'capitalisms matrix', distracted and struggling to articulate what we want (Klein, 2014).

Other structural factors can help explain why change does not necessarily follow crisis. Policy developments and choices are often shaped and constrained by path-dependent features including a country's constitution and past policies. Thus, once a government goes down a path, it is difficult to reverse, in part because doing so would challenge stakeholders' vested interests. Many studies of crisis stress the resilience of existing trajectories, finding little evidence that major natural or political shocks (including war, hurricanes and coup d'états) lead to lasting change in more developed political regimes (Castles, 2010). Strong path dependencies are indeed difficult to over-ride, 'humans tend to stick to what they know best', while policy-makers fall 'back on old habits' (Chung and Thewissen, 2011; Starke et al, 2013, p 10).

While responses to the pandemic crisis offered some 'glimpses of the future', the responses rarely challenged the core institutions of welfare capitalism. More often, accelerated policy momentums had some traction prior to the crisis (Hogan et al, 2021). The most important learning we can take from the study of crisis is to be ready and be organised. Proponents of transformation must have at the ready ideas for new policies, practices and rules of the game to be able to take advantage of the opportune – but often unpredictable – moments when change is possible (Levi, 2020). We need to be 'ready now'.

Framing narratives

The power of ideas

Ideas influence not only how problems are understood but how different societal actors define a problem, how they perceive different policy options to be effective, feasible and acceptable, or whether there are alternatives (Pomey et al, 2010). Ideas can also influence policy developments and choices and include knowledge (or evidence) based on empirical research, the informed opinion of experts and (less often) experiential knowledge of societal groups.

Indeed, 'availability of visible viable alternatives is a prerequisite of meaningful choices' (Kabeer, 2005). It is not unusual to see powerful actors contest the strength, validity and legitimacy of evidence provided by their opponents. We saw, for example, in COP 26 that the experiential knowledge of indigenous peoples is not fully valued. Reminding ourselves of structural power and the strength of the powerful, imagination is proactively curtailed or controlled by the powerful and wealthy interests which shape dominant values to suit their goals. They do this through media, advertising, celebrity culture, political discourse, religion, education, culture and arts.

We can distinguish three types of ideas: ideas as weapons, ideas as blueprints and ideas as cognitive locks embedding some ideas and preventing alternatives from emerging (Blyth, 2002). The relationship between mobilisation, alternatives and ideologies is crucial. Democratic processes and collective action enable people to own and understand the tension in competing demands, rather than be offered blueprints, or readymade packages of reforms or a pre-prepared manifesto for change. In this sense, ideas can evolve and progress while mobilising around and building alternatives. When this happens the process of engaging in ideology can be understood as imaginative or visionary (Beresford, 2020, p 12). Some old ideologies or traditional orthodoxies require reimagination in making sense of the future. 'A lot of mixing and matching, cutting and pasting, is now taking place' to 'develop a more unified approach from the new set of raw materials' (Cantillon, 2016, p 486), and this is not problematic. Feminist theory is key to this reimagination, focusing on an important dimension of collective identity and action that is relevant to both production and reproduction, while also speaking to intersectionality: the ways in which multiple forms of inequalities (based, for example, on gender, race/ethnicity, class, able-bodiness) interact to create new forms of inequalities (Folbre, 2021).

Values are key in framing narratives and are central motivators which underlie our beliefs, thoughts and actions, and define who we are and what individuals, groups and organisations stand for (Crowley, 2022). Many now work to rebalance cultural values to create a more equitable, sustainable and democratic society. Communication and campaign strategies consciously engage particular values that promote attitudes and behaviours that support work for social change (Crowley, 2022). The key, according to Common Cause (2022), is to 'champion and reflect the human values that underpin our care for one another and our living planet in mainstream culture, and to build a society in which key social institutions validate and reflect the values that most people prioritise'. Arts and culture are important vehicles through which alternative values are promoted and shaped and both UBS as arts and cultural services and institutions and PI as income support can promote people's engagement in shaping their own values and questioning those of the wealthy and powerful.

The importance of language

It is important who articulates, and what language is used to frame understandings of what is possible. Words need to connect with people, where they are, across many different places at different times. Language is developed in a context of structural power which contests and often weaponises words, turning them back against people as a tactic to undermine, disempower and fragment communities into sectoral interests. Framing is important as mental structures shape the way we view the world. As Lakoff (2004) shows us, when we hear a word, its frame or collection of frames is activated in our brain. Reframing is used in the political arena particularly well by conservatives and the political right to change what people view as commonsense or intuitively correct assessments of their reality, so that liberal economic narratives dominate our thought worlds and shape our social conversations (Jackson, 2021, p 3). Lakoff (2004) argues progressives should make more effective use of framing techniques to counter conservative arguments and reframe the debate. We need to consciously use words and images as metaphors to inspire change and follow Lakoff's advice 'to choose words and campaign demands wisely' – 'public investment' not 'public spending', 'tax justice' not 'more taxation' (Raworth, 2017).

Language is often inadequate to the task; the word 'care', for example, has to work hard, at least in the English language. The Irish have 40 shades of green, while there is a common myth that the Inuit people have 40–50 words for snow, yet humanity has few words that help us articulate care. This may be one of the reasons why definitions of care are often very expansive incorporating immediate bodily care, emotional care, health, education, as well as care of nature and the planet. When we see quite how fundamental the function of care is we can begin to imagine and articulate its importance and ultimate roles and central place in the alternatives to growth-dominated macro economy.

Language can also be co-opted. The ideas and frames that emerge from collective action have often been stolen or co-opted by the state and powerful actors. In the process, ideas are diluted, corrupted and become either meaningless or a source of confusion or conflict. The 'Green New Deal' movement has gained momentum across the Atlantic. It arose out of direct action in the US and was promoted along the lines of the New Deal of the 1930s. Direct action, such as that taken by the Sunrise Movement, including a high-profile occupation of former Democrat House Speaker Nancy Pelosi's office, demanded drastic public action to decarbonise the economy with an ambitious programme for social justice including public housing, new 'green' jobs, the revaluation of care work alongside racial justice and addressing legacies of slavery, colonialism and discrimination. Momentum around the Green New Deal has grown worldwide, however, the concept has also been diluted and co-opted and is now confused with efforts to 'green' growth and social policy as part of the mainstream environmental paradigm: green growth (Buch-Hansen and Carstensen, 2021). Some versions of a green new deal, like other co-opted terms including 'just transition' and 'green social investment', can be used in ways that entail no break with productivist forms of growth, and become a lowest common denominator or a force for division rather than a unifying concept (Mandelli, 2022).

Ecosocial language

Framing is crucial in the case of ecosocial policy and debates about economic growth where language can invoke what can be, for some, regressive images. Various literatures and initiatives to reconfigure the political economy or welfare state are framed as 'libertarian communism', 'communalism', 'communism' and 'ecosocialist'. The choice of such words runs the risk of presenting the ecosocial project as an overly developed policy agenda and may too narrowly frame ecosocial reforms as ideological projects or 'isms' that require advocates to be 'ists'. However, we do not aways have the words we need. Asking the reader to 'bear with me until we come up with better language', Solnit acknowledges that she uses phrases that are outdated, carry baggage and are often used pejoratively (2016, p 145).

Considerable effort went into the framing of the 2021 IPCC Report. Chapter 2 is entitled 'Framing Issues' and there is effective use of graphics throughout which enable readers to see the severity of the situation. Framing the ecosocial welfare project as a positive and open concept is crucial to its adoption by as wide a range of actors and interests as possible. In this space there are tensions between those who frame a 'degrowth' agenda, which, for some, has negative and regressive connotations, and is somewhat of a weapon word, and those who choose, what they see as, a more positive framing of 'post-growth' imaginaries (Murphy and Dukelow, 2022). However, even those using post-growth speculate that, eventually, 'we will find a better terminology to describe our world but, for today, "post-growth" is a necessary "thought word"' (Jackson, 2021, p xv). Following Lakoff's framing logic, a useful approach is to frame language and images to proactively message what we want people to hear, for example reinforcing the language of 'living within our limits' while remaining agnostic about, and limiting use of, growth-oriented words including degrowth or post-growth (Raworth, 2017).

It remains challenging to frame the concept of ecosocial in language and images that capture people's policy and political imagination. We need a 'more compassionate, kinder more lyrical politics' (Jackson, 2021, p 175), however the language of ecosocial policy does not particularly evoke passion, and for some sounds like an old-fashioned phrase from the 1970s. The merits of ecosocial and social-ecological are debated but what is core is that all evoke a political economy that values reciprocity, sociality and cooperation. Ideally such language and symbolism can and should come from the mobilisation process and reflect language people are using on the street to articulate what they want (Shenker, 2019). The logic that language will evolve through the process of action is consistent with Freire's observation that we make the road by walking. The struggle of and for ideas and political debate stops politics becoming managerial, likewise feminisation of politics is about changing the way politics is done and spoken, emphasising the importance of the small, the relational, the everyday, challenging the artificial division between the personal and the political and working for feminist, not feminised outcomes (Cullen and Murphy, 2020).

Sometimes language hides in plain sight and words and values that seemed out of fashion resurface to describe our futures and create conversations across generations and different interests. Much was made of the presence of faith groups augmenting the energy of youth groups at COP 26. Local language, and indigenous words, phrases, concepts and meanings can help us make sense of very specific challenges (Magan, 2020; Kirby, 2021). This language can and should evolve. While being very open to new language emerging, or old language re-emerging, in the meantime, as Jackson (2021) suggests, ecosocial policy (and its sister 'shecosocial') remains a necessary thought word, alerting us to the need to treat aspirations for equality and ecological sustainability in the same frame.

Irish imagination: transformation through values

Ireland's long anti-colonial history offers rich and, at times, inspirational examples of transformation which have been interpreted by many as a cause for hope. While the legacy of paternalism and conservatism is still evident in state responses to welfare, bio-political policy is increasingly and successfully challenged. Experiences of austerity have increased economic literacy, and recent transformative processes reinforce the younger generation's voice in the public sphere as well as feminist bio-political mobilisation that frame alterative imaginaries about care and participation. The recent pandemic has offered glimpses of the future, including remote working. All of this offers potential for climate crisis and equality mobilisation.

Ireland has demonstrated capacity to be innovative and creative. In 2002 a 15 cent tax per plastic retail bag (raised to 22 cent in 2007) was introduced with revenues funding waste management, litter prevention and other environmental initiatives. In 2004, Ireland became the first country in the world to implement legislation creating smoke-free enclosed workplaces that included bars and restaurants. A small state can offer inspiring leadership in climate change too (Robbins et al, 2020). However, most change is demanded from below, as, for example, Ireland's recent transformative changes in bio politics – the 2015 Marriage Equality Referendum and the 2018 referendum which removed a constitutional ban on abortion in Ireland – both of which were the outcomes of decades-long campaigns by activists which included direct action, coalition-building, mobilisation and legal strategy. Both referendums were preceded by deliberative forums: in 2013 a Constitutional Convention (CC) on Marriage Equality and in 2017 a Citizens' Assembly (CA) on the 8th Amendment (which prohibited abortion). These forums created space for policy imagination and transformative conversation between citizens, civil society, policy experts and the political elite. Such deliberative forums were first introduced in Ireland in the context of a failure of political institutions following the 2008 great financial crisis which resulted in the 2011 Irish bank guarantee and bailout. While welcomed by many, some remain cautious and ambivalent about their use and fear that such processes can be smoke screens to block or park debate about fundamental political reform, and that governments will agenda-set and effectively control what could be independent deliberative spaces.

Lessons on transformative change: kitchen table conversations

A referendum on 25 May 2018 approved the repeal of a constitutional ban on abortion by 66.4 per cent. The referendum campaign offers rich learning in relation to framing, narratives and storytelling. Pro-repeal focus group research had found that most people had fears and reservations about removing the 8th Amendment and about abortion more generally. Apprehensive that such a deeply contentious issue would be bitterly divisive, the campaign focused on the need for reasonable debate and time to think through the issue calmly. A reasonable and moderate tone was, therefore, necessary. The campaign organisation name, Together for Yes, was agreed upon by the civil society coalition partners as reflecting an inclusive broad-based national campaign that stood 'for' positive change rather than 'against' the past. Together for Yes was an example of a variety of civil society organisations coming together for a common purpose. The slogan, 'Choice, Compassion and Care', was used to frame the positive appeal of a yes vote. This was controversial, deliberately avoiding words like woman, right, abortion or reproductive rights, and to this day is a source of tension for many activists. However, if the result is the evidence of success, then the frame was effective and spoke as much to the broader theme of how Irish people wanted their society to be and believed it was.

Similar framing exercises underscored this approach in previous bio political referendums such as the right to divorce being positively framed as the 'right to remarry', and same sex marriage being framed as 'marriage equality'.

Personal stories were the bedrock of the campaign and a primary evidence-base as well as a key driver of campaign strategy. Preparing to campaign in the 2018 referendum, a 'Story Lab' identified existing and potential sources for personal stories and worked with and supported individual women and couples to prepare for media and other public events. An independent personal story initiative, called *In Her Shoes*, proved particularly impactful on social media. Rather than theoretical or abstract argument, the stories could reach people with their immediacy and authenticity, and were essential to grounding the credibility and integrity of the campaign. They informed, educated and raised public awareness, reinforcing key messages with a 'real-life' evidence base, establishing credibility and trust, and creating understanding and empathy. People talked, there was deep listening, opinions changed.

It is clear that green politics has absorbed lessons from this experience and applied it to climate change and ecosocial politics, not least in successfully campaigning for a CA on Climate Change in 2019 and a CA on Biodiversity Loss in 2022. The CA on Climate Change (discussed in Chapter 2) was credited with precipitating political momentum for a more ambitious climate change policy. The CA on Biodiversity Loss reported in late 2022 when its findings and recommendations were to be considered by government. Lessons from the process of campaigning for change highlight how communications is at the core of politics, both in traditional and online media, or 'air offensives', and mobilisation and canvassing, or 'ground offensives'. Conversation with undecided or 'middle ground' voters is key, as is mobilising and motivating supporters to act. Personal stories in the referendums discussed here helped explain the issues on the doorsteps and were the focus of intergenerational conversations at family dinner tables across Ireland. Change was seen as personally transformative.

Climate change is not yet salient enough to be a daily topic of conversation but how we talk about it and frame the problem is key. Translating the challenge into a social policy or welfare frame is part of the process of widening and deepening the conversation. A 2022 controversy on proposals to ban the use of domestic turf in Ireland highlighted how climate-related policy, if not carefully politically curated, has potential to be manipulated and weaponised. Irish people like to locate where you are from. Localising the story and relating it to the importance of place in people's lives offers opportunity for meaningful connections across diverse themes but this must be an inclusive conversation. Indigenous language can connect us to the specificities of place while also opening up the world (Cronin, 2019, p 9). Parallels are made between linguistic-diversity and biodiversity and how revival of endangered languages (like Irish) can enable new forms of knowledge of the non-human world; this can teach us skills for a more balanced future (Cronin 2019). That the Irish language has 32 words for field demonstrates the rich knowledge of natural landscape embedded in this ancestral language (Magan, 2020).

Changing the story isn't enough, but it has often been foundational to real changes. Making an injury visible and public is usually the first step in remedying it, and political change often follows culture, as what was long tolerated is seen to be intolerable, or what was overlooked becomes obvious. Which means that every conflict is in part a battle over the story we tell, or who tells and who is heard. (Solnit, 2016, p xiv)

In a Claiming our Future meeting in 2013 participants were captivated by the imagery of a hamster in a treadmill, constantly walking and never gaining any ground. This imaginative trope was created to encourage reflection on our lack of collective progress on climate change, but it also reflected back to participants the busyness of their own constant work. Civil society work is often geared towards the demands, timetables and agenda of the state, with a consequent lack of time for imagination, collaboration and work for transformation. While Chapter 9 reflects on the capacity of civil society to collaborate and join the dots for collective action, it is worth reflecting here on capacity of Irish civil society to imagine.

To date, a picture has emerged of a largely symbiotic civil society that is more policy focused than alternative focused and with no strong ideational force. However, the creativity more often found in culture and arts has bled into imaginative, innovative and creative alternatives in Ireland, from women's peace camps in the 1970s, to Parades of Innocence and campaigns against miscarriages of justice in the 1980s, Share the Wealth campaigns in the 1990s and the Spectacle of Defiance in the austerity era of the 2000s, to Extinction Rebellion in the 2010s. There were also imaginative and collective processes as diverse as Claiming Our Future (2011), Occupy (2012), Right to Change (2015) and One Future (2019) (Crowley, 2022).

9

Achieving change through high-energy democracy and coalition-building

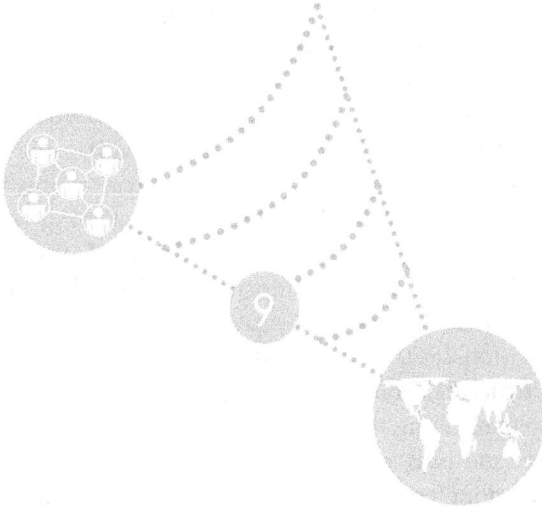

This chapter returns to the central theme of structure and agency. We organise collective decision-making through structural power and institutions that are often controlled by elites, while transformative change happens most often through the agency of people power, mobilisation and collective action. The relationship between the two is vital. The tremendous structural power of capital, corporations and elites has to be taken seriously, but so too does our own capacity and power as a force for transformation. Key to this force is the relationship between mobilisation and democratic institutions. Some forms of democratic structures are more enabling of agency. While there is no single transformative pathway to making ecosocial welfare happen, all pathways require two dimensions: more democracy (more equalising structures) and mobilised citizens (more agentic power).

The first section of the chapter briefly contextualises the structural power of capital, corporations and elites. It then addresses the importance of engagement of people in ideational debate in rich forms of participatory and deliberative democracy, what Unger (2011) calls a 'high-energy democracy'. The second section discusses strategies for collective mobilisation, arguing coalition-building and mobilisation around gender and social reproduction, environmental and traditional distributional concerns about income equality and public services could inspire a new politics or a triple movement (Fraser, 2013; Kishimoto et al, 2020). The chapter concludes by discussing Ireland from the perspective of movement-building, examining various constellations of actors and clusters of mobilisations.

Structure: contesting capital through high-energy democracy

The structural power of capital

Chapter 1 reflected on how 16th-century capitalism emerged as a form of political economy on the back of organised violence and systematic destruction of society through excessive profit and accumulation, and in processes of colonialisation, imperialism, war and famine (Polanyi, 1944; Folbre, 2021; Hickel, 2021, p 78). The ecological damage and structural inequality discussed in Chapters 2 and 3 relates to how 21st-century capitalism, in the form of neoliberalism and increasing financialisation, has narrowed ownership of wealth and assets (land, fossil fuels, nature, information technology, digital platforms, intellectual property), so they are concentrated in the hands of a small number of wealthy corporations and individuals (Jones, 2018, p 159; Razzouk, 2022). Economic violence occurs when structural policy choices are made for the richest and most powerful people, resulting in harm to everyone else, especially the poorest people, women and girls and racialised groups. The wealth of the world's ten richest men doubled since the pandemic began, while the incomes of 99 per cent of humanity are worse off because of COVID-19 (Oxfam, 2022).

Over decades there has been a significant erosion of the laws, regulations and social protection systems that protected the common person or sought to control the richest. We see this in international trade agreements with opaque international litigation processes designed for and by the richest (for example, the proposed Transatlantic Trade and Investment Partnership (TTIP) between the EU and the US and the more recent EU–Canada Comprehensive Economic Trade Agreement (CETA) which is contested in many EU states). Both include investor–state dispute settlement (ISDS) mechanisms, chilling international processes that facilitate investors to sue countries which introduce measures that limit profit-making or return on investments.

Economic inequality polarises society and democracy (Fleurbaey et al, 2018). Conscious politics has taken a strong polarising direction and democracy is under attack and hallowing out, while the institutions designed to protect society are weakened, including civil society, trade unions and media. Democracy itself has been captured and corrupted by elites and needs radical reform to pull it back, deepen it and expand it. New media can both contribute to and challenge democratic decision-making, but contemporary unequal ownership of new social media is strongly correlated to wealth inequality. It is very clear that the types of solutions proposed in this book will not be easily ceded by the grossly wealthy and powerful who will do all they can to protect growth and the status quo and fight against what is needed to achieve ecological and social sustainability. Razzouk (2022) points to the power of the fossil fuel industry as the most direct block on meeting climate change targets and argues these corporations need to be the focus of our action. With democracy weakening the future could see oligarchy, autocracy or international anarchy (Streeck, 2017).

Contesting inequalities through democracy

We need to use all the resources we can in the face of such gross wealth and power inequality. Oxfam (2022) powerfully argue in their annual Inequality Report that, despite such gross power inequality, we can radically redesign our economies to be centred on equality. This means deepening and widening democracy, so it is a more fitting base from which to contest the structural power of capital's wealthiest defenders. It also means using every bit of power society can muster, including the power of collective action and coalition-building, the power of ideas and creativity and the power of disruption, non-violent direct action and more (Malm, 2021). Previous chapters explored how the state and its welfare institutions might be reimagined as an ecosocial sustainable world. This chapter is concerned with strategies for making this happen. A key strategy is the focus on democracy and to reimagine the structures and institutions of democracy as a 'high-energy' process, in which we are engaged in deliberative, participative and representative mechanisms continually shaping the world we want to create (Klein, 2014; Solnit, 2016). We first expand on the concept of 'high-energy democracy', and then dispel some old myths to clear the way for greater mobilisation.

Villa El Salvador is a district in Lima, Peru that began in 1971 with the occupation of land by families in need of housing. I first heard of it as a final year undergraduate student in 1986 when it was proposed as a candidate for the 1986 Nobel Peace Prize by the International Commission for Human Rights. It was promoted as a model for a self-managing community. By 1986, with 300,000 inhabitants, mostly of Andean origin, it was the largest worker-owned housing experiment in 'town planning'. Residents built their own homes and streets (24 families formed a block and 16 blocks formed a neighbourhood), with land set aside for schools, markets, recreation centres and agricultural and industrial use. A high degree of democratic participation was encouraged through a self-managing model based on Andean tradition, where thousands of residents became leaders each year, with housing block leaders responsible for Health, Education, Commercialisation, Production and Services. Each neighbourhood chooses another eight representatives and ten people are appointed to form the Communal Executive Council, where the whole population is represented. I visited in 1988. The memory of the pride and joy people experienced in their high-energy democracy left a firm impression on my soul.

High-energy democracy

Unger's (2009) concept of 'high-energy democracy' envisages a state that enables a constant high level of organised popular engagement in politics – representative, participatory and deliberative. Participation is deepened, widened and 'melted' into, and becomes a natural part of everyday life. Politics maintains structure and organisation, but cumulative changes in practices, institutions and culture means people feel that they have effective agency. The demand for social justice and individual empowerment aligns with constructive transformative energy and perpetual innovation (Unger, 2009, p 82). Such collaboration happens alongside contestation and struggle (Moulaert et al, 2013).

In a mobilised form of democracy, a diverse range of institutions channel the energy of participation through effective use of old and new communication technologies and by regulating spaces through which power is mobilised. A high-energy democracy is also responsive to citizens through institutional rules facilitating younger people to vote and enabling recall votes and local or national plebiscites. Responsive subsidiarity principles are brought alive with strong devolved powers and networked collaborative governance. As many diverse actors as possible are engaged in locally designed and implemented solutions that can be quickly revised as circumstances change, so that everywhere experiences the constant power of experimental innovation (Unger, 2009, p 161).

A key question is how to shift from the low-energy democracy of most countries to a high-energy democracy and how mass mobilisation and social movements can engage with political society and the institutions of a high-energy democracy. The term 'institutional democracy' has been used to describe a widening of the scope of participatory democracy through lasting and often legal mechanisms to achieve the maximum practical involvement of people in decisions that affect their lives (O'Donnell, 2018, p 79). Simple measures can restore the power of the citizenry and make the political process more responsive to the population's needs and values (Fleurbaey et al, 2018). Effective structures are flexible, enabling diversity and agility in our forms of governance, and can include diverse policies including local government reforms, participatory budgeting, recall initiatives, plebiscites and referendums. Lowering the voting age to 16 can also mobilise more democratic participation.

Citizens' Assemblies (CAs) (discussed earlier in this book) and other deliberative forums, when appropriately designed, have potential to offer space and time to citizens and non-citizens to participate in policy processes. However, there must be careful attention afforded to who participates: should it be only citizens or all residents? Should politicians participate? Should participants be resourced or paid? How much participation is reasonable to expect? Who should set agendas? What experts should be invited? How should decisions be made? It is crucial to ensure that participative and deliberative processes have formal channels back to representative democratic processes. Successful deliberative and participative processes are usually leverage points in wider, longer campaigns which must sustain the relevant recommendations beyond the lifetime of the deliberative processes.

A high-energy democracy must be based on the principle of active and equal citizenship, in which everyone has a basic level of security (UBS and PI) and an adequate level of enabling resources and institutions. It can enable engagement in issues that are relevant to people's lives like health, care, transport, housing, parks and recreation. This requires time and navigational agency to enable participation, and a minimum capacity of education and personal empowerment to enable meaningful participation, equality of recognition and respect. Enhanced collective freedom can also mean more collective obligation; a requirement of reciprocal democratic care or stewardship could also be attached to citizenship and nurtured through state and social institutions.

Similar arguments are made by those calling for a new moral political economy focused on reciprocity and cooperation with institutions, mobilising strategies and governance arrangements that facilitate prosocial behaviour and overcome the divisions that block awareness of common interests (Levi and Ugolnik, 2023). Reclaiming democracy cannot happen without contending with power and the systematic root causes of exclusion and inequality. This means empowering people in their everyday lives, investing in the enabling institutions of civil society, the economy and the state, building public spheres that enable people to experience agency, resilience and collective action in their private lives and strengthening civil society through which people can learn the skills and practices of democracy and exercise power to influence sociopolitical outcomes (Han, 2020).

New forms of progressive power

Discussion of power and transformation in Chapter 7 argued that integrated and iterative strategies are needed to engage across the whole spectrum of power to generate a meaningful scale of transformative change. What institutions and approaches might sustain a high-energy democratic framework? Transformation requires power *over* as well as power *to, for, with* and *within*. Institutionalised participation of civil society actors in the political arena is all the more challenging when the political arena is increasingly hallowed out. At the same time, just transition requires democratic participation to enable compromises between different interests. Transforming existing democratic institutions towards a high-energy democracy has to involve both civil society and political parties, and engage representative politics alongside participative and deliberative politics. The dominant power of parties (*power over*) and transformative power of social movements (*power with, to* and *for*) need to coalesce in a new progressive future (Wainwright, 2018). Chapter 7 reflected on how this means valuing popular participation and informal, tacit or experiential knowledge and working through new forms of decentralised and networked organisation and with new forms of prefigurative and catalytic representation (Wainwright, 2018).

Examples of new progressive forms of integrating transformative politics and dominant power actors can be seen in processes of 'commoning' and 'community wealth building' (Guinan and O'Neill, 2019, p 1). While 'commoning' (discussed in Chapter 5) refers to a societal led collaborative and contributive practice, the latter is more a local state-led process. In line with Cumbers' (2018) call for plurality and diversity in economic democracy, both forms of public ownership, commoning and community wealth generation, are needed. Variously described as 'new local socialism' or 'remunicipalism', 'community wealth building' promotes local democratic participation and economic control, and works by mobilising the untapped power of the local public sector to build the local political economy (Jones and O'Donnell, 2017). While not yet scaled up to national impact, evidence of momentum in local politics is perhaps best exemplified in the 'Preston model' where the local economy has been re-energised around strong municipal governance and creative use of insourcing to support local economies and employment (Guinan and O'Neill, 2019, p 4). The question of how speedily such new paradigms can scale up may determine whether such change can be transformative in the sense of leading to a post-growth form of political economy. Yet in arguing for urgency we need to remain aware that the speed and scale of any transformation is a significant factor in social dislocation (Polanyi, 2001 [1944]). A human scale and speed of change is not an argument for incrementalism or gradualism but for accelerated transition to an ecosocial or post-growth world. The democratic nature of transition cannot be compromised.

Tactics for success: framing the debate

A *roly-poly toy* is a round-bottomed, doll-like image, usually egg-shaped, that tends to right itself when pushed at an angle, so that even when it looks like it should fall it just pops up again. There are a number of political roly-polies, arguments one might assume are dead but keep popping up again and again. We hear that inequality is natural and necessary, that some forms of transformation are unaffordable, others are technically unfeasible and beyond the bureaucratic capacity of state information technology (the computer says no), or that technology not yet invented will ease global warming (the computer says yes). These political roly-polies are constantly used by those who would lose most from redistributive politics and transformation towards a more sustainable and equal world. There is no doubt that combatting global warming and fundamentally overhauling infrastructure will be costly to both governments and citizens and will need to be funded by savings, borrowing and diverting spending on alternatives. However, we learned through the pandemic that the austerity-era insistence on balanced budgets and adherence to fiscal rules can be urgently and speedily overridden by political expediency, crisis conditions or emergencies. This approach to managing austerity was demanded by many but not politically delivered in the great financial crisis.

The money that could finance ecological transition exists and over the last decade has been channelled, through mechanisms of quantitative easing (QE), towards financial speculation leading to growing inequality. However, EU-level or state-led QE could provide funding for climate transition, but such expenditures, and others associated with addressing structural inequality, would need to be off the balance books and out of the calculation of the public deficit. The creation of an ecological bank as a subsidiary of the European Investment Bank could hasten these policies (Hessel et al, 2021). Similar proposals in the US context argue QE be used to buy out fossil fuel companies in a strategy described as 'QE for the planet' (Alperovitz, Guinan and Hanna, 2017, p 3).

Such proposals are important. Change requires that we are ready with viable and genuine solutions at the right time, it is about being 'ready now' (Alperovitz, Guinan and Hanna, 2017, p 3; Levi and Ugolnik, 2023). There is hope. It took only two weeks to decide on the framework of the original coal and steel union out of which the EU emerged, and a few months for Roosevelt to create a federal tax use (Alperovitz et al, 2017; Hessel et al, 2021). Kim Stanley Robinson creates such a scenario in the *Ministry for the Future* when he imagines the transformation of money as a key tool combining the transparency and accountability of technology, in this case blockchain technology, to enable a democratic form of QE to finance climate-specific policy interventions.

Fool me once, shame on you, fool me twice, shame on me. I was one of those anti-austerity protestors in 2008–2014 who, while clearly arguing against cuts that hit the most vulnerable, also tried to frame sensible arguments that bought into the deficit myth that there was no magic money tree, that governments would have to pay back borrowed money and that there were (sadly) limits to what could be done. This was largely in the context of EU monetary policy, Ireland's membership of the Euro zone and EU fiscal rules. The QE of the US and UK governments seemed to be politically impossible in the EU as Greek citizens were sacrificed, and many other EU citizens suffered. Recent EU experience has demonstrated that QE is a political possibility, feasible, viable and, in the long term, sustainable. While some economists directly link QE with hyper-inflation a more appropriately targeted QE used to invest in carbon-related policy, and democratically transparent and accountable, need not lead to inflation. This does not mean that money grows on trees, but it does mean that we can afford to pay the price needed to save our planet and our future.

So, transformation is fiscally and technically feasible. But what about political feasibility of an ecosocial welfare transformation? As Chapter 3 discussed, there is public support for ecosocial policy, but such support is relatively weak and very different perspectives inform such support. Some argue that good lives do not need to cost the earth and posit that ecosocial transformation can generate rich lives and wellbeing (Jackson, 2021, p 4). Such arguments can frustrate those who enjoy contemporary life and fear what they anticipate will be harsh realities of (even consensus) transformative adaptation. They believe such transformation has to be achieved and just want to get it over with. Both are on the same side of change, but do not necessarily share the same view of what the future will mean. This challenges us moving forward as part of the same politics of transformation.

Components of what is needed for climate change transition, such as retrofitting, carbon taxes, electric vehicles and locally-sourced (often more expensive) food are practically unaffordable for many individuals and households. As the gilet jaunes in France in 2020, or the turbulence in Kazakhstan in 2022, demonstrates, public acceptance of costs like higher fuel, for whatever (usually legitimate) reasons, is volatile. The consequences of the 2021 lorry strikes in the post-Brexit UK brought home to many the reality of lack of fuel, as did the Russian invasion of Ukraine in early 2022. People's fears are real, and the recent rises in the cost of living are sobering, reminding us of the fragility of many households and communities. Many cannot connect their lives with ecosocial transformation, and we cannot proceed without ensuring that no one is left behind in this post-growth future. This means realistically factoring existing inequality into our assessment of what needs to change and ensuring that what is proposed is realistic in the light of people's lived experience of inequality. This means listening and talking, even to those you might assume are on the other side.

'There is no such thing as a single-issue struggle, as we don't live single-issue lives' (Lorde, 1982). A grand coalition for a guaranteed minimum income as a universal safety net could be a way of expressing how we collectively value human dignity and freedom and of reclaiming a public language of morality (Klein, 2014). In this context, ecosocial welfare has potential to be politically salient. People have always used innate capacity for democratic deliberation to debate and reflect on diverse forms of social organisation, including welfare institutions (Graeber and Wengrow, 2021). However, welfare reform discussions can cause different groups to 'jockey for position' and press their own claims for resources, giving effect to the intersectional political economy (Streeck, 2017; Folbre, 2021). Bread-and-butter issues associated with welfare policy are often associated with and can promote self-interest over solidarity, they can lend themselves to policy argumentation where the attention is focused on trivial details and the big picture is lost. State and government power configurations create 'glass ceilings' for transformation (Jackson, 2021, p 151). Adaptability requires that we retire institutions that are tired or less relevant, however, welfare institutions also have their own political agency and power and will resist transformation (Daly and Rake, 2002). Understanding a new welfare settlement or an ecosocial welfare regime as a site of struggle with economic, cultural, social and other forms of power imbalances, means we cannot expect consistency or logic in such a political or policy domain (Daly and Rake, 2002, p 165). We do not need to be always right, the path to transformation will be a crooked and inconsistent path.

Agency: coalition-building and triple movements

Understanding how change happens is important but often difficult to articulate and the subject of heated debate, with arguments for building demand for change through coalition-building 'from moderates out', to more radical strategies involving direct action to match the urgency and scale of what is needed, or even targeted sabotage without interpersonal violence. Malm (2021, p 216) describes as inevitable the tension of co-organising in the context of a plurality of diverse tactics. I am personally wary of debates that force a dominant model of change in what is a very heterogeneous civil society. Tactical choices are rarely binary, multiple positions and tactics are necessary as are integrated and iterative approaches to power. The answer often lies in being 'strategically ambivalent', living and working with different theories of change, neither being precious nor getting in each other's way, thinking big and thinking small, 'while occasionally seeking to bring together coalitional strategies to back key leverage points' (O'Neill and Albas, 2020).

Much change from below occurs through collective action and a critical mass of mobilisation, and this has been the focus of this book. However, it can also come through smaller, more focused, processes. 'Social acupuncture' refers to small actions delivered in just the right place at just the right time which can have positive impacts that ripple through the system, 'picking the lock' to open and release the system to transform (Leicester, 2020, p 48), and enabling movement on to the next leverage point. A practical example of this approach is found in legal strategies for transformations which focus on lawsuits against oil companies, governments and nations. We already see examples of public order lawsuits against oil companies and the 'kids v climate' equal protection lawsuit against the US federal government. We can anticipate claims against nations that have profited from burning fossil fuels where those suffering climate change will seek direct reparations or liability as well as the cost of mitigation and adaptation (Wallace Wells, 2019, p 167). These forms of social acupuncture are welcome, however, for now we focus on the strategy of collective organising and coalition-building.

Necessity is the mother of coalition

People have the potential power of a 'sleeping giant' where civil society becomes a superpower in moments of rupture and when people find a 'we' that did not until then exist (Solnit, 2016, p xxiii). Habermas' theory of communicative action places civil society at the axis of change wherein an inclusive public sphere drives policy change and the political legitimacy of democracies is derived from their responsiveness to a dynamic public sphere. Power augments through intersectional coalition-building, working with the concept of collective power, or power *with* (see Chapter 7). The phrase 'necessity is the mother of coalition' speaks to the importance of organisation, solidarity and joint action, but also the urgency of now (Folbre, 2021). Transformation and participation are inextricably linked through the concepts of individual and collective agency, where, through collective discussion and deliberation, we develop a sense of responsibility towards others and experience a convergence of values.

More collective action is clearly needed, and we should not be complacent about the likelihood of engagement. Wallace Wells (2019, p 189) critiques the pursuit of conscious consumption and wellness as 'cop outs' rather than substitutes for collective political action, contentious politics or ideological dispute. Jackson (2021, p 160) challenges Greta Thunberg's assertion that 'real power belongs to the people', arguing the people 'must rouse from the conditions of their own inertia'. However, many people find politics off-putting, exhibiting a form of 'attention deficit' often preferring other diversions over political engagement (Berger, 2011, p 142). Hence the need for many diverse strategies and forms of social acupuncture, but also for civil disobedience and non-violent direct action as seen in many forms including anti-eviction campaigns, take back the street rallies, blockades and boycotts. Solnit challenges us to 'change our own imagination of change', so that political activism is not once-off or occasional, best kept for emergencies, but becomes a part of, and even 'a pleasure of everyday life'. In this sense, 'the journey is the aim not the destination, a politics of prefiguration will constantly inspire and catalyse change' (Solnit, 2016, p 62).

Pressing all the levers of collective action

People have always had to fight for transformative change (Solnit, 2016, p 92). The concept of 'triple movement' offers a strategy where disparate interests unite using new emancipatory tactics, narratives and political solidarities. It links across the triple crisis of 'capitalism, social reproduction and the environment' with a 'a triple movement' against the 'self-regulating market' that commodifies nature, labour and money (Fraser, 2013, p 62). The combined rejection of such forms of commodification is potentially transformative. Such a goal offers a strong vision and narrative for joining the dots and coalition-building. Effective framing offers potential to mobilise across a wide range of actors and enables people to see what unites them rather than what divides them. An ecosocial welfare regime, built on UBS and PI, offers such a uniting frame and narrative. The useful concept of 'triple movement' can be extended to include multiple movements, breaking down silos of fragmentation.

Coalescing across capitalism, social reproduction and the environment

There is also a need for strong realism in identifying the range of barriers that will need to be faced in the context of building coalitions for an ecosocial state (Jessola and Mandelli, 2022, p 249). While challenges of inclusive participation were discussed in Chapter 7, there are also generational challenges in working across old and new forms of power. Recent shifts to non-hierarchical decision-making, decentralised organising and deep community democracy can foster imagination, participation and adaptation. The metaphor of 'water' used to describe the tactics of pro-democracy activists in Hong Kong in 2019 resonates with the fluidity of such movements. A new form of power is emerging in the 21st century in a hyperconnected world where ideas and movements, such as #MeToo and BLM, spread with speed and with power to shape the future (Timms and Heimans, 2018). This 'new power' is understood to be open, participatory and peer driven. It works less in institutions and more as an energy, or a surge in channels. Old power values of formal governance are contested by new values of informality, collaboration, sharing, openness and transparency, conditional affiliation and participation. Participation takes new forms, new power behaviours enable sharing, affiliation, adapting, funding, producing and shaping (Timms and Heimans, 2018, p 71).

These new forms of power are challenged to coexist with old forms of power which affirm different values. In promoting collective mobilisation and power from below – the self-organisation of oppressed groups and non-hierarchical movements – we need to be mindful of limitations of structurelessness (Freeman, 1972). Working less in and through institutions and more in 'energy' can lead to absence of structure. There may be a lack of focus in leadership on longer term or sometimes harder to achieve political goals. The new participative movements are more able to 'walk the walk' but may be less able to 'talk the talk', or negotiate with old power to deliver policy change. New ground rules are required to facilitate old moderates and new self-organised radicalism to work together for transformation across feminist, labour and climate change movements (Klein, 2014, p 204). This can facilitate both hierarchical or vertical leadership as well as deliberative innovations that are highly structured and even in some cases state-controlled, for example, CAs. Space and permission are also needed for unnatural tactical alliances that arise not out of transformative participative processes but pragmatic and sometimes short-term engagement with corporations, elite policy makers and politicians (Klein, 2014).

Fred Hampton: joining the dots

Fredrick Allen Hampton Sr (1948–1969) was an American activist who came to prominence in Chicago as chairman of the Illinois chapter of the Black Panther Party (BPP). Motivated to stop fascism, he founded the antiracist, anti-class Rainbow Coalition, a prominent multicultural political organisation that initially included the Black Panthers, Young Patriots and Young Lords who respectively organised poor Blacks, whites and Hispanics, and an alliance among major street gangs to help them end infighting and work for social change. In 1967, the FBI identified Hampton as a radical threat, tried to subvert his activities, sowed disinformation among Black progressive groups and it is speculated that they assassinated Hampton and some colleagues. The deaths were found to be 'justifiable' homicides; however, a 1982 civil lawsuit was successful against the City of Chicago, Cook County, and the federal government.

Writing almost a decade ago, Klein (2014) was optimistic that climate change might be the focus for scaling up 'mass' mobilisation for winning big victories for social and economic justice. More recently, Fridays for Future, a climate strike movement of young people, led by Greta Thunberg, has captured public imagination, likewise have new forms of mobilisation including civil disobedience in new forms of horizontal movements like Extinction Rebellion. Young people and minority groups are increasingly visible and vocal, connecting the issues of climate change with other salient aspects of their lives including inequality, discrimination and freedom. The 2019 school strikes, non-violent civil disobedience, direct action and previous mobilisations had strong impacts, pushing climate change to the top of the World Economic Forum agenda (Shenker, 2019; Jackson, 2021, pp xii, 145–9). System-level changes will involve structural loss of trillions of dollars of wealth with real implications for elites, and for the likely scale of contestation and backlash. However, many are optimistic about the coming together of the great struggles of the civil rights movements, feminist movements and indigenous peoples, and imperialist movements to complete 'the unfinished business of liberation' (Klein, 2014, p 455). Both structure and agency must be enacted to generate a critical level of social mobilisation in a 'high-energy democracy'.

Ireland: joining the dots for ecosocial policy

Ireland as a republic is relatively weak in its promotion of the public sphere but has recently innovated deliberative public spheres and demonstrated capacity to generate at least a higher-energy democracy. Some state-led governance systems have captured the energy and creativity of some civil society, while there is also evidence of imaginative, innovative and experimental organising in new hyper-local and less institutional, more values-based collective actions and gatherings. Is there potential to join the dots across welfare politics, civil activists, feminists' focus on social reproduction, productivist politics and ecological or environmental activism, to generate a triple movement (Fraser, 2013)? The following reflection on five distinctive spheres of mobilisation in Ireland (visualised in Figure 9.1) assesses potential for breaking down silos and fragmentation to join the dots for transformation and system change towards an ecosocial welfare regime.

Work and welfare

Those pursuing productivist justice or income equality through paid work or welfare reform, including trade unions and welfare-oriented non-government organisations, often focus on incremental symbiotic change, doing things now and leaving it open to more in the future. However, sometimes compromises mean accepting parasitic forms of incremental change or reforms that can reinforce neoliberalism, for example arguing for narrow tax reliefs that can only meet the needs of a particular group. Such change, more incremental than transformational, is often pursued through institutional corporatist structures or social dialogue. Since 2008, when the government stood down institutional corporatist social partnership structures, many CSOs refreshed traditional membership or representative mobilisation strategies including industrial action, strikes, coalition-building and advocacy and have made efforts to build public spheres, particularly evident in mobilisation against austerity.

Attempts at 'joining the dots' are hampered by an absence of consensus about how to frame key distributional and environmental policy. This was particularly evident in the reaction to the introduction of domestic water charges in 2014, considered by some to be a missed opportunity to join the dots across distributive and ecological coalitions (Crowley, 2022). The anti-water charge mobilisation is heralded by some as a positive political dynamic constituted from outside mainstream politics. Others in the environmental movement, following the EU environmental 'polluter pays' logic and focused on achieving wider environmental targets, saw the movement as destructive. Within the alliance of left civil and political society who opposed water charges, there were also difficulties in wider coalitional-building. The 2015 Right to Change movement mobilised over 100 candidates in the 2016 General Election behind a set of policy principles but had little post-election traction, and were outflanked by radical left political parties manoeuvring, leading the participating trade unions to review their involvement. Some trade unions, ICTU, for example, offered logistical support to the Irish schools' climate strike movement (Gold, 2020), and some trade unions are key members of the Just Transition Alliance launched in 2022. Anti-poverty and equality interests have, with some exceptions (for example, Social Justice Ireland, TASC, NERI and EAPN), been slow to initiate climate policy-related welfare reforms, but have supported the Just Transition Alliance.

Care and social reproduction

The involvement of women's groups in coalition and alliances to advance social reproduction in care equality, reproductive rights and violence against women provide distinct insights into new power, new politics and new political opportunity structures. Women's reproductive rights have long been considered a 'wicked problem'. The learned capacity to root policy analysis in lived experience is a growing feature of campaigns for gender

Figure 9.1: Five civil society spheres

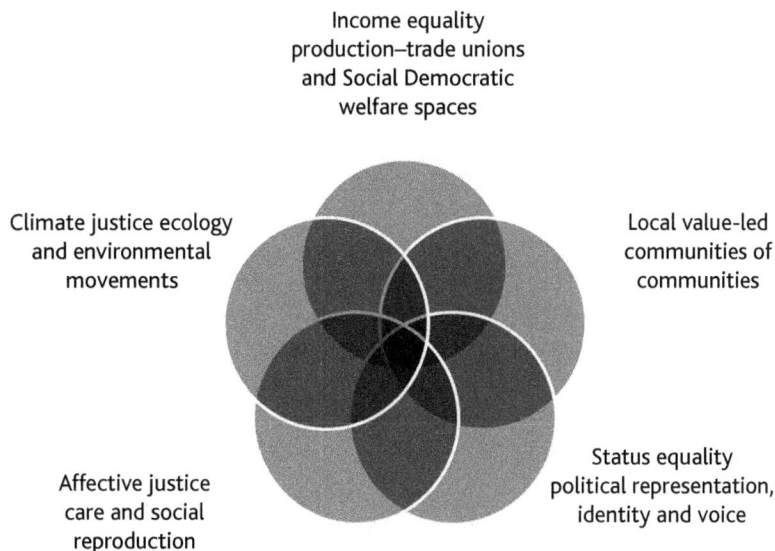

Income equality
production–trade unions
and Social Democratic
welfare spaces

Climate justice ecology
and environmental
movements

Local value-led
communities of
communities

Affective justice
care and social
reproduction

Status equality
political representation,
identity and voice

equality. The lessons from the Repeal movement (see Chapter 8) are more visible in campaigning methods of CSOs in future referendum campaigns. These include the use of social media, but also the power of conversations and one-on-one dialogues and debates within families, making the political personal. Women's agency has been visible and powerful with considerable momentum concerning gender-based and sexual violence, and childcare. The National Women's Council (NWC) is a central fulcrum connecting many, but not all, groups, and themes around gender equality. Using insider and outsider strategies, the NWC mediates an ambivalent relationship with the state and civil society, simultaneously working with and campaigning against governments, while also maintaining a diverse membership of women's groups and individuals. While there are challenges in this approach, there is also much to be gained. Alliances across productivist and social reproduction agendas include a campaign for a four-day working week by the trade union, Fórsa. Campaigns about the distribution of work, care and time have a clear ecological dimension, and speak to the post-capitalist visions articulated in Chapter 3, but there is less articulation of class and welfare issues. The potential of eco-feminism will advance through a recent NWC and Community Work Ireland initiative to progress a feminist approach to Climate Action. This is crucial to ensure ecosocial is framed as a shecosocial vision, avoiding a hecosocial articulation that disregards gender and care.

Ecology and environment

Irish environmental protest has often mobilised against the local environmental impacts of eco-modernisation, for example, in relation to planning energy infrastructure (Mercier et al, 2020). Some campaigns follow ruptural theories of change, including the 1970s Carnsore campaign against nuclear energy, the 1990s Glen of the Downs campaign against environmentally destructive road building, the Shell to Sea Campaign against fossil fuel extraction, and recent campaigns in Tarbert and Leitrim (Gorman, 2021), as well as direct-action strategies of the Irish branch of Extinction Rebellion. The Irish ecological and environmental movement has also followed a prefiguration pathway. Cloghjordan Eco Village celebrated '20 years a-growing' in 2020 (Kirby, 2020). Focusing on ecological building standards, district heating and a sustainable food system as well as a democratic community practicing reciprocity, creativity, culture and education, it has created cross-conversations with equality and anti-poverty actors (on social housing) and the agricultural community (on food and permaculture). Twenty-six environmental groups comprise the Environmental Pillar, the insider organising mechanism for the sector's participation in social partnership and Social Dialogue (as outlined and Chapter 3). Green Party-political pathways have ebbed and flowed, including the recent electoral success, discussed in Chapter 1, in an insider-insider strategy. The growing global awareness of climate emergency and long-term domestic citizen mobilisation has been recently captured in Extinction Rebellion, Fridays for Future and strategic legal challenges (O Neill and Alblas, 2020). An unprecedented and significant increase in activity from 2015 includes Coalition 30 (60 diverse civil society organisations focused on the United Nations SDGs), and recent work by the Stop Climate Chaos network to coordinate the One Future campaign (Gold, 2020). Aligned with Extinction Rebellion, Fridays for Future and school's strike mobilisations have brought a powerful imaginative and collaborative dynamic to the climate change movement. Older insiders-outsiders may struggle to cope with the growth in strength of new outsider-outsider groups who are more critical of dominant eco-modernisation frames (Gold, 2020). New alliances continue to grow, including the 2022 Just Transition Alliance.

Status equality

Fraser (2014) identifies an important focus on identity-based oppression alongside mobilising for political representation, identity, voice and personal freedoms. Ireland has a long history of campaigns that focus on civil rights, and the tension between the rights of citizens and others including those focusing on partition. Many focus on the practice of the state(s) and other actors including religious denominations, which seek to control people's freedom and/or to oppress people. Recent focus of civil liberty campaigns included redress for those oppressed by the abuse experienced in Mother and Baby Homes, Magdalene Laundries and Industrial Schools. Civil liberty issues relating to Traveller oppression, and conditions experienced by undocumented workers and asylum seekers, have also been a focus of campaigns over the last decade as have campaigns against racism. The last decades have heard significant discourse on freedom in the context of social media and surveillance regulation, the right to dissent and in relation to migration including refugee and asylum policy. During the pandemic, the focus was on protecting civil liberties in the context of the erosion of freedoms to curtail social mixing, and as society mediated new limits on personal freedoms in exchange for collective security and wellbeing.

New local communities of communities

Common calls for solidarity are not new, but the practice of solidarity can be reimagined. New forms of campaigning often follow hyper-local, values-led, bottom-up, grass roots mobilisation strategies and self-organisation of communities. There are also contemporary international mass mobilisations along intersectional coalitions of oppressed groups. #MeToo and #BLM, the most recent high-profile international examples, had presence in Irish mobilisations. The key difference between these and earlier mobilisation around civil rights is the degree to which people mobilise on an intersectional basis and recognise the shared experience of oppression across identity, class, race or other status. The local nature of many agendas reflects an often-rural focus on protecting the environment. Increasingly there are urban community perspectives that unite diverse actors, often in less institutional forms of alliances when various groups unite to campaign about public land use, planning issues and the quality of urban life, for example in the vibrant cultural group 'Dublin is Dying', which combines urban planning, culture, music and lifestyles. Local spaces will be increasingly important as sites of struggle (Mercier et al, 2020).

'Dublin is Dying' campaign

The 'Dublin is Dying' campaign is a grass roots movement set up in November 2021 to oppose the destruction of culturally significant buildings and venues across Dublin to make way for more hotel rooms, build-to-rent and student accommodation and commercial space for multinational corporations. Most notably, the campaign was central to preventing the redevelopment of the famous traditional Irish music hub, the Cobblestone bar as well as saving Dublin's iconic Merchant's Arch, also under threat at the time. The erosion of cultural spaces was a key motivation for the group which organised a protest outside Dublin City Council's offices at which traditional Irish musicians played on the steps of the offices. Planning permission was ultimately declined, and the developer withdrew objections to the refusal amid public pressure. Dublin is Dying shows the power of mobilisation in preserving important cultural hubs and joining the dots across culture, planning, urban development and local democracy.

Beyond the usual suspects

Other sectors are important for mobilisation and joining the dots. The importance of the culture and arts sector was discussed in Chapter 8 as crucial in pioneering imagination towards change. The agency within this sector prompted the Irish artists basic income pilot discussed in Chapter 6. The development sector has strong overlaps with other sectors and makes a crucial contribution in building public awareness of the impact of both inequality and climate change on the Global South. There is considerable mobilisation capacity as demonstrated, for example, in the Peoples Vaccine Campaign, tax campaigns and the Oxfam annual Inequality Report. The sector, through its second-hand shops, is also a considerable presence in Ireland's growing circular economy. This third sector, the 'sustainability sector' of renewable energy, small social enterprises and businesses, often overlaps with interstitial spaces of the ecological or environmental movement. While often in the shadowlands of civil society, these are important sites for local innovation, awareness-raising, mobilisation and activism as are community-based renewable energy projects (Watson, 2020). Faith groups had a significant presence in COP 26 in Glasgow and recent leadership across churches in Ireland was evidenced in Our Common Home project (Gold, 2020, p 280; JCHJ, 2020).

These progressive movements need to engage in broader political coalition-building and encompass a wide range of interconnected social and political interests. Change will happen but the real issues are what the change will be and who will determine that change (Solnit, 2016). Inclusive mobilisation will determine a just change.

A message from the Future 1 and 11

Warm, safe homes, meaningful jobs with living incomes, liveable communities, preventative health services, free public transport, universal child, adult and elder care are all part of a vision of the future. But how can people imagine this future? Intercept's Messages from the Future videos demonstrate how culture can animate a vision of the future in a way that enables people to make sense of what needs to be done to get there and excites them to be part of making that future happen.

The 7-minute film,[1] *Messages from the Future 1*, illustrated by Molly Crabapple (a New York-based artist), is set in a can-do, climate-fiction utopian future where progressive politicians joined with grassroots movements to launch the 'Decade of the Green New Deal', successfully battling poverty, injustice and climate disruption all at the same time. Viewed more than 12 million times, and nominated for an Emmy, its success convinced the Intercept team of the need for more progressive art that offers hope and meaning and giving insight into how people's agency and contestation could enable a sustainable future to evolve from a steep and perilous path.

Following this a second 2020 9-minute video, 'Message from the Future: Part 11'[2] by Molly Crabapple, Avi Lewis, Opal Tometi and Nnimmo Bassey began by illustrating how the world moved from the pandemic to, in 2023, super droughts and mega floods and what seems an inevitable future of burning cities and forests, a highly contagious and deadly virus and deep pollution destroying human health. Having evoked fear, anger and despair, the latter half of the video turned to a message of hope when people finally realised they could not keep patching up the old system.

Using examples of viral rent strikes, essential workers' strikes and public protest, the video demonstrated how, over time, society's agency could eventually achieve a focus on Repairing the Future, where society collectively creates a new equal, diverse and sustainable world which extended into reparations for historical injustices within and between territories. The focus on repair is a thread that weaves together a story of struggle across different interest and themes, effectively joining the dots. Over time the video shows societal action created a system of care and repair where no one is sacrificed, and everyone is essential, and happier. The ultimately hopeful film was launched alongside a diverse coalition of groups and networks that are using the films as vehicles to educate and organise.

Conclusion: The case for systemic transformation

This book began by reflecting on Naomi Klein's candid admission that she came late to climate change politics. Rebecca Solnit has also reflected on how she realised it was time to shift her priorities and make her 'mild engagement with climate something larger and fiercer', and challenges us to find our place in engagement with climate change, 'not just changing what you do, it means being part of the demand for systemic change' (Solnit, 2016, pp 135–6). This book echoes that challenge, identifying a clear problem and proposing an ecosocial solution as part of a broader transformative agenda to a post-growth world. It also sketched a political strategy for making it happen. In this conclusion these propositions are interrogated to test whether they are coherent and convincing arguments.

Restating the urgent problems and solutions

Problem

The UK legal contestation of a third runway at London's Heathrow airport and the December 2022 UK decision to open a new coalmine in Whitehaven, Cumbria that will produce annually 400,000 tonnes of greenhouse gas emissions, throws into sharp light the inherent conflict between growth driven by ever-increasing consumption and profit, and the climate emergency which threatens our very existence. Both highlighted the link between high levels of inequality, needless consumption, excessive travel, use of fossil fuels and carbon emissions. We can no longer think about climate crisis, economic inequality and never-ending consumerism in isolation. Tackling them requires action now to develop new ecosocial policies to enable us to reduce consumption by collectively meeting our needs. This means moving ultimately to a post-growth economy and society. Recent COPs and IPCC reports shine a nuanced light on inequality and climate injustice but make clear that the rich are the major contributors to worsening climate change, mainly in the Global North, but with rapidly rising numbers in the Global South (Sweeney, 2020). Developed countries, as perpetrators of such inequality and suffering, need to step up and bear their disproportionate responsibility.

Chapters 1 to 3 made the link between ecological destruction and social inequality as two sides of the same coin. Inequality of income, resources, power and wealth are unequally experienced across different groups in society. Inequality also impacts on the ecological crisis, increasing wants and fuelling consumption in the Global North while leaving countries and people in the Global South vulnerable to poverty and ill-equipped to meet the challenges that climate change is already presenting. This is particularly true for women and girls who bear the worst impacts of both inequality and climate change. The crisis is now beyond urgent, and any solution or strategy requires accelerated action and impacts. Real solutions to climate crisis are also our best hope of building a much more equitable economic system (Klein, 2014, p 125). System change, not climate change.

Solution

The focus for solutions has to be multifaceted but must include action to meet needs within planetary limits, including through a social guarantee composed of essential services and a minimum guaranteed income. Everyone should have access to UBS – services which are universal, sufficient and without cost. Enabling universal access to health, education, childcare and public transport is estimated by the OECD to cost 4–5 per cent of GDP, while having the potential to reduce income inequality by 20 per cent (Coote, 2022). UBS generates and strengthens solidarity and secure employment, as well as ecological sustainability, and prevents harm to health and social wellbeing. The role of the state is central to the provision of quality basic universal services and must be focused on funding those services, ensuring entitlement and equality of access, and regulating for quality. They can then be delivered by a range of actors – public, social and community – with less possibility for profit-driven market providers than at present. Service delivery needs to relate to citizens and service users, not in an authoritative fashion, but in a facilitative way, enabling citizens to maximise their own wellbeing and practice their own just transition. The UN SDGs provide a framework to prioritise investment in services. The strapline, *leave no one behind*, means starting with those most marginalised, an approach taken in a feasibility report on an EU Child Guarantee. Gender and care are at the centre of a recast model of welfare that takes both equality and environmental goals seriously. Just as austerity and the decimation of public services has profoundly gendered impacts, a focus on UBS has significant potential to drive gender and wider intersectional equality.

The provision of UBS and a social guarantee needs to include a form of complementary income support that is delivered in the form of a Minimum Income Guarantee. This income needs to be preferably universal or, if tactically necessary, it should be targeted at a high enough income threshold to ensure it can be delivered without stigma. Institutions, rules and norms play an important role in incentivising behaviour, and a payment can prompt, support, encourage or incentivise desired socially-useful activity. This could target a range of socially useful activities, for example, a greater sharing of care between men and women, more comprehensive engagement in democratic deliberation or direct environmental activity. This can be done in two ways: offering a PI to those who meet a minimum income threshold who are willing to engage in socially useful activity and/or offering institutional mechanisms to enable such activity, for example, local government ecological programmes, civil society projects or social enterprises. It may also be useful as an interim, transitional or bridging measure to consider encouraging or incentivising participation in democratically-defined, socially-useful activity in the form of obligations for reciprocity attached to income support. While there are reasonable theoretical arguments that this may be administratively unfeasible, Hiilamo (2022) argues recent advances in digitalisation and co-creation of services means a PI may be more feasible than assumed. What may not work in theory, may well work in practice. This form of PI is only justifiable in the context of sufficient supports and safeguards against exploitation or stigmatisation. Reciprocal activity or participation requirements may also add to the political feasibility of ecosocial welfare reform, easing fears of those who worry that people 'might get something for nothing' while also opening the possibility of incorporating more actors, including trade unions, in pro-reform coalitions and movements. We should not be precious, engaging in the minutiae of policy debate about income support is not what is needed now, and should not distract from the bigger challenge of coalition-building and joining the dots. It may well be that a partial or targeted PI are the first steps towards a longer transition to a UBI.

Ireland was offered as an anchor case to illustrate the need for an ecosocial welfare future, to examine how the contemporary welfare state might offer some 'seeds of the future' to nurture towards an ecosocial transition, and to explore the political challenges of getting there. Some challenges Ireland faces are peculiar to Ireland, but others can be generalised to Western European countries and experiences, and enable examination of how different welfare capitalist models are situated in the context of ecosocial transition (Dryzek, 2008; Koch and Fritz, 2014). While not normally associated with strong municipal governance of social democratic regimes, Ireland is associated with corporate, collaborative, networked and deliberative governance in common with other regimes experimenting with enabling participation including Netherlands, Finland, Denmark and Scotland (Larruffa et al, 2021). Ecosocial challenges will generate new interest constellations and conflicts and Ireland offers some interesting examples of emerging generational and urban/rural cleavages. The Irish artists basic income pilot discussed in Chapter 6 offers an interesting example of how new political cleavages emerge in times of challenges, when ecological interests overlap with cultural and precarious workers, mixing material and post material cleavages.

Strategy: contesting power and joining the dots

In the words of the playwright Beckett (1983, p 1), 'Ever tried. Ever failed. No matter. Try Again. Fail again. Fail better'. We have to keep doing and hoping. Any strategy must be capable of contesting power across representative and participatory forms of democracy and cannot be naïve of the corporate context within which the unequal fight for a new world is being fought. As discussed in Chapters 1, 2 and 9, corporations work hard and proactively to maintain the status quo, to divide and conquer, to confuse and deny. O'Neill and Alblas (2020, p 70) are correct in their assessment that 'complex socio-economic transitions require new and bold thinking, driven by evidence, innovation and imagination along with political courage and new forms of political mobilisation and institution-building'.

Any strategy of change underpinning a just ecosocial welfare policy needs to deliver urgent change. This means raising ambition and developing new narratives of change that are grounded in connections with people and with what they value. Rather than dispute which theory of change is most appropriate, the approach offered is to work through many pathways, some radical, others more incremental, some insider, many outsider, but all urgent. Significant change often happens in response to crisis but only in the context of prior leadership, evidence and concerted campaigns. More progressive eco-political movements and broader political coalition-building can encompass a wider range of social and political interests, and these are best coalesced around shared values.

Chapter 8 discussed the importance of imagination. Sustainable welfare has the capacity to generate the social provisioning to meet human need as it relates to concepts of equality and collective, as well as individual, freedom. Framing such a reform agenda can create a narrative that captures public support. The language used should not come from academic theory or past ideologies but should reflect and build from everyday language and should speak to the sustainable and equal future we need to build together. We need to forget perfection, avoid the narcissism of small differences or being caught up in micro details (Solnit, 2016). The focus needs to be not on blueprints, but on directions of change and making the first steps in these directions. These first and subsequent steps need to happen quickly.

Learning from past and contemporary examples of non-capitalist societies' institutional flexibility, and often seasonal adaption between different forms of social organisation reminds us that there may be no single solution other than flexibility, adaptability, oranisational or institutional openness, and constant deliberation about what is needed at transition points (Graeber and Wengrow, 2021). In this sense the seeds of the future are in our past and present, and we can grow them into our future. The issue of language, knowledge and framing is a common theme across many advocating an ecosocial future (Klein, 2014; Raworth, 2017; Jackson, 2021). For example, Shenker (2019) argues that the 'new politics of the people' means that as many people as possible need to be involved, from the ground up, using language that reflects their own lives and experiences, in developing knowledge and frames (Beresford, 2020).

And what of the 'high-energy democracy' and the type of democratic and enabling welfare institutions needed to achieve such transformation? While national political institutions are diverse, our contemporary political and state institutions have insufficient capacity to develop and implement the type of policies envisaged. In recent years we have seen the benefits of deliberative and consensus decision-making and experimentation with participation in co-production and co-design of services, but much still needs to change culturally and institutionally. Local is where people are, and where people live their lives. Devolving real power to local government can ensure that UBS works for people while empowering local communities. This can facilitate new forms of local leadership where local people as consumers, workers, residents and service users can participate. Lowering the voting age to 16 can strengthen young people's voices and lever the participation of this vital and vibrant age group.

Transformation requires mobilisation, inclusive participation and forms of movement coalition-building which can join the dots across diverse peoples and groups. This means listening to and respecting each other's understanding of how change happens and traditions of action. It means not getting in each other's way and recognising when and where to join the dots. Contemporary movements are challenged by what agendas might trigger inclusive participation across disparate identities and geographies. However, we can agree significant values and transformational goals. These can be as diverse as a Minimum Income Guarantee, banning fossil fuels, four-day working weeks or free universal public transport. Rather than imposing present and often ineffective ideologically-informed positions, we need to promote more participative ways so that people can decide for themselves what they believe is necessary.

Triple movement

Reversing capitalism's core organising principal of 'commodification' towards 'decommodification' requires changing the fundamental growth-based profit-seeking logic of capitalism. A focus on capitalism and climate can unite people across production (inequality), social reproduction (care) and ecology (nature) (Fraser, 2013; 2014; Klein, 2014). The economic rules that govern capitalist societies can and should be rewritten to free people from the control that the market exerts over our future (Stiglitz, 2015; Konczal, 2021). The strategy must address the cojoined problems of social and ecological destruction. This means planning and managing our lives to reflect our goals and values, rather than accepting that this can be left to the magic of the market (Klein, 2014, p 40). Inclusion, fairness and leaving no one behind points to the importance of coalition-building and mobilisation for a new politics or a 'triple movement' (Fraser, 2013; Kishimoto et al, 2020).

Stressing participation and enabling institutions does not necessarily imply that all will be rosy in this high-energy democracy. There will always be politics and power at play, and there will always be contestation as well as division, exclusion and antagonism. Many of the deliberative and participative experimental institutions such as participatory budgeting or citizens' assemblies have been critiqued as unresponsive to citizens' needs, as expert controlled, as exclusionary and contested. Concepts of participatory and deliberative democracy will always be difficult to translate into reality and many 'mini publics' do not meet the need for mass participation. This is especially the case beyond the local level. We have less sense of what future national and supranational institutions are necessary, but such institutions are crucial for scaling up transformation and tackling wealth inequality (Bradley, 2012).

The challenges outlined in Part I of this book cannot wait for crisis to trigger change. We know that crisis generally acts as an accelerant of existing change, where it acts as a 'bulldozer' clearing the path ahead, but it does not necessarily open new paths to transformation (Hogan et al, 2022). Crisis-induced change may accelerate society in the wrong direction, towards more autocratic, unequal or technocratic states. It is crucial, therefore, to be facing in the right direction prior to crisis. Our political and governance mechanisms must also accelerate positive forms of transformative change without the pressure of crisis. Democratic politics must be 'a machine for the permanent invention of the future', or a 'high-energy democracy' (Unger, 2009, p 78). The challenge is to unleash the power of civil society and people, or power from below, towards creative transformation and empowerment (Klein, 2014; Solnit, 2016). This means shifting how key actors engage with governance mechanisms. It requires civil society to reimagine their own traditional organisational structures to understand the needs of key vulnerable groups and to enable new forms of inclusive participation in a more horizontal form of civil society (Timms and Hiemans, 2018). Chapter 4 discussed the relationship between reciprocity and freedom, and the need to recast demands for freedom, not in terms of individual liberties, but in terms of collective freedoms, and to understand reciprocity, mutual aid and welfare as ways of constituting collective freedom. The aim here is not simply greater inclusiveness but a new emancipatory project, reconnecting the legitimate concerns about emancipation, social protection and freedom through a new paradigm of ecosocial welfare.

Having made the case not for welfare reform but for paradigmatic transformation, an ecosocial welfare regime offers a step towards transformation and a world partially built on UBS, Participation Income, and enabling and reinforcing institutions. These combine to nurture interdependent reciprocity and flourishing, active and equal citizens. Hope is a political position, so I end on a hopeful note that, in the Irish language, 'Is Feidir Linn', we can do this.

Ireland

This appendix offers readers who are unfamiliar with Ireland a brief introduction to the 100-year-old Irish state and its institutional features. Understanding Ireland's distinct social ecology and how it impacts on the functioning of politics, administration and economy is important to make sense of the case study sections at the end of each chapter. Apart from its openness and peripherality, three features of the Irish state merit particular attention from the perspective of transformation: the small size of the state (approximately 5.1 million in 2022); its highly centralised distribution of power; and the scale and speed of recent change.

Institutions

Irish public and policy institutions have evolved in a relatively consensus-oriented democracy characterised by a centralised multi-party system with a two-chamber parliament and a prime minister (Taoiseach) with a moderate amount of influence. The institutional and policy context is characterised by the paradox of a strongly centralised state and weak local government, alongside a political culture dominated by strong localism that is reinforced by a proportional national electoral system organised around 41 constituencies. A growth in agencies is fracturing central power and creating new veto points which pose challenges for climate and social policy implementation (Torney, 2020). While local county loyalty is strong, sub-national or 'county'-level power in Ireland is weak, with low density populations and one-off housing creating consequences for institutional capacity, planning and governance (Dekker, 2020). The local autonomy index (Ladner et al, 2015) ranks Ireland as one of the weakest countries in Europe with respect to local autonomy, with strong limiting consequences for the potential role of local government in local procurement and regional planning. In comparative terms, Ireland is grouped with countries with unitary governance and weak local autonomy including Portugal, Romania and Slovenia.

The relatively unique electoral system – proportional representation through a single transferable vote (PR-STV) – reinforces a pre-existing political culture of brokerage and clientelism and fosters localism and a strong sense of local community and loyalty which was a strong asset in the context of pandemic responses and is potentially an anchor for societal responses to climate change. An Irish form of voluntary corporatism, known as 'social partnership', was a feature of Irish politics and policymaking from 1986 to 2008 when successive governments privileged particular sectors (unions, business, farming, community and voluntary, and environmental organisations) and is associated with developmental characteristics of the Irish state. While this was replaced by a relatively weak process of social dialogue in 2008, a relatively consensus-oriented culture remains among many, but not all, societal actors.

Political and policy dynamics

Originally a patriarchal state with strong theocratic origins, Ireland was predisposed towards conservative and paternalistic policies. There have been significant advances in progressive bio-politics (divorce, marriage equality, abortion), but less progression on social and economic rights (Cullen and Murphy, 2020), and Ireland remains 'a careless state'. Women have been traditionally underrepresented in national and local political, and business leadership. Even in the context of a 30 per cent national gender candidate quota in 2020 (which rose to 40% in 2023), only 23 per cent of parliamentary seats in the lower house are held by women following the 2020 General Election, with only slightly more at the local level. Social conservatism is still evident in distributional politics with a male bread winner tax and transfer system, a poor care infrastructure and high levels of occupational segregation.

A low level of tax effort is a core feature of the Irish political economy. Consequently, there is poor public service provision, with a market-oriented, low-paid and gendered essential economy, associated with the characteristics of a competition state. In the austerity context, alongside male-dominated decision-making, a gender-blind approach was taken to management of the economic crisis contributing to rising female and family homelessness, lone parent poverty, a divisive gender pension gap and gender pay gaps (Barry, 2021). Alongside the state's ideological resistance to investment, social disinvestment during a period of deep austerity has limited the opportunities for social movement mobilisation and created an inhospitable political context for intersectional claims (Cullen and Murphy, 2017).

Irish political culture and political party formations mean, up to 2022, there is a relative absence of hard-right populism or significant *overt* anti-immigrant sentiment in party political terms. Party politics may lead to a different reform dynamic than in a more majoritarian political culture, smaller parties (including the Green Party) often participate in coalition government. In the context of weak local government, there have been numerous experiments in networked governance including local social partnership,

Table A.1: Election outcomes, 2011 to 2025

Political party	Seats 2011	Seats 2016	Seats 2020	Seats 2025
Fine Gael	77	50	34	?
Fianna Fail	21	43	37	?
Labour Party	37	7	6	?
Sinn Féin	14	23	36	?
ULA (2011) AAA PBP (2016)	7	6	6	?
Social Democrats	–	3	6	?
Green Party	0	2	12	?
Independent Alliance	–	6	–	?
Independents	14	15	21	?
New Party	–	–	–	?

that some describe as 'a deliberative miracle' (O'Donnell, 2021). Attempts to deepen and widen democracy can also be seen in the deliberative democratic experimentation of constitutional conventions and citizens' assemblies. The political dynamics over recent elections, influenced by the 2008 economic crisis and resulting austerity, and mirroring similar shifts across the globe, shifted the party system, with a decline in the traditional dominance of the two large centre-right parties of Fine Gael (FG) and Fianna Fáil (FF). The dynamics of growth and crisis has implications for the political salience of climate change, as higher political salience is associated with high economic growth and low unemployment (Little, 2020).

The results of the most recent General Election (GE) (see Table A.1) in February 2020 shook Ireland's political foundations and for the first time produced a three-horse race for which would be the largest party, with FF and FG demoted to 37 and 35 seats respectively, and with SF winning 36 seats. A novel coalition arrangement saw the previously opposed civil war parties sharing less than 50 per cent of the vote enter government with the rising GP. This, for many, signalled the demise of 'civil war' politics in Ireland and the beginning of the end of dominance of FF and FG. The related rise of SF charts an emerging more typical left/right cleavage; this includes some championing of ecosocial policy by left party People before Profit. Irish politics are in a state of transition and hope can thrive in conditions of uncertainty (Solnit, 2016).

Irish welfare state

Ireland has been described as a 'most unwilling caring state' (Daly and Rake, 2002, p 171). Its origins lie in a poor, peripheral, colonised and underdeveloped political economy. The newly independent state was led by the 'most conservative of revolutionaries' who, for the first 30 years of its existence, adopted a relatively isolationist strategy where Church and State contrived to implement macro and micro controls of society in Ireland, particularly on women and the most vulnerable, many of whom remain deeply scarred by time spent in Church and State institutions such as industrial schools, mother and baby homes, and Magdelene laundries. Exposure of these experiences challenged and undermined those in power, including the historically omnipotent Catholic Church. Emigration was a fact of life. By 1961, 45 per cent of all those born in Ireland during the years 1931–1936 and 40 per cent of those born during 1936–1941 had emigrated. This level of emigration was a political, economic, cultural and social safety valve. It was also a force of welfare imagination as emigrants saw and relayed what was possible elsewhere.

Ireland is shaped by its colonial history, and often associated with liberal welfare states and political economies of Western Europe. However, it is not 'a pure type' welfare regime, but a hybrid, or a 'mongrel', having grown over time from a relatively rudimentary welfare state dominated by Church-based provision of education and health to the post-World War 2 era of incremental development of a 'Beveridge' (UK) liberal welfare state. While embedded in a liberal regime trajectory characterised by more centralised power, Ireland is considered more social democratic than the UK's more liberal marketisation regime with a more muted, centrist and consensus-oriented Irish discourse (Dukelow, 2021).

The Irish system of working-age income support or institutional design of the policy architecture were largely built around social insurance and social assistance payments (with some universal payments in childhood and old age). Most changes have been piecemeal and incremental following a largely path-dependent regime. Historical pay-related benefits have been de-emhasised in favour of the now more dominant means-tested social assistance, but may be soon revived.

Historical development

From the late 1950s Ireland modernised its economy to the extent that globalisation began to dominate its political economy and society benefited from an era of liberation. Some strong developmental institutions, including the Industrial Development Authority (IDA) have continued to contribute to Ireland's successful record of attracting foreign direct investment, at once a strength and weakness of the Irish political economy. Multiple factors drove the development of welfare change in Ireland, including interest group mobilisation and politics, demographic factors and social development. International policy transfer and dynamics have influenced Irish welfare policy. EU membership was considered pivotal in augmenting existing domestic mobilisation for gender equality as the late 1970s and early 1980s began a period of welfare expansion and modernisation. Deeply eroded in the 1980s economic crisis, a decade of economic growth known as the Celtic Tiger period (1996–2006) was a period of catch-up in social investment in services and more generous income supports. This was interrupted by the GFC. Over the 2010–2013 period, Ireland was at risk of defaulting on its debt and was loaned €67.5 billion by the European Commission, European Central Bank and the International Monetary Fund (the 'Troika'). Local elites favoured and influenced the 2010–2013 conditionalities associated with the loan. These copper-fastened specific neoliberal welfare reforms including privatisation and marketisation (Dukelow, 2015; Hick, 2016).

Ireland has also experienced transformative levels of inward migration over the last two decades (interrupted by the more traditional form of outward emigration over the 2008–2014 GFC period). Social policy choices are contextualised by monetary and fiscal policy, and Ireland's membership of the EU and Eurozone, the fiscal and monetary preconditions of which impacts on sovereign borrowing and debt, with consequences for Ireland's capacity to absorb extra social investment. Ireland's status as a relatively low revenue jurisdiction and, until recently, a tax haven, means Ireland lacks a sustainable taxation base. This leads to arrested development of and underinvestment in public services. Similarly developed states meet social and economic goals through higher revenue and expenditure without imperilling economic performance.

During the last 30 years, Ireland has arguably over-invested in income supports at the expense of underinvestment in services. A conscious rebalancing is needed to achieve a better equilibrium between the two. Citizens are demanding health, housing, care and public transport as Universal Basic Services. Aspects of a Minimum Income Guarantee or a PI are hiding in plain sight in Ireland's categorial income support system which already provides income for those participating in care, cultural and community-based work including environmental work through Community Employment Programmes and the local government active labour market programme, TUS.

An all island eco state?

In assessing the potential to transform Ireland's welfare architecture towards an ecosocial-welfare regime we need to understand both new and old challenges in the context of an all-island frame, incorporating both the Republic of Ireland and Northern Ireland (NI) in our welfare imaginary. The Republic of Ireland and NI have been separate and distinct jurisdictions for over 100 years. The most formidable challenge facing both Ireland and Northern Irish/Irish welfare regimes is the climate crisis (Robbins et al, 2020). An all-island office in the Department of An Taoiseach (Prime Minister) has commissioned several reports and facilitated north–south dialogues on climate change on the island of Ireland. A welfare imaginary could visualise a future trajectory where this discussion expands to the best path for sustainable welfare policy. Civil society and academic communities north and south are also coming together more frequently.

At the heart of republican theory lies the concept of 'public' – a collective sharing of public goods. A core value of republicanism is Pettit's absence of domination: this requires a symmetry of power between equals, and that people have the power of contestation to challenge the actions of the state. The post-Brexit constitutional future of both Britain and Northern Ireland will create key political dynamics with implications for welfare on the island of Ireland. These will likely play a role in sparking our collective sociological imagination about how climate change and related issues of poverty and inequality will be addressed in the future of the island. Post-Brexit, the UK is undergoing immense constitutional pressure with campaigns for border polls in Northern Ireland and an independence referendum in Scotland. In this context the Scottish government has articulated and communicated a counter-hegemonic welfare state imaginary (Wiggan, 2017) that feeds into future constitutional and social democratic visions. Devolution has led to 'laboratories of democracy' in social security policy in Scotland, and in Wales an agenda for social security devolution is now emerging. A north–south social security 'laboratory of democracy' could feed collective welfare imaginaries and inform future constitutional debate on the island of Ireland.

Irish civil society

Power, wealth and economic resources are highly concentrated in Ireland. This structural reality of golden circles and state capture by a domestic and international elite sets an important context for those seeking to animate transformational change (TASC, 2015). Much is expected of 'power from below' (Fox Piven, 2008).

Over the mid-1800s, pre-independent Ireland experienced a period of mass mobilisation in the Catholic Emancipation Movement, and innovated Monster Meetings, large outdoor political rallies. The late 1800s was a period of intense civil society agitation that provided the foundations of what would become the independent Irish state in 1922. While much of civil society, particularly the voluntary sector, is now service-oriented and organised as fragmented, siloed sectors, civil society also remains a source of political active citizenship in a variety of public spheres. These, while not unique to Ireland, are nonetheless popular and include cultural, political and policy-based summer schools, mind fests and talk forums, and arts and culture (Crowley, 2022). As discussed, Ireland has also experimented with national, regional and local deliberative forms of collaborative governance including local environmental spheres (JCFC, 2020).

However, the Irish state exhibits a passive-aggressive relationship with civil society, espousing partnership and deliberation while also suppressing and inhibiting advocacy (Harvey, 2014), leading to campaigns for the right to dissent. Irish environmental groups face the highest legal costs in the EU and are often threatened with funding cuts when they pursue legal action against the state. In 2021, the Irish Council for Civil Liberties lead the Coalition for Civil Society Freedom, seeking legal reform to lift prohibitions on civil society actors fundraising for legitimate advocacy work. While the political opportunity structure for Irish civil society is changing, opening possibilities for coalition-building, inclusive participation remains a challenge. Enabling inclusion and participation of the diverse migrant population (with over 13 per cent of the population not born in Ireland), as well as indigenous minorities (Travellers were recognised as an ethnic minority in 2017), women as the majority gender, people with disabilities and people in the LGBTI+ community are key to generating a high-energy, representative, participative and deliberative democracy. While there is reason for 'sober optimism', this has to be tempered with a realistic sense of the challenge involved in breaking down silos and raising the temperature and demand for transformation.

Ireland has demonstrated significant capacity to embrace transformative change in bio-political terms, but such dynamics have not yet translated into distributional politics and climate transition. The bleak years of austerity and societal responses to austerity budgets and cuts have increased economic literacy across the population. The quick and often imaginative policy responses to the pandemic offers glimpses of the future and a realisation that, when there is political will, most change is possible. Civil society can collectively shape the nature of that change by developing new welfare imaginary for a republic that recently commemorated its 100th anniversary.

Quo vadis

The recent fragmentation of the old cleavages of the political party system and 'civil war politics' offers new opportunities and prospects of new alliances between political society and civil society (broadly defined). Writing in late 2022, two years ahead of a February 2025 general election, it seems likely that the next election will contribute to a further dissolution of old politics. Whether it will be open to more potential for a new political dynamic capable of transformative policy is less obvious, but arguably there is momentum and demand from society for equality and sustainability. Sinn Féin, the main contender for government, which is questioning the legitimacy of Ireland's current Climate Action Plan 2020–2030 and carbon tax regime, may be incompatible with a Green Party who may be positioned to choose between a right and left constellation and determine who forms the next government. Whatever mix of parties, the post-2025 government will be faced with significant challenges in implementing 'the heavy lifting' required to deliver back-loaded 2030 carbon emissions reduction targets, reaching EU Lisbon equality and poverty targets and developing a sustainable future for all. This political tension intensifies the need for sustainable welfare and ecosocial welfare policy. Ready now.

Notes

Introduction

[1] A number of theorists provide particular inspiration and are drawn from more than once including with respect to discussions about eco-political economy (Polanyi, 1944; Kirby, 2020), ecological sustainability (Fitzpatrick, 2014; Raworth, 2017; Graeber and Wengrow, 2020), post-growth (Hickel 2020; Jackson, 2021), feminism (Fraser, 2013; Folbre, 2021), sustainable provision of needs (Koch and Mont, 2016; Gough, 2017; Coote and Percy, 2020) and transformative change (Wright, 2013; Klein, 2014; Green, 2016; Solnit, 2016).

[2] Known as mycorrhizal-networks (https://www.sciencefocus.com/nature/mycorrhizal-networks-wood-wide-web/).

Chapter 1

[1] https://podcasts.apple.com/us/podcast/the-most-important-book-ive-read-this-year/id1081584611?i=1000500763227

[2] https://theconversation.com/housing-is-both-a-human-right-and-a-profitable-asset-and-thats-the-problem-172846

[3] https://ec.europa.eu/commission/presscorner/detail/en/IP_16_2923

[4] For updates on the appeal, see Commission v Ireland and Others (Case C-465/20 P) available at https://curia.europa.eu/juris/liste.jsf?num=C-465/20&language=en [accessed 14 January 2023].

Chapter 2

[1] It is calculated using national share of territorial emissions (1850–1969) and consumption-based emissions (1970 to 2015) (Hickel, 2021, p 114).

[2] www.carbonbrief.org

[3] Four of which are already overshot – climate change, biodiversity loss, deforestation, biogeochemicals – while a fifth, ocean acidification, is at its tipping point (Hickel, 2021, p 124).

Chapter 3

[1] Arguing that meeting material needs is a central value, human nature is understood as fluid, social and reciprocating, not isolated but interdependent, not calculative but approximate, not dominating nature but deeply embedded in the web of life. However, Raworth is also wary of an overfocus in literature and research of values that reflect WEIRD (western, educated industrialised rich and democratic (2017, p 94).

Chapter 4

[1] The Indigenous peoples of the Americas, also known simply as Native Americans or American Indians, are the inhabitants of the Americas before the arrival of the European Settlers in the pre capitalist 15th century, and the ethnic groups who now identify themselves with those peoples.

[2] Indeed, one of the principal attractions of a dominant alternative to the present welfare paradigm – Universal Basic Income – is that it has no conditional obligations (discussed further in Chapter 6).

[3] Koch and Fritz (2014) examine public support for sustainable welfare and the related political feasibility of reform agendas and conclude that there is evidence of public demand, so policy makers and politicians could be bolder in attempts to form political

coalitions around ecosocial policy strategy. Otto and Gugushvili (2020) highlight a need for investment in education and rural areas where ecosocial scepticism is highest. Emilsson (2021) find a 'frame dilemma' in their assessment of how social movements frame the environment, economic growth and welfare. Both environment and welfare are framed as positive, and it is unclear how people differentiate them.

Chapter 5

[1] https://www.gov.scot/groups/minimum-income-guarantee-steering-group/
[2] https://livingincome.org.uk/uploads/files/living-income-pamphlet.pdf
[3] https://www.gov.ie/en/campaigns/09cf6-basic-income-for-the-arts-pilot-scheme/

Chapter 6

[1] https://www.powercube.net

Chapter 7

[1] Solar Punk, which emerged alongside an increased awareness of social injustices, impacts of climate change and inextricable economic inequality, is concerned with technology; it also embraces low-tech ways of living sustainably such as gardening, positive psychology and do-it-yourself ethics. Its themes may reflect on environmental philosophies such as bright green environmentalism, deep ecology and ecomodernism, as well as punk ideologies such as anti-consumerism, anti-authoritarianism and civil rights.
[2] https://www.oxfamireland.org/sites/default/files/survival_of_the_richest-full_report.pdf

Chapter 8

[1] https://theintercept.com/2019/04/17/green-new-deal-short-film-alexandria-ocasio-cortez/
[2] https://theintercept.com/2020/10/01/naomi-klein-message-from-future-covid/

References

Acheson, N. and Visser, A. (2019) 'Making a difference to public policy and facing the challenge to advocacy work by community and voluntary organisations in 2019. What can new research on Ireland's Advocacy Initiative tell us about its long-term lessons ten years on', *Dublin Science Gallery* [conference] 4 April 2019.

Afri (2012) *Ireland, Irish Finance and the Nuclear Weapons Industry*, Dublin: Afri.

Ahmed, S. (2010) 'Killing joy: Feminism and the history of happiness', *Signs: Journal of Women in Culture and Society*, 35(3): 571–94.

Alston, P. (2020) 'Statement by Professor Philip Alston, United Nations Special Rapporteur on extreme poverty and human rights, on his visit to Spain', available from https://www.ohchr.org/en/statements/2020/02/statement-professor-philip-alston-united-nations-special-rapporteur-extreme [Accessed 14 July 2022].

Allen, M. (1998) *The Bitter Word*, Dublin: Poolbeg Press.

Alperovitz, G., Guinan, J. and Hanna, T. (2017) 'The policy weapon climate activists need' [online], *The Nation*, Available from https://www.thenation.com/article/archive/the-policy-weapon-climate-activists-need/ [Accessed 30 September 2022].

Anderson, E. (2004) 'Welfare, work requirements, and dependent-care', *Journal of Applied Philosophy*, 21(3): 243–56.

Arendt, H. (1958) *The Human Condition*, Chicago: University of Chicago Press.

Arnstein, S. (1969) 'A ladder of citizen participation', *Journal of the American Institute of Planners*, 35(4): 216–24.

Atwood, M. (2013) *Maddaddam: A Novel*, New York: Doubleday.

Atkinson, A.B. (1996) 'The case for a participation income', *The Political Quarterly*, 67(1): 67–70.

Attwood, M. (2013) *Maddaddam*, London: Bloomsbury.

Avaaz (2021) 'The Glasgow Equity and ambition Pact A Code Red for Humanity to Address the Climate Emergency', available from https://secure.avaaz.org/campaign/en/cop26_peoples_climate_deal_11/?fpla [Accessed 11 July 2022].

Barry, U. (2021) *The Care Economy, COVID-19 Recovery and Gender Equality – A Summary Report*, Brussels: European Commission.

Baumberg, B. (2015) 'The stigma of claiming benefits: a quantitative study', *Journal of Social Policy*, 45(2): 181–99.

Beck, U. (2000) *The Brave New World of Work*, Cambridge: Polity Press.

Beckett, S. (1983) *Worstward Ho*, New York: Grove Press.

Bednar, J. (2023) 'Governance for human social flourishing' in Levi, M. and Farrell, H. (eds) *Special Issue on Moral Political Economy Daedalus*, 152(1).

Beresford, P. (2016) *All Our Welfare: Towards Participatory Social Policy*, Bristol: Policy Press.

Beresford, P. (2020) *Participation and Ideology Social Policy*, Bristol: Policy Press.

Bregman, R. (2017) *Utopia for Realists, and How We Can Get There*, London: Bloomsbury.

Berger, B. (2011) *Attention Deficit Democracy: The Paradox of Civic Engagement*, New Jersey: Princeton University Press.

Blyth, M. (2002) *Great Transformations, Economic Ideas and Institutional Change in the Twentieth Century*, Cambridge, Cambridge University Press.

Bohnenberger, K. (2020) 'Money, vouchers, public infrastructures? A framework for sustainable welfare benefits', *Sustainability*, 12(2): 596.

Bohnenberger, K. and Fritz, M. (2020) 'Making welfare resilient. Creating stable & sustainable welfare systems in times of declining economic growth. Transformation Policy Brief #2', ZOE Institute for Future-Fit Economies.

Bonvin, J. and Laruffa, F. (2022) 'Towards a capability-oriented ecosocial policy: Elements of a normative framework', *Social Policy and Society*, 21(3): 484–95.

Bookchin, M. (1991) *Libertarian Municipalism*, London: Green Perspectives.

Boucher, G. and Watson, I. (2017) 'Introduction to a visual sociology of smaller nations in Europe', *Visual Studies*, 32(3): 205–11.

Boyle, M. (2013) *The Moneyless Man*, London: Oneworld Publications.

Bradley, K. (2012) 'Book review perspectives: *Understanding the Environment and Social Policy* by Tony Fitzpatrick (Editor)', *Sutainability: Science, Practice and Policy*, 8(1): 116–23.

Browne, C. and Diehl, P. (2019) 'Conceptualising the political imaginary: An introduction to the special issue', *Social Epistemology*, 33(5): 393–97.

Brundtland, G.H. (1987) *Our Common Future: Report of the World Commission on Environment and Development*, Geneva, United Nations.

Buch-Hansen, H. and Carstensen, M.B. (2021) 'Paradigms and the political economy of ecopolitical projects: Green growth and degrowth compared', *Competition & Change*, 25(3–4): 308–27.

Buckingham, S. (2020) *Gender and Environment*, 2nd edn, London: Routledge.

Button, D. and Coote, A. (2021) *A Social Guarantee: The Case for Universal Services*, London: New Economic Foundation.

Callinicos, A. (2004) *Making History: Agency, Structure, and Change in Social Theory*, 2nd edn, London: Brill.

Cantillon, S. (2016) 'The political economy landscape: in conversation with Nancy Folbre', *Review of Radical Political Economics*, 48(3): 485–93.

Carson, R. (1962) *The Silent Spring*, Boston, MA: Houghton Mifflin.

Castles, F.G. (2010) 'Black swans and elephants on the move: the impact of emergencies on the welfare state', *Journal of European Social Policy*, 20(2): 91–101.

Coates, D. (2017) *Reflections on the Future of the Left*, London: Agenda Publishing.

Connaughton, B. (2021) 'Committees and the legislature' in Hogan, J. and Murphy, M.P. (eds) *Policy Analysis in Ireland*, Bristol: Policy Press.

Christophers, B. (2020) *Rentier Capitalism: Who Owns the Economy and Who Pays for It?*, London: Verso.

Chung, H. and Thewissen, S. (2011) 'Falling back on old habits? A comparison of the social and unemployment crisis reactive policy strategies in Germany, the UK and Sweden', *Social Policy & Administration*, 45(4): 354–70.

Citizens' Assembly (2018) *Third Report and Recommendations of the Citizens' Assembly: How the State can make Ireland a leader in tackling climate change*, Dublin: Citizens' Assembly.

Citizens' Assembly (2022) 'Citizens' Assembly Recommends Constitutional Amendment To Protect Biodiversity', 27 November [online] available from https://www.citizensassembly.ie/en/news/press-releases/citizens-assembly-recommends-constitutional-amendment-to-protect-biodiversity.html [Accessed 13 December 2022].

Clasen, J. and Clegg, D. (2007) 'Levels and levers of conditionality: measuring change within welfare states', in J. Clasen and N. Siegel (eds) *Welfare State Change: The Dependent Variable*, Cheltenham: Elgar, pp 166–97.

Claassen, R. (2018) *Capabilities in a Just Society: A Theory of Navigational Agency*, Cambridge: Cambridge University Press.

Collins, M. and Walsh, M. (2011) 'Tax Expenditures, Revenue and Information Forgone. The experience of Ireland', TEP Working Paper No. 1211 August 2011, Dublin: TCD.

Common Cause (2022) https://www.commoncause.org/ [Accessed 12 July 2022].

Community Platform (2022) 'Towards a progressive model of collaborative governance: a Community Platform discussion paper', Dublin: Community Platform.

Connor, S. (2011) 'Structure and agency: A debate for community development?', *Community Development Journal*, 46(2): 97–110.

Coote, A. (2015) 'People, planet, power: Toward a new social settlement', *International Journal of Social Quality*, 5(1): 8–34.

Coote, A. (2022) 'Towards a sustainable welfare state: The role of universal basic services', *Social Policy and Society*, 21(3): 473–83.

Coote, A. and Percy, A. (2020) *The Case for Universal Basic Services*, London: Polity.

Coote, A. and Yazici, E. (2019) *Universal Basic Income: A Union Perspective*, Geneva, Public Services International.

Craig, L. (2008) 'Valuing by doing: Policy options to promote sharing the care,' *Journal of the Association for Research on Mothering*, 10(1): 45–56.

Cronin, M. (2019) *Irish and Ecology – An Ghaeilge agus an Éiceolaíocht*, Dublin: FÁS.

Crowley, N. (2022) *Civil Society for Equality and Environmental Sustainability: Reimagining a Force for Change*, Dublin: TASC.

Cullen, P. and Gough, S. (2022) *Different Paths, Shared Experiences: Ethnic Minority Women and Local Politics in Ireland*, Dublin: NTWF and AkiDwA.

Cullen, P. (2021) 'Trade union mobilization and female-dominated care work in Ireland: Feminised and/or feminist?', *Politique Europeenne*, 74: 136–63.

Cullen, P. and Murphy, M.P. (2017) 'Gendered mobilisations against austerity, Special Issue: Gender equality and "austerity": Vulnerabilities, resistance, and change', *Gender, Work and Organization*, 24(1): 83–97.

Cullen, P. and Murphy, M.P. (2020) 'Responses to the COVID-19 crisis in Ireland: From feminized to feminist', *Gender, Work and Organisation*, Feminist Frontiers. Advance online publication. doi: 10.1111/gwao.12596.

Cumbers, A. (2018) 'Rethinking public ownership as economic democracy', in Jones, B., and O'Donnell, M. (eds) *Alternatives To Neoliberalism: Towards Equality and Democracy*, Bristol: Policy Press, pp 209–27.

Daly, H.E. (2007) *Ecological Economics and Sustainable Development: Selected Essays of Herman Daly*, Cheltenham: Edward Elgar.

Daly, M. and Rake, K. (2002) *Gender and the Welfare State*, London: Polity.

De Schutter, O. (2010) 'Sovereignty-plus in the era of interdependence: Towards an international convention on combating human rights violations by transnational corporations', *CRIDHO Working Papers*, Louvain.

Dekker, S. (2020) 'Responding to climate change: The role of local government' in Robbins, D., Torney, D. and Brereton P. (eds) *Ireland and the Climate Crisis*, Basingstoke: Palgrave Macmillan, pp 109–28.

De Wispelaere, J. and Stirton, L. (2018) 'The case against participation income: political, not merely administrative', *Political Quarterly*, 89(2): 262–67.

Dryzek, J.S. (2008) 'The ecological crisis of the welfare state', in Gough, I., Meadowcroft, J., Dryzek, J., Gerhards, J., Lengfield, H., Markandya, A. and Ortiz, R. (eds) *JESP Symposium: Climate Change and Social Policy*, *Journal of European Social Policy*, 18: 325.

Dukelow, F. (2015) 'Pushing against an open door: Reinforcing the neoliberal policy paradigm in Ireland and the impact of EU intrusion', *Comparative European Politics*, 13(1): 93–111.

Dukelow, F. (2021) 'Recommodification and the welfare state in re/financialised austerity capitalism: Further eroding social citizenship?', *Social Policy and Society*, 20 (1): 125–41.

Dukelow, F. (2022) 'What role for activation in ecosocial policy?', *Social Policy and Society*, 21(3): 496–507.

Edelman Ireland (2022) *Edelman Trust Barometer Findings Ireland*, Dublin: Edelman.

Emilsson, K. (2021) 'Urban sustainable welfare survey study'. Technical Report. Lund, Sweden: Lund University.

EPA (2022) *Ireland's Greenhouse Gas Emissions Projections 2021–2040*, Dublin: EPA. Available from https://www.epa.ie/publications/monitor ing--assessment/climate-change/air-emissions/EPA-Ireland's-GHG-Proj ections-Report-2021-2040v4.pdf [Accessed 7 July 2022].

Fisher, B. and Tronto, J. (1990) 'Toward a feminist theory of caring', in Abel, E. and Nelson, M. (eds) *Circles of Care: Work and Identity*, Albany: SUNY Press, pp 35–62.

Fitzpatrick, T. (2004) 'A post-productivist future for social democracy?', *Social Policy and Society*, 3(3): 213–22.

Fitzpatrick, T. (2014) *Climate Change and Poverty. A New Agenda for Developed Nations*, Bristol: Policy Press.

Fleurbaey, M., Bouin, O., Salles-Djelic, M., Kanbur, R., Nowotny, H., Reis, E. and Sen, A. (2018) *A Manifesto for Social Progress: Ideas for a Better Society*, Cambridge: Cambridge University Press.

Folbre, N. (2021) *The Rise and Decline of Patriarchal Systems An Intersectional Political Economy*, New York: Verso.

Fox Piven, F. (2008) 'Can power from below change the world?', *American Sociological Review*, 73(1): 1–14.

Fraser, N. (2013) 'A triple movement? Parsing the politics of crisis after Polanyi', *New Left Review*, 81: 119–32.

Fraser, N. (2014) 'Can society be commodities all the way down? Post-Polanyian reflections on capitalist crisis', *Economy and Society*, 43(4): 541–58.

Freeman, J. (1972) 'The tyranny of structurelessness', *Berkley Journal of Sociology*, 17: 151–65.

Galbraith, J.K. (1958) *The Affluent Society*, Boston, MA: Houghton Mifflin.

Galgóczi B. (2022) 'From a "just transition for us" to a "just transition for all"', *Transfer: European Review of Labour and Research*, 28(3): 349–66.

Galgóczi, B. and Pochet, P. (2022) 'Introduction: Welfare states confronted by the challenges of climate change: A short review of the issues and possible impacts', *Transfer: European Review of Labour and Research*, 28(3): 307–16.

Gaventa, J. (2006) 'Finding the spaces for change: A power analysis', *IDS Bulletin*, 37(6): 23–33.

Gaventa, J. (2021) 'Linking the prepositions: Using power analysis to inform strategies for social action', *Journal of Political Power*, 14(1): 109–30.

Gaventa, J. and Petitt, J. (2010) *Power and Participation in Political and Civic Leadership*, London: Sage.

Garavan, M. (2007) 'Resisting the costs of "development": Local environmental activism in Ireland', *Environmental Politics*, 16(5): 844–63.

Gold, L. (2020) 'The changing faces of the climate movement in Ireland' in Robbins, D., Torney, D. and Brereton, P. (eds) *Ireland and the Climate Crisis*, Basingstoke: Palgrave Macmillan, pp 269–86.

Gopnik, A. (2023) 'Caregiving in philosophy, biology, and political economy', *Daedalus*, 152(1).

Gorman, J. (2021) 'Rooting and reaching: insights from Love Leitrim's successful resistance to fracking in Ireland', *Community Development Journal*, 57(1): 17–39.

Gough, I., Meadowcroft, J., Dryzek, J. Gerhards, J., Lengfeld, H., Markandya, A. and Ortiz, R. (2008) 'Climate change and social policy', *Journal of European Social Policy*, 18(4): 325–44.

Gough, I. (2017) *Heat, Greed, and Human Need: Climate Change, Capitalism, and Sustainable Wellbeing*, Northampton: Edward Elgar.

Gough, I. (2022) 'Two scenarios for sustainable welfare: A framework for an ecosocial contract', *Social Policy and Society*, 21(3): 460–72.

Government of Ireland (2021) *National Climate Action Plan*, Dublin: Government of Ireland.

Graeber, D. and Wengrow, D. (2021) *The Dawn of Everything: A New History of Humankind*, London: Allen Lane.

Green, D. (2016) *How Change Happens*, Oxford: Oxford University Press.

Guinan, J. and O'Neill, M. (2019) 'From community wealth building to system change: Local roots for economic transformation', *IPPR Progressive Review*, 25(2): 382–92.

Hall, D. and Hobbs, C. (2017) 'Public ownership is back on the agenda in the UK' in Petitjean, O. and Kishimoto, S. (eds) *Reclaiming Public Services*, Brussels: TNI.

Han, H. (2020) 'Fixing democracy demands the building and aligning of people's motivation and authority to act', *Stanford Social Innovation Review*, 18(1): A5–A6.

Harvey, B. (2014) *Are We Paying for That? Government Funding & Social Justice*, Dublin: Advocacy Initiative.

Harvey, F. (2018) 'Mary Robinson launches new feminist fight against climate change', *The Guardian*, 24 July [online] https://www.theguardian.com/environment/2018/jul/24/mary-robinson-launches-new-feminist-fight-against-climate-change [Accessed 10 December 2022].

Hay, C. (2004) 'Ideas, interests and institutions in the comparative economy of great transformations', *Review of International Political Economy*, 2(1): 204–26.

Hearne, R. (2017) *A Home or a Wealth Generator? Inequality, Financialisation, and the Irish Housing Crisis*, Dublin: TASC.

Held, D., McGrew, A., Goldblatt, D. and Perraton, J. (1999) *Global Transformations: Politics, Economics and Culture*, Stanford: Stanford University Press.

Hessel, A., Jouzel, J. and Larrouturou, P. (2021) *A Climate Pact for Europe How to Finance the Green New Deal*, Bristol: Bristol University Press.

Hick, R. (2018) 'Enter the troika: The politics of social security during Ireland's bailout', *Journal of Social Policy*, 47(1): 1–20. doi: 10.1017/s0047279417000095.

Hick, R. and Murphy, M.P. (2021) 'Common shock, different paths? Comparing social policy responses to COVID-19 in the UK and Ireland', *Social Policy Administration*, 55(2): 312–25.

Hickel, J. (2020) 'What does degrowth mean? A few points of clarification', *Globalisations*, 18(7): 1105–11.

Hickel, J. (2021) *Less is More How Degrowth Will Save the World*, London: Cornerstone.

Higgins, M.D. (2021) 'Recovering possibilities: Discovering the rich promise of a moral foundation to economy & society', *Irish Journal of Sociology*, 29(3): 274–81.

Hiilamo, H. (2022) *Participation Income: An Alternative to Basic Income for Poverty Reduction in the Digital Age*, Cheltenham: Edward Elgar Publishing.

Hiilamo, H. and Komp, K. (2018) 'The case for a participation income: Acknowledging and valuing the diversity of social participation', *Political Quarterly*, 89(2): 256–61.

Hirvilammi, T. and Koch, M. (2020) 'Editorial: Sustainable welfare beyond growth', *Sustainability*, 12(5): 1824.

Hirvilammi, T. (2020) 'The virtuous circle of sustainable welfare as a transformative policy idea', *Sustainability*, 12(1): 391.

Hirvilammi, T., Häikiö, L., Johansson, H., Koch, M. and Perkiö, J. (2023) 'Social policy in a climate emergency context: Towards an ecosocial research agenda', *Journal of Social Policy*, 1-23 [online] doi: 10.1017/S0047279422000721.

Hogan, J., Howlett, M. and Murphy P. (2022) 'Re-thinking the coronavirus pandemic as a policy punctuation: COVID-19 as a path-clearing policy accelerator', *Policy and Society*, 41(1): 40–52.

Hogan, J. and Murphy, M.P. (2021) *Policy Analysis in Ireland*, Bristol: Policy Press.

Hogan, J., Howlett, M. and Murphy, M.P. (2021) 'Re-thinking the coronavirus pandemic as a policy punctuation: COVID-19 as a path-clearing policy accelerator', *Policy and Society*, 41(1): 40–52.

Howard, M. (2020) 'Select Committee on Economic Affairs: Uncorrected oral evidence: The economics of Universal Credit', House of Lords [online] available from https://committees.parliament.uk/oralevidence/123/pdf/ [Accessed 10 December 2022].

Huesemann, M.H. and Huesemann, J.A. (2011) *Technofix: Why Technology Won't Save Us or the Environment*, Canada: New Society Publishers.

IPCC (2014) *Climate Change 2014: Synthesis Report. Contribution of Working Groups I, II and III to the Fifth Assessment Report of the Intergovernmental Panel on Climate Change: Summary for Policymakers*, [Core Writing Team, R.K. Pachauri and L.A. Meyer (eds)]. Geneva, Switzerland: IPCC.

IPCC (2018) 'Summary for Policymakers' in *Global Warming of 1.5°C. An IPCC Special Report on the Impacts of Global Warming of 1.5°C above Pre-industrial Levels and Related Global Greenhouse Gas Emission Pathways, in the Context of Strengthening the Global Response to the Threat of Climate Change, Sustainable Development, and Efforts to Eradicate Poverty* [Masson-Delmotte, V., Zhai, P., Pörtner, H.-O., Roberts, D. and Skea, J., et al (eds)], Geneva, Switzerland: World Meteorological Organization.

IPCC (2021) 'Summary for Policymakers' in *Climate Change 2021: The Physical Science Basis. Contribution of Working Group I to the Sixth Assessment Report of the Intergovernmental Panel on Climate Change* [Masson-Delmotte, V., Zhai, P., Pirani, A., Connors, S.L., Péan, C. and Berger, S., et al (eds)], Cambridge and New York: Cambridge University Press.

IPCC (2022a) 'Summary for Policymakers' [Pörtner, H.-O., Roberts, D.C., Tignor, M., Poloczanska, E.S., Mintenbeck, K. and Alegría, A., et al (eds)] in *Climate Change 2022: Impacts, Adaptation, and Vulnerability. Contribution of Working Group II to the Sixth Assessment Report of the Intergovernmental Panel on Climate Change* [Pörtner, H.-O., Roberts, D.C., Poloczanska, E.S., Mintenbeck, K., Tignor, M. and Alegría, A., et al (eds)]. Cambridge and New York: Cambridge University Press.

IPCC (2022b) *Climate Change 2022: Impacts, Adaptation, and Vulnerability. Contribution of Working Group II to the Sixth Assessment Report of the Intergovernmental Panel on Climate Change* [Pörtner, H.-O., Roberts, D.C., Tignor, M., Poloczanska, E.S., Mintenbeck, K. and Alegría, A., et al (eds)]. Cambridge: Cambridge University Press.

Jackson, T. (2021) *Post-growth Life After Capitalism*, London: Polity.

Jackson, W.A. (2005) 'Capabilities, culture, and social structure', *Review of Social Economy*, 63(1): 101–24.

Jameson, F. (2003) 'Future City', *New Left Review*, 21(22): May/June.

JCFJ (2020) *Integral Ecology: Five Years On. Working Notes No 86*, Dublin: Jesuit Centre for Faith and Justice.

Jessoula, M. and Mandelli, M. (2022) 'Eco-social mobilization at the supranational level? The case of "The Right to Energy for All Europeans' coalition" in Schoyen, M.A., Hvinden, B. and Leiren M.D. (2022) *Towards Sustainable Welfare States in Europe Social Policy and Climate Change*, Cheltenham: Edward Elgar, pp 238–57.

Johnston, H. (2022) 'Basic income in Ireland: The development of two pilots', *European Journal of Social Security*, 24(3): 243–56.

Jones, B. and O'Donnell, M. (2018) *Alternatives to Neoliberalism: Towards Equality and Democracy*, Bristol: Policy Press.

Just Transition Alliance (2022) Joint Declaration, [online] available at https://ictu.ie/sites/default/files/publications/2022/Just%20Transition%20Alliance%20Joint%20Declaration_1.pdf [Accessed 15 December 2022].

Kabeer, N. (2005) 'Gender equality and women's empowerment: A critical analysis of the third millennium development goal 1', *Gender and Development*, 13(1): 13–24, doi: 10.1080/13552070512331332273.

Khan-Cullors, P. and Bandele, A. (2017) *When They Call You a Terrorist: A Black Lives Matter Memoir*, New York: St Martin's Press.

Killian, S. (2015) 'On responsibility and tax policy: An exploration based on Ireland and Malawi', in Healy, S. and Reynolds, B. (eds) *Measuring Up Ireland's Progress Past Present and Future*, Dublin: Social Justice Ireland.

Kimmerer, R.W. (2020) *Braiding Sweetgrass: Indigenous Wisdom, Scientific Knowledge and the Teachings of Plants*, London: Penguin.

Knijn, T. and Kremer, M. (1997) 'Gender and the caring dimension of welfare states: Toward inclusive citizenship', *Social Politics: International Studies in Gender, State and Society*, 4(3): 328–61. doi: 10.1093/oxfordjournals.sp.a034270.

Kirby, P. (2020) 'Cloghjordan eco village community led transitioning to a low carbon future' in Robbins, D., Torney, D. and Brereton P. (eds) *Ireland and the Climate Crisis*, Basingstoke: Palgrave Macmillan, pp 287–303.

Kirby, P. (2021) *Karl Polanyi and the Contemporary Political Crisis: Transforming Market Society in the Era of Climate Change*, London: Bloomsbury.

Kirby, P. and O'Mahony, T. (2018) *The Political Economy of the Low-Carbon Transition: Pathways Beyond Techno-Optimism*, Basingstoke: Palgrave Macmillan.

Kirby, P. and Murphy, M.P. (2011) *Towards a Second Republic: Irish Politics after the Celtic Tiger*, London: Pluto Press.

Kishimoto, S., Steinfort, L. and Petitjean, O. (2020) *The Future is Public: Towards Democratic Ownership of Public Services*, Amsterdam: TNI.

Kitchin, R., O'Callaghan, M., Boyle, M., Gleeson, J. and Keaveney, K. (2012) 'Placing neoliberalism: The rise and fall of Ireland's Celtic Tiger', *Environment and Planning*, 44(6): 1302–26.

Klein, N. (2014) *This Changes Everything*, London: Allen Lane.

Klein, N. (2017) *No is Not Enough*, Canada: Knopf Publishers.

Koch, M. and Mont, O. (eds) (2016) *Sustainability and the Political Economy of Welfare*, London: Routledge.

Koch, M. (2022) 'Social policy without growth: Moving towards sustainable welfare states', *Social Policy and Society*, 21(3): 447–59.

Koch, M. and Fritz, M. (2014) 'Building the eco social state: do welfare regimes matter', *Journal of Social Policy*, 43(4): 679–703.

Konczal, M. (2021) *Freedom from the Market: America's Fight to Liberate Itself from the Grip of the Invisible Hand*, New York: The New Press.

Ladner, A., Keuffer, N. and Baldersheim, H. (2015) *Self Rule Index for Local Government*, Brussels: European Commission.

Lakoff, G. (2004) *Don't Think of an Elephant! Know Your Values and Frame the Debate: The Essential Guide for Progressives*, London: Chelsea Publishing Company.

Larragy, J. (2016) *Asymmetric Engagement: The Community and Voluntary Pillar in Irish Social Partnership (Irish Society)*, Manchester: Manchester University Press.

Laruffa, F. (2020) 'What is a capability-enhancing social policy? Individual autonomy, democratic citizenship and the insufficiency of the employment-focused paradigm', *Journal of Human Development and Capabilities*, 21(1): 1–16.

Laruffa, F., McGann, M. and Murphy, M.P. (2021) 'Enabling participation income for an ecosocial state', *Social Policy and Society*, 21(3): 508–19.

Le Guin, U. (2014) 'Ursula K Le Guin's speech at National Book Awards' [online] *The Guardian*, available from https://www.theguardian.com/books/2014/nov/20/ursula-k-le-guin-national-book-awards-speech [Accessed 10 December 2022].

Leicester, G. (2020) *Transformative Innovation: A Guide to Proactive and Policy for System Transformation*, 2nd edn, Milton Keynes: Triarchy Press.

Lelkes, O. (2021) *Sustainable Hedonism: A Thriving Life that Does Not Cost the Earth*, Bristol: Policy Press.

Levi, M. (2020) 'Frances Perkins was ready', [online] available at https://www.socialsciencespace.com/2020/03/frances-perkins-was-ready [Accessed 10 December 2022].

Levi, M. and Ugolnik, Z. (2023) 'Mobilising in the interest of others' in Levi, M. and Farrell, H. (eds) *Special Issue on Moral Political Economy Daedalus*, 152(1).

Lima, L., Hearne, R. and Murphy, M.P. (2022) 'Housing financialisation and the creation of homelessness in Ireland', *Housing Studies*. doi: 10.1080/02673037.2022.2042493.

Lister, A. (2020) 'Reconsidering the reciprocity objection to unconditional basic income', *Politics, Philosophy & Economics*, 19(3): 209–28.

Little, C. (2020) 'The party politics of climate change in Ireland' in Robbins, D., Torney, D. and Brereton, P. (eds) *Ireland and the Climate Crisis*, Basingstoke: Palgrave Macmillan.

Lombardozzi, L. (2020) 'Gender inequality, social reproduction and the universal basic income', *The Political Quarterly*, 91: 317–23.

Lorde, A. (1982) 'Learning from the 60s', talk delivered at the Malcolm X Weekend, Harvard University, https://www.blackpast.org/african-american-history/1982-audre-lorde-learning-60s/ [Accessed 10 December 2022].

Lukes, S. (2004) *Power: A Radical View*, 2nd edn, New York: Red Globe Press.

Lynch, K. (2022) *Care and Capitalism*, London: Polity Press.

Magan, M. (2020) *Thirty-two Words for Field,* Dublin: Gill.

Malm, A. (2021) *How to Blow Up a Pipeline: Learning How to Fight in a World on Fire.* London: Verso.

Mandelli, M. (2022) 'Understanding ecosocial policies: a proposed definition and typology', *Transfer: European Review of Labour and Research*, 28(3): 333–48.

Mandelli, M., Sabato, S. and Jessoula, M. (2021) 'EU economic governance and the socio-ecological transition: Towards a more sustainable European semester?' *Politiche Sociali, Social Policies*, 3: 619–38.

Massey, D. (2013) 'Vocabularies of the economy' in Hall, S., Massey, D. and Rustin, M. (eds) *After Neoliberalism the Kilburn Manifesto*, London: Soundings L.W. Books, pp 1–16.

Matthies, A.L. (2017) 'The conceptualisation of ecosocial transition' in Matthies, A.L. and Närhi, K. (eds) *The Ecosocial Transition of Societies: The Contribution of Social Work and Social Policy*, Routledge: Routledge Advances in Social Work, pp 17–35.

Mazzucuto, M. (2013) *The Entrepreneurial State: Debunking Private v Public Sector Myths*, London: Anthem.

Meadowcroft, J. (2007) 'Building the environmental state: What the history of social welfare tells us about the future of environmental policy', *Alternatives Journal*, 33(1): 11–17.

Meadows, D.H., Meadows, D.L., Randers, J. and Behrens, W. (1972) *The Limits to Growth: A Report for the Club of Rome's Project on the Predicament of Mankind*, New York: Universe Books.

Mercier, S., Bresnihan, P., McIlroy, D. and Barry, J. (2020) 'Climate action via just transitions across the island of ireland: Labour, land and the low-carbon transition' in Robbins, D., Torney, D. and Brereton, P. (eds) *Ireland and the Climate Crisis*, Basingstoke: Palgrave Macmillan, pp 249–68.

McGann, M. (2021) 'The political economy of welfare in a time of coronavirus: Post-productivism as a state of exception', *Irish Journal of Sociology*, 28(2): 225–30.

McGann, M. (2021) '"Double activation": Workfare meets marketisation', *Administration*, 69(2): 19–42.

McGann, M. and Murphy, M.P. (2021) 'Income support in an ecosocial state: The case for Participation Income', *Social Policy and Society* [online] doi: 10.1017/S1474746421000397

Mills, C.W. (1967) *The Sociological Imagination*, Oxford: Oxford University Press.

Moulaert, F. MacCallum, D., Mehmood, A. and Hamdouch, A. (2013) *The International Handbook on Social Innovation: Collective Action, Social Learning and Transdisciplinary Research*, Cheltenham: Edward Elgar.

Mudge, S.L. (2008) 'What is neoliberalism?', *Socio-Economic Review*, 6(4): 703–31.

Murphy, M.P. and Dukelow, F. (eds) (2016) *The Irish Welfare State in the 21st Century Challenges and Change*, Basingstoke: Palgrave Macmillan.

Murphy, M.P. and Dukelow, F. (2022) 'Building the future from the present: Imagining post-growth, post-productivist ecosocial policy', *Journal of Social Policy*, 51(3): 504–18.

Murphy, M.P., Maher, M. and Irwin, A. (2020) *Winners and Losers: The Social Marketisation of Civil Society; Impact of Commissioning and Procurement on Irish Civil Society Advocacy and Service Delivery*, MUSSI: Maynooth University.

NESC (2020a) *Addressing Employment Vulnerability as Part of a Just Transition in Ireland, Report number: 149*, Dublin: NESC.

NESC (2020b) *The Future of the Irish Social Welfare System: Participation and Protection, Report number 151*, Dublin: NESC.

NESC (2022) *The COVID-19 Pandemic: Lessons for Irish Public Policy*, Dublin: NESC.

Nussbaum, M.C. (2005) 'Women's bodies: Violence, security, capabilities', *Journal of Human Development and Capabilities*, 6(2): 167–83.

Obersteiner, M., Azar, C., Kauppi, P. et al (2001) 'Managing climate risk', *Science*, 294(5543): 786–87.

OECD (2009) *Privatisation in the 21st Century: Recent Experiences of OECD Countries*, Paris: OECD.

OECD (2014) 'Trends in income inequality and its impact on economic growth', OECD Social, Employment and Migration Working Papers, No. 163, OECD Publishing. http://dx.doi.org/10.1787/5jxrjncwxv6j-en [Accessed 10 December 2022].

O'Donnell, M. (2018) 'The democratic deficit: institutional democracy' in Jones, B. and O'Donnell, M. (eds) *Alternatives to Neoliberalism: Towards Equality and Democracy*, Bristol: Policy Press, pp 79–96.

O'Donnell, R. (2021) 'The social partners and NESC: From tripartite dialogue via common knowledge to network knowledge' in Hogan, J. and Murphy, M.P., *Policy Analysis in Ireland*, Bristol: Policy Press.

O'Neill, S. (2022) 'Environmental justice in Ireland: Key dimensions of environmental and climate injustice experienced by vulnerable and marginalised communities', Community Law and Mediation [online] [nd], available from https://communitylawandmediation.ie/wp-content/uplo ads/2022/03/Environmental-Justice-in-Ireland-230322-1.pdf [Accessed 8 July 2022].

O'Neill, D.W., Fanning, A.L., Lamb, W.F. and Steinberger, J.K (2018) 'A good life for all within planetary boundaries', *Nat Sustain*, 1: 88–95.

O'Neill, S. and Alblas, W. (2020) 'Climate litigation politics and policy change lessons from Urgenda and climate case in Ireland' in Robbins, D., Torney, D. and Brereton, P. (eds) *Ireland and the Climate Crisis*, Basingstoke: Palgrave Macmillan, pp 57–72.

Ó Riain, S. (2014) *The Rise and Fall of Ireland's Celtic Tiger: Liberalism, Boom and Bust*, Cambridge: Cambridge University Press.

Ó Riain, S. (2020) 'Ireland's COVID-19 crisis response: Perspectives from social science' [Oral Presentation], *Navigating COVID-19 in a Small Open Economy*, Dublin: Geary Institute, UCD.

Ostrom, E. (2015) *Governing the Commons*, Cambridge: Cambridge University Press.

O'Sullivan, K. (2022) 'EU official castigates Government over environmental court costs', *Irish Times*, 21 January.

O'Sullivan, K. (2021) 'Climate in 2021: Beyond the "blah, blah, blah" of Cop 26', *Irish Times*, 24 December.

Otto, A. and Gugushvili, D. (2020) 'Ecosocial divides in Europe: public attitudes towards welfare and climate change policies', *Sustainability*, 12(1): 404.

Oxfam (2021) *The Inequality Virus*, Oxford: Oxfam International.

Oxfam (2022) *Inequality Kills*, Oxford: Oxfam International.

Oxfam International (2023) *Survival of the Richest*. Nairobi: Oxfam, Available from https://www.oxfamireland.org/sites/default/files/survival_of_the_richest-full_report.pdf [Accessed 16 January 2023].

Oxfam and Trocaire (2021) 'Sustainable food systems: Steps Ireland can take to become a global leader', Oxfam and Trocaire [online], July 2021, available from https://trocaire.org/wp-content/uploads/2021/07/Sustainable-Food-Systems_Aug.pdf?type=policy [Accessed 8 July 2022].

Panitch, V. (2011) 'Basic income, decommodification and the welfare state', *Philosophy and Social Criticism*, 37(8): 935–45.

Peck, J. (2010) *Constructions of Neoliberal Reason*, Oxford: Oxford University Press.

Perez, A.C., Grafton, B., Mohai, P., Hardin, R., Hintzen, K. and Orviset, S. (2015) 'Evolution of the environmental justice movement: Activism, formalisation, and differentiation', *Environmental Research Letters*, 10(10): 1–13.

Penn, H. and Lloyd, E. (2014) *Start Strong 'Childcare': Business or Profession?* London: University of East London.

Pérez-Munoz, C. (2016) 'A defence of participation income', *Journal of Public Policy*, 36(2): 169–93.

Pérez-Munoz, C. (2018) 'Participation income and the provision of socially valuable activities', *Political Quarterly*, 89(2): 268–72.

Petitjean, O. and Kishimoto, S. (2017) *Reclaiming Public Services*, Brussels: TNI.

Pierson, C. (2021) *The Next Welfare State? UK Welfare after COVID-19*, Bristol: Policy Press.

Polanyi, K. (2001) [1944] *The Great Transformation: The Political and Economic Origins of Our Time*, Boston: Beacon Press.

Pomey, M.P., Morgan, S., Church, J., Forest, P.G., Lavis, J.N., McIntoch, T. and Dobson, S. (2010) 'Do provincial drug benefit initiatives create an effective policy lab? The evidence from Canada', *Journal of Public Health Politics, Policy, and Law*, 35(5): 705–42.

Piketty, T. (2014) *Capitalism in the 21st Century*, Cambridge, MA: Harvard University Press.

Raazzouk, A. (2022) *Saving the Planet Without the Bullshit: What They Don't Tell You About the Climate Crisis*, London: Atlantic Books.

Raworth, K. (2017) *Doughnut Economics. Seven Ways to Think Like a 21st-century Economist*, London: Random House.

Rees, J. (2014) 'Public sector commissioning and the third sector: Old wine in new bottles?', *Public Policy and Administration*, 29(1): 45–63.

Robbins, D., Torney, D. and Brereton, P. (eds) (2020) *Ireland and the Climate Crisis*, Basingstoke: Palgrave Macmillan.

Robinson, Z.P., Catney, P., Calver, P. and Peacock, A. (2022) 'Universities as living labs for climate praxis' in Howarth, C., Lane, M. and Slevin, A. (eds) *Addressing the Climate Crisis Local Action in Theory and Practice,* Basingstoke: Palgrave Pivot, pp 129–40.

Rockström, J., Steffen, W., Noone, K., Persson, A., Stuart II Chapin, F., Lambin, E. et al (2009) 'Planetary boundaries: Exploring the safe operating space for humanity', *Ecology and Society*, 14(2): 32.

Runciman, D. (2021) *Confronting Leviathan: A History of Ideas*, London: Profile Books.

Schoyen, M.A., Hvinden, B. and Leiren M.D. (2022) *Towards Sustainable Welfare States in Europe Social Policy and Climate Change*, Cheltenham: Edward Elgar.

Sen, A. (1999) *Development as Freedom*, New York: Alfred Knopf.

Shearer, J.C., Abelson, J., Kouyaté, B., Lavis, J.N. and Walt, G. (2016) 'Why do policies change? Institutions, interests, ideas and networks in three cases of policy reform', *Health Policy and Planning*, 31(9): 1200–11.

Shenker, J. (2019) *Now We Have Your Attention: The New Politics of the People*, London: Bodley Head Press.

Slevin, A. (2016) *Gas, Oil and the Irish State: Understanding the Dynamics and Conflicts of Hydrocarbon Management*, Manchester: Manchester University Press.

Slevin, A., Barry, J., Hill, T., Orr, J., O'Flynn, P. and Sullivan, L. et al (2022) 'Local climate praxis in practice: Community climate action in Belfast' in Howarth, C., Lane, M. and Slevin, A. (eds) *Addressing the Climate Crisis Local Action in Theory and Practice*, Basingstoke: Palgrave Pivot, pp 3–13.

Smith, A.M. (1998) *Laclau and Mouffe: The Radical Democratic Imaginary*, London: Routledge.

Smith, N.J. (2005) *Showcasing Globalisation? The Political Economy of the Irish Republic*, Manchester: Manchester University Press.

Solnit, R. (2009) *A Paradise Built in Hell: The Extraordinary Communities that Arise in Disasters*, London: Penguin.

Solnit, R. (2016) *Hope in the Dark*, London: Cannongate.

Stamm, M.A., Hirilammi, T. and Narhi, K. (2020) 'Combining labour market and unemployment policies with environmental sustainability? A cross national study on ecosocial innovations', *Journal of International and Comparative Social Policy*, 36(1): 43–56.

Stanley Robinson, K. (2021) *The Ministry of the Future*, New York: Orbit.

Stiglitz, J. (2015) *Rewriting the Rules and Agenda for Growth and Shared Prosperity in the American Economy*, Washington DC: Roosevelt Institute.

Stone, L., Montes de Oca, G. and Christie, I. (2022) 'A commoners' climate movement' in Howarth, C., Lane, M. and Slevin, A. (eds) *Addressing the Climate Crisis Local Action in Theory and Practice*, Basingstoke: Palgrave Pivot, pp 27–39.

Starke, P., Kaasch, A. and van Hooren, F. (2013) *The Welfare State as Crisis Manager: Explaining the Diversity of Policy Responses to Economic Crisis*, Basingstoke: Palgrave Macmillan.

Streeck, W. (2014) 'How will capitalism end?' *New Left Review*, 87 (May/June).

Streeck, W. (2017) *How Will Capitalism End? Essays on a Failing System*, London: Verso.

Swaton, S. (2018) 'For an ecological transition income', Green European Journal [online] 17 October, available from https://www.greeneuropean journal.eu/for-an-ecological-transition-income/ [Accessed 8 July 2022].

Sweeney, J. (2020) 'Climate change in Ireland, Science impacts and adaptation' in Robbins, D., Torney, D. and Brereton, P. (eds) *Ireland and the Climate Crisis*, Basingstoke: Palgrave Macmillan, pp 57–72.

Szolucha, A. (2018) 'Anticipating fracking: Shale gas development and the politics of time in Lancashire UK', *The Extractive Industries and Society*, 5(3): 348–55.

TASC (2015) *The Distribution of Wealth in Ireland*, Dublin: TASC, authored by Cormac Staunton.

The Care Collective (2020) *The Care Manifesto, The Politics of Interdependence*, London: Verso.

The Commission on Care Centered Transition (2023) *Daring to Care*, Berlin: Hot or Cool.

Thompson, J. (1984) *Studies in the Theory of Ideology*, London: Polity Press.

Thunberg, G. (2019) Speech, UN Youth Climate Summit, New York, 21 September 2019.

Timms, H. and Heimans, J. (2018) *New Power: How it is Changing the 21st Century and Why You Need to Know*, Basingstoke: Pan Macmillan.

Torney, D. (2020) 'The politics of emergency? Ireland's response to climate change', *Irish Studies in International Affairs*, 31: 13–26.

Torney, D. and O'Gorman, R. (2019) 'A laggard in good times and bad? The limited impact of EU membership on Ireland's climate change and environmental policy', *Irish Political Studies*, 34(4): 575–94.

Unger, R. (2009) *The Left Alternative*, London: Verso.

Unger, R. (2011) 'The future of the left', *The European* [online] 24 October, available from https://www.theeuropean.de/en/roberto-unger--2/6041-the-future-of-the-left [Accessed 8 July 2022].

UN (2020) *From Insights to Action: Gender Equality in the Wake of COVID-19,* Geneva: United Nations.

Utting, P. (2018) 'Achieving the sustainable development goals through social and solidarity economy: Incremental versus transformative change', Geneva: UNRISD [online] 24 April, Available from https://www.unrisd.org/en/library/publications/achieving-the-sustainable-development-goals-through-social-and-solidarity-economy-incremental-versus [Accessed 8 July 2022].

van der Zwan, N. (2014) 'Making sense of financialization', *Socio-Economic Review,* 12(1): 99–119.

Wainwright, H. (2018) *A New Politics from the Left,* London: Polity.

Wallace Wells, D. (2019) *The Uninhabitable Earth Story of the Future,* London: Allen Lane.

Watson, C. (2020) 'Community engagement and community energy', in Robbin, S.D., Torney, D. and Brereton, P. (eds), *Ireland and the Climate Crisis,* Switzerland: Palgrave Studies, pp 205–29.

White, S. (2010) 'The left and reciprocity', *Soundings,* 46: 18.

Wiggan, J. (2017) 'Contesting the austerity and "welfare reform" narrative of the UK Government: Forging a social democratic imaginary in Scotland', *International Journal of Sociology and Social Policy,* 37(11–12): 639–54.

Wilkinson, R.G. and Pickett, K. (2009) *The Spirit Level: Why More Equal Societies Almost Always Do Better,* London: Allen Lane.

Wilkinson, R.G. and Pickett, K. (2018) *The Inner Level: How More Equal Societies Reduce Stress, Restore Sanity and Improve Everyone's Well-being,* London: Penguin.

World Bank (2015) *Poverty Report,* Washington DC: World Bank.

Wright, E.O. (2013) *Envisioning Real Utopias,* London: Verso.

Index

References to figures and tables appear in *italic* type. References to endnotes show the page and chapter number and the note number (231ch2n3).

www.ingramcontent.com/pod-product-compliance
Lightning Source LLC
Chambersburg PA
CBHW062108040426
42336CB00042B/2563